Public Schools That Work

Critical Social Thought

Series editor: Michael W. Apple
John Bascom Professor of Curriculum and Instruction and
    Educational Policy Studies, University of Wisconsin-Madison

Already published

Critical Social Psychology Philip Wexler
Reading, Writing and Resistance Robert B. Everhart
Arguing for Socialism Andrew Levine
Between Two Worlds Lois Weis
Power and the Promise of School Reform William J. Reese
Becoming Clerical Workers Linda Valli
Racial Formation in the United States Michael Omi and Howard
    Winant
The Politics of Hope Bernard P. Dauenhauer
The Common Good Marcus G. Raskin
Contradictions of Control Linda M. McNeil
Social Analysis of Education Philip Wexler
Keeping Them Out of the Hands of Satan Susan D. Rose
Primary Understanding Kieran Egan
Capitalist Schools Daniel P. Liston
The New Literacy John Willinsky
Becoming a Woman Through Romance Linda Christian-Smith
Growing Up Modern Bruce Fuller
Getting Smart Patti Lather
Teacher Education and the Social Conditions of Schooling Daniel P.
    Liston and Kenneth M. Zeichner
Teachers and Crisis Dennis Carlson
Views Beyond the Border Country Dennis L. Dworkin and Leslie
    G. Roman (eds)
I Answer With My Life Kathleen Casey
Japan and the Pursuit of a New American Identity Walter Feinberg
Race, Identity and Representation in Education Cameron McCarthy
    and Warren Crichlow (eds)

Public Schools That Work

Creating Community

Edited by
GREGORY A. SMITH

ROUTLEDGE
New York • London

Published in 1993 by

Routledge
29 West 35 Street
New York, NY 10001

Published in Great Britain by

Routledge
11 New Fetter Lane
London EC4P 4EE

Copyright © 1993 by Routledge

Printed in the United States of America on acid free paper.

Library of Congress Cataloging-in-Publication Data

Public schools that work : creating community / edited by Gregory A. Smith.
    p.   cm. — (Critical social thought)
Includes bibliographical references and index.
ISBN 0-415-90577-X
    1. School environment—United States.   2. School management and organization—United States.   3. Social networks—United States.
4. Educational sociology—United States.   I. Smith, Gregory A.
II. Series.
LC210.5.P83   1993
370.19′3—dc20   93-24205
                                                            CIP

British Library Cataloguing-in-Publication Data also available.

Contents

Contents

Series Editor's Introduction

In the 1980s, when William Bennett was what some of us called the "Secretary of War on Education," the federal government was deeply enamored both with wall charts that plotted out comparative achievement scores and with little booklets that told all of us "what works." The meaning of these two words—what works—was constructed in a particular way. It centered largely around an unquestioning acceptance of conservative definitions of the academic (and vocational) curriculum as the only useful ones. It believed that achievement test scores were the primary measure of a good environment. And standing behind it was actually an attack on the very idea of the public. By and large, whatever was public was bad. Private was good.

This attack on the public has not abated. In fact, even with a different administration in Washington (and perhaps in part because of it), conservatives have redoubled their efforts to gain power at local, regional, and state levels. This has met with no small measure of success.

Conservatives of various kinds tell us that public schools can't work. These institutions are simply "black holes" into which money is poured to little or no effect. Only voucher or choice plans, or only privatization and marketization, will restore initiative. Absent that, we must have increasingly tighter control over curricula, teaching, and evaluation. Run schools like factories; make them efficient producers of the human capital required by international economic competition. Thus, the usual choices presented to the public are either turning our schools over to market forces or increasing the mechanisms by which we "guarantee appropriate results."

Yet it is not only the conservative coalition that has criticized the daily realities and results of schooling. Over the past two decades there has been a veritable explosion of critical literature on what schools may be doing from progressive voices. Some of this has focused on the role of schooling in producing inequalities around race, gender, and class and in creating conditions that sever the connections between student knowledge and "official" knowledge (see, e.g., Apple, 1985; Apple, 1988; Apple, 1990). Others have been more popular, and very powerful, in documenting the awful conditions that exist in many of our inner-city schools.

Thus, for example, in *Savage Inequalities,* Jonathan Kozol presents a compelling indictment of the reality of schools in our poorest urban areas: insufficient resources, decaying buildings, students and teachers in crisis, disintegrating communities, a school funding apparatus that seems to be nearly consciously designed to increase the already wide disparities between the poor and the affluent (Kozol, 1991). If anything, in our urban and rural areas these conditions seem to be worsening, driven by the results of years of destructive and punitive policies in the economy, in social welfare, in culture, and in education.

Many of the criticisms leveled at our educational institutions by conservative populists, however, should not be dismissed. Indeed, while the solutions proposed by the rightist populist agenda—funding for private and religious schools and academies, home schooling, a more "Christian" curriculum that is based on irredentist readings of the Bible, and so on—may lead in dangerous directions (Rose, 1988), the criticisms themselves do point to a school system that is often highly bureaucratic, out of touch with its local community, and alienating to many of its students. As Dennis Carlson has shown, these characteristics have had truly damaging effects on the lives and hopes of teachers as well (Carlson, 1992).

But, is it all bad? Are there public schools of various kinds that are *now* in existence that work, not only on those ubiquitous standardized achievement tests but in a broader sense than these limited and deceptive measures can gauge?

It is crucial that those of us committed to defending *and* restructuring *public* education know about the successes as well as the more widely publicized failures, for this is a very perilous time in the history of American education. The vast experiment of a school for all of the people (one that has been acted on only very partially, of course) is in danger of collapsing into privatized or marketized schools for the affluent and decaying "holding tanks" for the children of the poor and dispossessed.

As I have argued at considerable length in *Official Knowledge* (Apple, 1993), what is at stake here is the very idea of citizenship. The conservative movement aims at radically transforming what it means to be a citizen, what it means to participate in the institutions of our society. It wants to evacuate politics from the educational world and transform the citizen into simply a *consumer*. What an odd metaphor. We are thus either stomachs or furnaces (Apple, 1990). The world becomes a vast supermarket and—just as with real supermarkets—some people will go in and buy lots of goods and others will remain outside, unable to do more than stare. In essence, under these conditions of market-based plans, choice simply becomes a code word for conditions of educational apartheid (see Education Group II, 1991).

But there are different, more democratic, senses of citizenship, ones based on the formation of caring communities, not on the possessive individualism that stands behind the ideal of the person as only a consumer. And they have been institutionalized in schools that work.

What we have been prevented from seeing are those publicly funded schools that, even under what are at times very difficult conditions, are doing exceptional things with and for their students. We need detailed pictures of the actual practices of these more democratic schools at work. This is what Gregory Smith gives us in *Public Schools That Work*.

Each of the schools portrayed here is built around ideas of establishing community. This includes two elements: the school itself is a community, and the walls between the school and the local community are torn down. These schools are about the politics of official knowledge as well. They seek to redefine what counts as legitimate knowledge in schools by consciously making the students' own culture the object of serious study.

Among the examples are: innovative vocational education programs that seek to go well beyond the all too current emphasis on equipping students with "flexible job skills" needed by industry; inner-city elementary schools that have developed unique bilingual approaches and that have a greater emphasis on parental involvement; schools grounded in social action curricula, where students focus on projects that make a difference in their own lives as well as their community's. There are other emphases as well.

Public Schools That Work brings together representative exemplars of a wide range of schools. The book is valuable for a variety of reasons, but two stand out in my mind especially. First, it helps to transform our sense of what it means to say something "works." It widens our concerns well beyond the limited sensibilities embodied in the conservative restoration. In so doing, it returns some of our history to us. That is, it enables us to once more reflect on what public schooling can and should be at a time when so many forces conspire to stain the values that we supposedly hold most dear about our children and their present and future lives. Second, the volume restores our sense of what is possible. It gives us hope, a rare commodity in a time of great difficulty in education and the larger society.

Taken together, these attributes make Gregory Smith's book a welcome antidote to the cynicism and despair that characterize so much of the discussion of public schools today. Let us not be romantic, however. Building programs such as those described here will not be easy; indeed, even defending their existence may require a good deal of effort. Yet the fact that they do exist—and work—should provide us with some of the imaginative resources necessary to keep those who would privatize, those who wouild turn schooling into simply one more market, at bay.

Educators, community members, researchers, and policymakers who are deeply concerned with the pressing issues of student alienation and dropouts, more community-centered education, and more responsive and engaging curricula and teaching within our public schools will find much to ponder and much to excite them here.

Michael W. Apple
University of Wisconsin-Madison

References

Apple, M. W. (1985). *Education and Power*. New York: Routledge.

Apple, M. W. (1988). *Teachers and Texts*. New York: Routledge.

Apple, M. W. (1990). *Ideology and Curriculum*. 2d. edition. New York: Routledge.

Apple, M. W. (1993). *Official Knowledge: Democratic Education in a Conservative Age*. New York: Routledge.

Carlson, D. (1992). *Teachers and Crisis*. New York: Routledge.

Education Group II (1991). *Education Limited*. London: Unwin-Hyman.

Kozol, J. (1991). *Savage Inequalities*. New York: Crown.

Rose, S. (1988). *Keeping Them Out of the Hands of Satan*. New York: Routledge.

Introduction: Schools and the Maintenance of Community

Gregory A. Smith

Mainstream educators are becoming increasingly concerned about establishing a deeper sense of community within schools. It is not uncommon, for example, to see elementary schools labeling themselves as educational communities. Much of the literature about school improvement also points to the need for school staff to develop a shared sense of vision and purpose upon which to ground their interactions with one another and their students and families (Brandt, 1992; Edmonds, 1982; Sizer, 1992). The school choice movement, despite its divisive and fragmenting characteristics, is to some extent predicated on a concern about community building by suggesting that parents, as well as teachers, should be drawn into this process. More recently, the development of broader professional communities to support school change has become part of our common discourse (Lieberman, 1992). In this introduction, I would like to consider why these communitarian concerns may be emerging at this point in our shared history, discuss factors within schools that may impinge on efforts to change their nature, and examine promising directions that could guide us in our efforts to help children feel connected to one another and to their teachers as they journey through the educational process.

It is the absence of this sense of connectedness that now seems so problematic in much of our public life (Bellah et al., 1985; Ketcham, 1987). Spun in myriad directions by our jobs, the media, and education,

Gregory A. Smith

we find little to pull us together. Without this sense of shared existence, our ability to function as democratic citizens is impaired. In the late twentieth century, growing social fragmentation inhibits our ability to recognize how the lives of all our neighbors impinge on our own well-being. Instead of acting in ways supportive of the common good, the economically able display a growing tendency to direct their attention to the protection of their own interests and those of people like them. The privatization of schools, community services such as garbage disposal and sewage treatment, and police and fire protection threatens to divert both public monies and public will from the provision of communal supports required by everyone (Scherer, 1992). In such "lifestyle enclaves" (Bellah et al., 1985), there is talk of community, but this talk is narrowly focused rather than inclusive. Given the gravity and universality of the environmental, economic, and social problems we now face, it seems essential that we create ways to help our children understand what they share with others if we are to deal successfully with factors in our common life that threaten us all.

Spurred on by concerns such as these, my wife and I took positions at a small Quaker boarding school in northern California more than a decade ago. In a small alternative school that self-consciously functioned as an educational community, we hoped to discover ways to cultivate for both ourselves and our students a deeper experience of interdependence and social responsibility. Our experience there was largely what we had hoped to find, and it has shaped my understanding of the possible. Located in the foothills of the Sierra Nevada mountains, the John Woolman School offered us an opportunity to live and work with a group of committed staff and a diverse range of students, many of whom were at the school because of educational or personal difficulties they had encountered prior to joining us. Our six years at this school were intense, often difficult, but remarkably fulfilling.

We were instructors to our students and colleagues to other staff, but our relationships went far beyond this. Students in my courses on classical Greek literature or creative writing were the same people who would drop by the house after learning that a parent needed another cancer operation or would involve us in efforts to shake their need for drugs. The variety of interactions we experienced on a daily basis allowed for the sharing of parts of ourselves normally excluded from most formal educational settings. We learned with one another as complete people, and it was this that I came to realize was so important about what we shared.

At this school, in part because of those relationships, I saw students

2

grow and develop in remarkable ways. Visitors to the school frequently commented on how our students seemed much more mature, self-assured, and caring than many other high school students they had encountered. Although the school can be faulted for the way in which our lives were to some extent enclosed within the boundaries of our own community, college recruiters who visited us would note our students' finely tuned sense of social consciousness. During the 1980s when most students they met seemed preoccupied with careers that would bring them large salaries, our students were more concerned with issues related to social justice, peacemaking, and protecting the earth. Given the school's Quaker heritage, such preoccupations were certainly what we hoped our students would take from their time with us. What was surprising was simply the fact that when so many of their peers elsewhere were turning inward, they were directing their attention to the needs of the world around them. Our students were experiencing their lives not in isolation from one another but as deeply connected—as were we ourselves.

My experience at the John Woolman School pointed to one way young people might be drawn into community and helped to live lives characterized by a recognition of interdependence and mutual obligation. In my years at this school, I became convinced that one of the keys to the revitalization of American education—and perhaps American communities—may lie in the construction of educational settings similar to what I had known there, settings, however, that would be located within the home communities of students rather than removed from them. Although I knew it would be impossible to provide all students with the same depth of community experience that can come with living in a boarding school, I suspected that this liability would be offset by the opportunity to apply lessons learned about community building and social interdependence within the school itself to the experiences students encountered every day outside its walls. In this way it might also be possible to avoid the danger of turning school into just another "lifestyle enclave."

After leaving the John Woolman School, I sought answers to these questions while pursuing a doctoral degree at the University of Wisconsin-Madison. While there, I became involved in a nationwide study of alternative public school programs created for students at risk of not completing the work required to graduate from high school. The results of this study are reported in *Reducing the Risk: Schools as Communities of Support* (Wehlage et al., 1989). Many of the programs our research team investigated featured elements that paralleled those I

Gregory A. Smith

had encountered at the John Woolman School. These schools also demonstrated a similar impact on their students in terms of immediate personal relationships and, on occasion, their broader social commitments.

During this time I also had the opportunity to meet educators working in a variety of alternative schools across the United States who were addressing similar issues. Although few of these educators were necessarily motivated by the same concerns as myself, what I saw happening in their schools confirmed much of what I had seen both at the John Woolman School and the schools we had studied as part of our research. In a period when there is growing concern about the creation of an educational process that confirms community, turning to schools where educators have already begun this process could provide useful guidance. Before moving on to an overview of some of the central characteristics and foci of these schools, however, it seems important to explore why the current concern about communities and schooling is emerging in the way it is now and why schools have been so inhospitable to such an orientation in the past. Unless we consider reasons behind the marginality of the efforts of alternative educators, we may remain blind to factors that will inhibit the development of the communitarian ethos and behaviors now being called for by spokespeople throughout the educational establishment.

The Emergence of Communitarian Concerns

Throughout much of American history, the health of our communities has been taken for granted by most U.S. citizens. How healthy these communities in fact were is worth debate, but the vision of some halcyon era of small-town America remains part of our common mythology. Its power was expressed vividly in the Republican campaigns of the 1980s, and to some extent was tapped in Bill Clinton's successful bid for the presidency in 1992. In their recent book *The Good Society* (1991), Robert Bellah and his associates point out the almost iconographic significance of "Main Street" in the imaginative worlds created by the Disney corporation in California and Florida. They suggest that it is this vision of our common life that acts as the ground bass upon which the improvisations of modernity have been played out. It is a vision, however, that is being sorely pressed by current realities.

What has been neglected in our understanding of that common life are warnings such as those presented by Alexis de Toqueville over a century and a half ago about the disintegrating impact of another fundamental component of our national mythology: individualism. Toqueville suggested that the myopic focus on concerns related to the individual or individual families eventually might threaten the commitment of U.S. citizens to the health of their collective life. More recent analysts have elaborated on Toqueville's concerns and shown how closely our preoccupation with the individual is tied to assumptions that lie at the heart of what can be called the American experiment.

Going back to theories that lie behind the political and economic systems of the United States, C. B. MacPherson suggests that Thomas Hobbes's view of the individual as the fundamental building block of society coupled with John Locke's celebration of private property has given rise to the possessive individual. Possessive individuals see themselves not as members of larger social wholes but as owners of themselves. It is through this ownership with its "freedom from dependence on the wills of others" and "proprietors[hip] of their own capacities" that people in our society are able to realize their full potential (Mac-Pherson, 1962: 3). For wage earners rather than independent producers, the possession of unique skills, knowledge, and dispositions is a critical component to successful participation in a market economy. Survival in such a social environment is dependent upon one's ability to compete against other individuals for the work needed to purchase the necessities of daily life. In earlier social formations, survival was predicated on group membership. In such situations, personal welfare was linked not to setting oneself apart from others but to the nurturing of relationships and patterns of mutual aid (e.g., gift giving) which could be drawn upon in times of need.

Given this view of the individual as an isolated and competitive social atom, Hobbes and Locke envisioned the state not so much as the protector of the commonweal as the protector of the individual's pursuit of personal development and property. For them, the aim of government is to allow for the free play of individual initiative as long as it does not impinge upon the initiative of other individuals. Government itself is defined negatively as a necessary evil rather than as a means for ameliorating our common life (Ketcham, 1987). Although this depiction of the Lockean state is simplistic, it embodies much of the philosophy of the Republican administrations that until recently have dominated U.S. life since 1980. Without referring to MacPherson or Ketcham, Bellah and his associates follow their lead in asserting that the Lockean view of the individual and the state has contributed to an institutional impasse in the United States that is leading to the unraveling of the social ties and obligations we depend upon for our common welfare.

During the long era of economic expansion enjoyed in the United States since the end of World War II, it became possible for an ever-increasing proportion of U.S. citizens to experience for themselves the economic and social independence that lies at the core of this vision of social life. In *The Urban Villagers* (1962) and *Middle-American Individualism* (1988), Herbert Gans describes how this process has taken place. Prior to 1950, most people in the United States remained tied to more traditional human groupings, either in small towns or the ethnic enclaves that made up most U.S. cities. The maintenance of such alliances was essential because of the general unpredictability of the national economy as a whole. Although U.S. history has been characterized by a growing middle class, it was not until the middle of the twentieth century that industrial productivity made it possible for large numbers of people to assume this economic status and the prerogatives associated with it. Those prerogatives included the ability to leave family and friends to seek new jobs, new housing, and new friends and acquaintances. Gans asserts that it is this freedom that lies at the heart of what it means to be middle-class.

This process led to the creation of Levittown and all the other suburban developments that have followed it. It led as well to the ability of people to leave family and friends without the threat of impoverishment or physical harm. In an era when the physical frontier had become history, a growing economy allowed for a continued playing out of the nineteenth-century pioneers' search for independence and financial prosperity. It led, too, to the growing cosmopolitanism and tolerance of Americans and the diminished power of conventional moral restraints. In the late twentieth century, liberation from the ideological, behavioral, and economic inhibitions placed upon individuals in traditional communities became available for the majority. Much of the energy and excitement of twentieth-century America as well as the appeal of the United States to the immigrants who continue to seek this country out can be tied to the promise it holds for individuals willing to break molds and take advantage of entrepreneurial opportunities. The downside of this vision of social reality has been the way in which people who do not succeed are pushed to the margins of our collective consciousness and blamed for their failure to compete (Hacker, 1992; Sennett and Cobb, 1972).

When a majority of American citizens were entering the middle class or believed their children would be able to make this leap into increased levels of economic security and personal freedom, the diminished health of our public life and communities could be more safely disregarded. It was possible to continue to believe that "the rising tide would lift all ships." With declining economic productivity, the growth of an increasingly disenfranchised underclass, and the deterioration of the infrastructure upon which our national well-being depends, however, it is becoming apparent that the peculiar working relationship Americans had established between the needs of individuals and the needs of communities may be dysfunctional in ways we had not previously imagined. Much of the current discourse about community may be tied to this recognition and the need to find ways once more to protect ourselves collectively from the vagaries of an uncertain world. When most citizens believed they could succeed in the competitive market economy that dominates our lives, a focus on individualism was tolerable. As the possibility of success becomes more questionable, however, it is not surprising that we have turned our attention once more to the need to construct communities where our well-being is more likely to be assured.

Factors Impinging on Schools as Communities

One of the consequences of the growth of the middle class and the independence associated with it has been the deterioration of the smaller human groupings and voluntary associations encountered in well-functioning communities (Berger and Neuhaus, 1977; Bronfenbrenner, 1986). Places where children might learn what it means to become responsible participants in adult society have become scarce. Schools remain one of the few sites in our society where children are able to experience an ongoing social relationship with a group of people that extends beyond their immediate family and friends. As neighborhoods, churches, and even nuclear families have become more ephemeral and less significant in the lives of children in the United States, there are fewer and fewer places where the continuous and close relationships that characterize well-functioning communities can be encountered in our common life. If children are to learn what it means to live in interdependent and successfully functioning groups, schools may be one of the few places where these lessons can be mastered.

This was certainly John Dewey's hope. In *School and Society* (1899/1959), Dewey argued that modern educators should prepare the young

7

for adult responsibilities in a manner that imitated and extended the experience they would have had in premodern villages. They should thus be exposed to the range of occupations linked to meeting basic human needs and learn to be effective citizens by sharing in decision making about the school community. While Dewey can be criticized for his preoccupation with membership in the Great Community (see Dewey, 1927) rather than students' membership in their more immediate communities, the process he proposed remains viable and worth consideration. It focuses on a form of lived practice that stands in contrast to the isolation and individualism that have become too common in most American schools. Rather than presenting learning as an activity aimed at increasing students' value as individuals in a competitive labor market, Dewey sought to place education within a broader communal context.

As schools have developed in the twentieth century, however, few have been structured to accomplish this end. Sociologists such as Talcott Parsons (1959) and Robert Dreeben (1968) have persuasively argued that schools actually fulfill a contrasting function in modern societies by helping children acquire norms associated with the more gesellschaft requirements of contemporary economic and political institutions, norms that in many respects are the antithesis of those associated with community membership. These norms include independence, an achievement orientation, universalism, and specificity. Independence refers to the development of self-reliance and self-sufficiency, dispositions essential if children are to become successful wage earners in positions that will require them to fulfill tasks upon which their performance as workers or future workers will be judged. Achievement points to the disposition to believe that one can have an impact on one's environment by competing against some external standard of excellence. Universalism includes the willingness to set aside group loyalties in interactions with others. Finally, people who have acquired the norm of specificity deal with others not as complete human beings but as the purveyors of specific services and skills. Dreeben suggests that these norms cannot be learned within the family with its more particularistic and supportive forms of relationship and that some new institution had to be invented to transmit them to the young.

Schools draw children into an acceptance of these norms not so much through specific instruction as through induction into a social milieu more typical of modern bureaucracies than mutually supportive communities. To begin with, schools teach students new patterns of interaction with the adults from whom they are expected to learn about the world. Instead of the diffuse and caring relationships they would be expected to encounter in healthy homes, they are drawn into relationships characterized by emotional flatness, continuous evaluation, and transiency. Students quickly learn that their teachers have little room for their needs as complete people. They are simply learners whose job is the acquisition of the behaviors, knowledge, and skills seen as important by the school. Furthermore, their success in school is closely tied to their willingness to comply with its expectations. Little tolerance is shown to students who fail to learn the school's lessons, especially those lessons tied into institutional conformity (Jackson, 1968).

With the adults they meet in school, children must acquire the ability to display a level of emotional distance that would be inappropriate in the home. Even though they may naturally come to experience a degree of attachment to their teachers—especially at the elementary school level—such attachment is systematically broken on an annual basis, mirroring the pattern of detachment often expected of young adults as they enter the job market or leave their homes upon the completion of their formal education. As indicated earlier, such detachment is an accepted part of our own way of life; however, it remains highly problematic in other societies. Among the Amish, for example, it is grounds for ostracization. In rural Alaska, as well, teachers' common expectation that successful students must leave their villages runs counter to parents' desire and need for their children to remain close by to help fulfill important tasks related to subsistence economic activities and the support of vital community functions.

Children in school must furthermore learn to submit to a continuous process of evaluation by their teachers that has little to do with their relationships with others. Many come to believe that their value lies not so much in who they are as in what they can do. Certainly, parents demonstrate a similar concern about the acquisition of socially desirable skills and behaviors, but their relationship with their offspring is predicated more on kinship than on performance. In healthy families, care and support derive from membership; in school, this kind of concern is often denied children whose level of achievement does not meet the school's expectations or whose behavior challenges the school's authority. Through their adaptation to such relationships, children who succeed in school learn the norms of independence and achievement and come to recognize that their well-being depends not on social membership but on their ability to meet standards of achievement determined not by those closest to them but by impersonal and seemingly inescapable educational and economic institutions.

Schools also induct children into new patterns of interaction with one another. In school, for example, they learn to be alone in a crowd (Jackson, 1968). Rather than being allowed to interact freely with one another as members of the same community, their inclination to converse and play with friends is systematically inhibited. They are shown instead that their success is tied to their ability to work quietly and by themselves, complying with the expectations of their teachers rather than the interests of their group. Students are furthermore led to believe that achievement is predicated on their ability to do better than their peers in a competition for the school's scarce rewards. Only a certain proportion of students in a class will be seen as able or gifted and talented; the remainder will be viewed as more mediocre or even deficient. From early on, students are encouraged to position themselves against one another and helped to develop identities based not on group membership but individual capacity. Not all students become willing participants in this social creation, but those who do not tend to be viewed by the school and often themselves as failures.

In terms of their relationship with the institution as a whole, children are essentially taught that they occupy a subservient position to their teachers and that their primary responsibility lies in their acquiescence to the school's behavioral norms and standards of achievement. As Philip Jackson (1968) noted over two decades ago, school tends to initiate children into the "life of the company," where they must do work determined by others and obey their teacher as their first boss. There is little room to learn what it means to share actively in the construction and maintenance of a healthy community and nearly no opportunity to participate in its governance.

In regard to the content of what they learn in school, children must accept the school's definition of important knowledge, even though the curriculum may seem foreign to their own experience and unrelated to their more pressing concerns. This is especially problematic because of the instrumental as opposed to expressive nature of what is taught in school. The abstract and detached skills and knowledge children learn from their teachers often have little to do with the developmental tasks they must accomplish in the process of becoming adults. Issues related to personal identity, moral choices, ultimate purposes, and their relationship to the broader community are rarely if ever dealt with. As churches have come to play a diminished role in the lives of more and more students, there is no place where these matters can be raised. Basil Bernstein (1975) has suggested that in the absence of opportunities to consider these fundamental questions, children and youth are forced to create their own answers. This may in part be one of the reasons that youth culture has become more dominant and strident in industrialized nations than in most other societies from the past. In a sense, adults in twentieth-century America have failed in their effort to impart to children what should be most important in their lives. In doing so, they have neglected the transmission of the social orientation and values that have been critical to the maintenance of most civilizations in the past.

Finally, schools contribute to the erosion of community most obviously and yet most subtly because of their simple isolation from the rich texture of existence and work that goes on beyond their walls. Prior to our own era, children learned the skills and dispositions needed to function successfully as adults from their relatives and neighbors. Now, those skills are learned from strangers. This means that children's dependence upon the people closest to them for their own future economic survival is reduced, and the lessons learned at home are less significant. In contrast, for example, children in Amish families still learn the skills needed to run their farms and homes from parents committed to their instruction (Hostetler and Huntington, 1971). These skills are quickly translated into valued economic activities as they grow into late adolescence and young adulthood. The same is true in Alaskan villages where subsistence hunting and gathering remain the central form of economic activity. In each instance, however, public schooling jeopardizes the transmission of these abilities and the social values of cooperation and sharing associated with them, weakening the bonds of interrelationship that undergird the strength of these communities. Although in the case of the Amish and Alaska Natives the corrosive impact of public education on community strength is obvious, schools everywhere have a similar impact.

What all of this suggests is that schools as they are currently constructed are poorly designed to foster the experience of community. They are instead primarily aimed at positioning children to compete as best they can in a market society that offers little support or encouragement to those whose talents, dispositions, or backgrounds are viewed with disinterest or suspicion. If schools are to provide the support and guidance young people need to become responsible and engaged adults motivated by a concern for the common good, they will need to be reformulated in ways that counter the disintegrative impact of their present organizational and governance structures as well as their curricula. More than discourse about educational communities and shared visions will be needed to bring about this change.

Gregory A. Smith

Promising Directions: Lessons from Alternative Schools

Reasserting the link between communities and schools will at the outset require a reconceptualization of the educational goals that have resulted in the institutional structures and practices described in the preceding section. Instead of seeing schooling as a vehicle by which individuals can advance their own economic well-being, we need to reinvent an educational process that enables children to discover and cultivate their talents not for themselves alone but for the people who are touched by their lives. The acquisition of knowledge and skills needs to be framed in communal terms as an obligation by which one is able to support and advance the welfare of others. This is the role that education has traditionally played in premodern societies. In the past when children in Athabaskan villages learned to trap beaver or marten, tan hides and make parkas, smoke salmon and dry berries, and pass on the songs and dances of their people, they assured, as much as was humanly possible, the continued survival of the tribe. They mastered their culture in an effort to provide for both themselves and their neighbors. It is important to note that this process was not insensitive to the unique attributes of individuals. Skillful hunters, creative singers and storytellers, boatbuilders and netmakers, among others, were given the space to develop their own potential, but that potential was directed to the community rather than individual aggrandizement. Furthermore, without the opportunity to share talents within the group, the development of individuals would have become stripped of meaning and purpose, since it is within the context of that sharing that personal actions are imbued with value.

Once this link between the education of individual students and the communities to which they belong is clarified, then educators can begin to shape programs built on that relationship. Instead of extracting children from surrounding social environments, schools could strive to integrate children into richer and more varied encounters with the life of their community. Doing so, however, will require confronting the tension between the culture of the school and the culture of local communities that has been one of the salient characteristics of American education at least since the early 1900s (Waller, 1932/1967). Instead of ignoring or denigrating local culture, as has often been the case in schools serving nonmainstream students, teachers must strive to make that culture pivotal to students' learning activities. Crafting educational programs such as this, however, demands paying attention to traditions generally viewed by the school as peripheral rather than central to its primary educational activities. Although there is always the risk of parochialism in focusing too narrowly on the local or regional, this danger can be avoided if the local is studied in conjunction with the cultures of other regions.

There are multiple examples of educators who are now moving in this direction. The Foxfire project and its many offshoots are perhaps the most widely recognized. The strength of this approach lies in the way it has directed students to the richness of their own traditions and their own people. Carol Stumbo (1989) has written tellingly of the impact of her use of this approach in a small mining town in West Virginia. Students who had been minimally engaged by the school became aware of their own power as historians and storytellers after they began to view their parents and grandparents as people who were worth listening to rather than disregarding. One of the grave dangers of public schooling from its inception has been its tendency to lead children to neglect or even condemn the wisdom of their elders. This is a story which continues to be played out on a daily basis in rural Alaska. Schools that honor children's own culture by making it the focus of serious study do much to reverse the corrosive effect of a curriculum detached from their experience.

Two schools that have sought to overcome the division between the classroom and the home are the New Fratney School in Milwaukee, Wisconsin (chapter 2), and the Denali Elementary School in Fairbanks, Alaska (chapter 3). Much of their current work has evolved from a lively and sustained collaboration between educators, parents, and interested community members. At the New Fratney School in Milwaukee, teachers and parents have crafted an educational program that builds on the strengths, interests, and unique cultural backgrounds of its diverse students. One of the school's most striking features is a Spanish/English program in which all students receive instruction across the curriculum in Spanish and English. This has meant that students whose home language is Spanish are not at a disadvantage but instead have significant skills to offer to students for whom English is generally their first and only language. These children now actively turn to Spanish-speaking peers as they strive to acquire a second language. The school has also sought to create a multicultural curriculum that acknowledges in more than a superficial manner the cultural traditions of its various student groups. Rather than being disregarded, those traditions are made a focal point of the school's program in the same way that children's parents have been brought directly into the school's decision-making process rather than marginalized by it.

At the Denali School, this collaboration has led to the adoption of a new curricular focus that emphasizes allowing children to learn in school in the same way they learn at home, through a process of discovery. Part of this school's success has been tied to the manner in which educational activities spill beyond the school into projects like a community garden available to neighborhood families as well as the infusion of an ongoing stream of volunteers from the community into the school. At Denali as well, Alaska Native elders provide regular instruction in Athabaskan traditions and crafts to all students. In each of these schools, the wisdom of children's parents is no longer ignored; it shapes what happens.

Within the school itself, much can also be done to draw students into the behaviors and dispositions associated with community membership. Such "habits of the heart" do not develop by accident, something that has become only too apparent in our own society. Instead, they need to be cultivated with attention and care. Educators in a number of alternative public schools are now taking steps to do just this. Among their concerns are the creation of structures that help children experience mutual support and learn how to assume responsibility for their actions and the health of the social groups in which they live.

One school that has sought to self-consciously build community is the Alternative Community School in Ithaca, New York (chapter 4). Now close to twenty years old, ACS has developed a variety of means to draw its students into an experience of interconnectedness and interdependence with one another and their teachers. Through a combination of regular whole-school projects such as the building of a yurt retreat center and day-to-day structures that allow for more sustained adult-student relationships, teachers at this school have been able to create an institutional environment that directs all school members to what they have in common. In doing so, they have created a small functioning community that exemplifies much of what Dewey (1899/ 1959) believed schools must do in modern societies: provide opportunities for children to experience community membership within a contained environment before confronting the more disparate social relations of the broader society.

Much of the success of the Alternative Community School has depended on its size. The achievement of identity and purpose within a school becomes more difficult after it grows much beyond 400 students (Gregory and Smith, 1987; Meier, 1992). Past this number, establishing and maintaining the face-to-face relations upon which a deep sense of shared identity is based is inhibited. In fact, as public interest in the Alternative Community School has increased and its waiting list grown, rather than simply absorbing more students into one school, ACS is now planning a second sister program.

Also tied into the success of this and other alternative public schools is the way they provide students with an opportunity to work with a small group of teachers over an extended period of time. Rather than being run past a series of instructors whose names and faces are often forgotten, students work with teachers for several years. What is often forgotten in American schools is the close link between motivation and affective relations. Studies of at-risk youth have shown how their level of academic achievement often improves dramatically when they are placed with teachers who encourage the formation of more personal ties (Wehlage et al., 1989). By reducing the number of teachers students must get to know, it may also be possible to foster more of the interpersonal bonding that seems to underlie educational success.

In addition to cultivating interpersonal bonds between younger and older members of the school, the development of community also requires the formation of bonds among students. These student communities, however, must be distinguished from the student peer groups encountered in many schools. Most student peer groups tend to be fragmented and exclusionary; few direct their attention to the school community as a whole or the broader social environment in which it is embedded. In many respects, these groups stand in opposition to the competitive and isolating social relationships presented by most schools (Cusick, 1973; Willis, 1977). The creation of integrated and purposeful school communities requires the cultivation of more cooperative and supportive patterns of interaction among students. Setting aside the competitive nature of most classroom work and evaluation promises one route to the achievement of this end. Making students themselves responsible for the health of the broader school community is another.

At the Jefferson County Open School outside of Denver, Colorado (chapter 5), students are encouraged to develop this kind of awareness and responsibility by being drawn into the process of governing their school. This school holds weekly governance meetings during which students and staff make many of the institutional decisions normally reserved for administrators, including the hiring of new teachers. Students who wish to facilitate these meetings must enroll in a leadership class that provides training in group process skills essential for the management of this kind of decision making. Students, furthermore, are given the responsibility for planning the school's many trips to sites of educational interest across the United States. Routes, meals, and housing arrangements for fifteen or more people must be planned, again giving young people a chance to grapple with what it means to administer human endeavors. In such a situation, students are placed in positions where they must acknowledge the needs of an entire school and the desires of the diverse individuals within it. In doing so, they are required to think beyond their own or their own peer group's narrow perspective and consider their membership within a more extensive and inclusive social environment.

In addition to helping students become cognizant of their responsibility to others in the school community, educators in many alternative schools also ask their students to become much more responsible for the shaping of their own education. Such a process can be extraordinarily liberating when students realize that learning is not something that is done to them but is instead a vehicle for realizing their own goals and dreams. At the High School Redirection in Denver (chapter 6), a group of innovative educators sought to apply some of the curricular principles from the Jefferson County Open School to a school created for potential dropouts. Their four-year experiment, financed by a U.S. Department of Labor grant, reconnected students who had given up on schools to the potentialities of their own education. High School Redirection's curriculum focuses on the development of both character and intellect by asking students to fulfill a wide-ranging set of fourteen graduation expectations in areas such as knowledge of inner resources, caring for self and others, persistence/commitment, sense of history/political power/global awareness, and expressive arts. Students make many of their own curricular decisions and play an important role in the creation and even teaching of the school's offerings. Although the recipient of positive reviews from accrediting agencies and accolades from parents and students, High School Redirection was recently closed by the Denver Board of Education. Reopened under private auspices, it is continuing in its efforts to show students minimally touched by conventional schooling that they have the capacity and power to shape their own education in ways that foster both self-realization and service to the broader community.

Other schools have taken an even more direct approach to demonstrating the link between school and community. While focusing on the construction of highly supportive and communitarian school environments, educators in these institutions have extended learning to occupational settings outside the classroom. In doing so, they have done much to initiate students into membership in the communities they will join as adults. For young people who feel marginalized by mainstream society, such experiences can be very rewarding.

The Partnership Academies model in California exemplifies this approach. In these innovative vocational programs, students continue to take a full range of academic courses in their conventional school but are provided with ongoing opportunities to interact either in class or in the field with professionals in occupational areas such as medicine, media, banking, food processing, and electronics (Dayton et al., 1992). The Media Academy, in Oakland, California (described along with the Health Academy in chapter 7), is one of these academies. It enrolls students with a history of low academic achievement but an interest in media professions in a three-year program that prepares them for entry-level jobs or postsecondary training in this field. Students in the Media Academy have an opportunity to work closely with a small and supportive group of teachers and students over their high school careers. During this time they hone their skills as editors, reporters, video producers, or design artists both on school publications and in internship opportunities in local media establishments. In this process they learn to contribute their own efforts to a common product and find themselves excelling for rather than against one another (Wehlage et al., 1989).

The International High School in New York City (chapter 8) provides another example of a program that draws its students into an experience of community within the school and yet helps them make the transition to the larger community beyond it. This school enrolls a population of immigrant students all of whom have been in the United States for less than four years. Most do not speak English as their first language, and two-thirds come from families whose incomes are below the poverty level. For one trimester during each of their three years at the International High School, students venture into businesses and social service agencies where they work half days with adults who take the time to induct them into the world of work. What was foreign becomes familiar for most of these students, eighty-five percent of whom go on to college. As at the Peninsula Academies, learning is not circumscribed by the school; the school acts instead as a conduit through which students are given access to community experiences that otherwise might be beyond them.

It is important to recognize, however, that there is no guarantee that adopting a more communitarian orientation within schools or even bridging the gap between school and community will necessarily foster the deeper sense of civic responsibility and citizenship discussed earlier in this introduction. The tendency of Americans to create "lifestyle enclaves" (Bellah et al., 1985) remains strong. As Robert Everhart (1985, 1988, and chapter 9 in this volume) has persistently warned, this form of inward turning can infect the efforts of progressive educators. If we are to help our children break out of this tendency, we must guard against the development of educational environments characterized by self-absorption or self-congratulation. Teachers must instead help their students make connections between the way in which various commonly accepted factors in our shared economic and political lives serve to marginalize or give privileges to certain members of our communities. Responsible community participation requires that such processes be illuminated and challenged. Community building from this perspective must be a political as well as a social process, a process that involves resisting and overcoming practices that threaten the common good.

Although examples of this more critical and active form of education are not common, educators in numerous schools around the country are demonstrating what can happen when students are encouraged to become participants in the making of political, economic, and cultural decisions in their communities rather than remain mere observers. In her book *Kid's Guide to Social Action* (1991), Barbara Lewis recounts the work of a class of elementary school students in Utah. During a unit on the environment, one boy noted that he passed by a lot that contained rusting barrels on his way to school. Not long afterward, the class took a field trip to the lot and observed that several barrels were leaking. Concerned, they sought the identities of the owners of the property and quickly found themselves embroiled in a political controversy. Unintimidated, they approached sympathetic members of the Utah assembly and helped frame legislation that resulted in more stringent regulations governing waste disposal. In this instance, students were provided with experiences that demonstrated the power of concerned and persistent citizens to take steps to improve their own communities.

Student energy and intelligence can also be directed to the realm of economics and community development. Educators in a number of schools throughout the United States are now striving to involve their students in projects aimed at strengthening the local economic base and generating occupational opportunities for young adults once they have graduated from high school (chapter 10). Although few of these projects are the focus of an entire school, they are indicative of the way in which school/community interaction can lead to the creation of entrepreneurial activities attractive enough to convince students to remain in their home town. Schools that play this role can contribute to the regeneration of communities undercut by broad economic trends in the 1970s and 1980s that have resulted in the migration of jobs to selected urban and suburban centers or out of the United States altogether. In schools where these programs have been initiated, teachers and students have begun to give back to the community the support the community has shared with them. When this happens, the experience of interdependence that is at the heart of communal membership is played out in the very relationship between school and community. Both give and take from one another. Involvement in programs predicated on this ideal helps students embody in their present experience what it means to be full and participating citizens able and willing to reconstruct the socioeconomic and cultural contexts in which they lives their lives.

Conclusion

By providing a place where children are given the experience of communal membership and are helped to understand in a personal rather than abstract way their relationship to communities beyond the classroom, educators can begin to overcome the sense of alienation and loss that too often undermines student learning. In the study of programs for at-risk youth referred to earlier, my fellow researchers and myself found that this experience of membership often made the difference between school success and failure (Wehlage et al., 1989). A similar experience of membership is encountered in many alternative schools and may be one of the primary contributing factors to their success.

Over and beyond the impact that community building within schools or the strengthening of ties between school and community has on the lives of individual students, however, is the potential effect of this process on the quality of our common life. Although it would be incorrect to assume that most alternative public schools actively seek to address this issue (Raywid, chapter 1, this volume), practices encountered in many of them promise to nurture a level of communal membership, civic awareness, and activism too often ignored in conventional schools. For many children growing up in today's society, the possibility of community seems farfetched, something from another era not realizable in their own. This was the case with many students I encountered during my years at the John Woolman School. Months of living closely with their peers and a set of caring adults, however, altered their perspective, and many began to realize that they could be participants in the shaping of healthy communities.

Gregory A. Smith

One might hope that comparable alternative schools are generating a similar sense of possibility. In doing so, they may be helping children understand their connections to one another and the broader society in ways that will lead to informed and committed public involvement. Although there remain ongoing questions about the degree to which schools can influence broader social movements rather than simply reflect them, in a period when the state and the gigantic commercial institutions that dominate our lives have become less and less able— and in some instances increasingly less inclined—to foster the well-being of communities, it may be incumbent upon people at the local level to once more assume responsibility and power over their economic and political lives. Such efforts are almost certain to inspire resistance or derision, something that has been too common an experience among those who attempt to create alternative schools.

Persisting in such activities, however, seems imperative if we are to build a society in which our children will be able to make and act upon the decisions needed to sustain the social and natural environments upon which our lives depend. Doing so will require that we help them develop the inclination to join with others to accomplish these tasks. It will also require a familiarity with the decision-making processes and obligations that undergird the activities of well-functioning communities. Schools in which students have the opportunity to learn these lessons and build communal ties may in the end do more than work for themselves. They will be working for us all.

References

Bellah, R., Madsen, R., Sullivan, W., Swidler, A., and Tipton, S. (1985). *Habits of the heart: Individualism and commitment in American life*. New York: Harper and Row.

Bellah, R., Madsen, R., Sullivan, W., Swidler, A., and Tipton, S. (1991). *The good society*. New York: Vintage.

Berger, P., and Neuhaus, R. (1977). *To empower people: The role of mediating structures in public policy*. Washington, D.C.: American Enterprise Institute for Policy Research.

Bernstein, B. (1975). *Class, codes, and control, Volume 3: Towards a theory of educational transmission*. London: Routledge and Kegan Paul.

Brandt, R. (1992). On building learning communities: A conversation with Hank Levin. *Educational Leadership* 50 (1): 19–23.

Bronfenbrenner, U. (1986). Alienation and the four worlds of childhood. *Phi Delta Kappan* (February): 430–36.

Cuban, L. (1992). What happens to reforms that last? The case of the junior high school. *American Educational Research Journal* 29 (2): 227–52.

Cusick, P. (1973). *Inside high school: The student's world.* New York: Holt, Rinehart, and Winston.

Dayton, C., Raby, M., Stern, D., and Weisberg, A. (1992). California Partnership Academies: Remembering the "forgotten half." *Phi Delta Kappan* (March): 539–45.

Dewey, J. (1899/1959). *School and society.* In M. Dworkin (ed.), *Dewey on education: Selections.* New York: Teachers College Press. 33–90.

Dewey, J. (1927). *The public and its problems.* New York: Holt and Company.

Dreeben, R. (1968). *On what is learned in school.* Reading, Mass.: Addison-Wesley.

Edmonds, R. (1982). Programs of school improvement: An overview. *Educational Leadership* 40 (3): 4–12.

Everhart, R. (1985). On feeling good about oneself: Practical ideology in schools of choice. *Sociology of Education* 58 (October): 251–60.

Everhart, R. (1988). *Practical ideology and symbolic community: An ethnography of schools of choice.* London: Falmer.

Gans, H. (1962). *The urban villagers: Group and class in the life of Italian-Americans.* New York: Free Press.

Gans, H. (1988). *Middle-American individualism: The future of liberal democracy.* New York: Free Press.

Gregory, T., and Smith, G. (1987). *High schools as communities: The small school reconsidered.* Bloomington, Ind.: Phi Delta Kappa.

Hacker, A. (1992). *Two nations: Black and white, separate, hostile, unequal.* New York: Scribner.

Hostetler, J., and Huntington, G. (1971). *Children in Amish society: Socialization and community education.* New York: Holt, Rinehart, and Winston.

Jackson, P. (1968). *Life in classrooms.* New York: Holt, Rinehart, and Winston.

Ketcham, R. (1987). *Individualism and public life: A modern dilemma.* Oxford: Basil Blackwell.

Lewis, B. (1991). *Kid's guide to social action: How to solve the social problems you choose and turn creative thinking into positive action.* Minneapolis: Free Spirit Publishing.

Gregory A. Smith

Lieberman, A. (1992). The meaning of scholarly activity and the building of community. *Educational Researcher* 21 (6): 5–12.

MacPherson, C. B. (1962). *The political theory of possessive individualism: Hobbes to Locke.* London: Oxford University Press.

Meier, D. (1992). Reinventing teaching. *Teachers College Record* 93 (4): 594–609.

Parsons, T. (1959). The school class as a social system: Some of its functions in American society. *Harvard Educational Review* 29 (4): 297–318.

Sarason, S. (1982). *The culture of the school and the problem of change.* Boston: Allyn and Bacon.

Scherer, M. (1992). On savage inequalities: A conversation with Jonathan Kozol. *Educational Leadership* 50 (4): 4–9.

Sennett, R., and Cobb, J. (1972). *The hidden injuries of class.* New York: Knopf.

Sizer, T. (1992). *Horace's schools.* Boston: Houghton Mifflin.

Stumbo, C. (1989). Teachers and teaching. *Harvard Educational Review* 59 (1): 87–97.

Waller, W. (1932/1967). *The sociology of teaching.* New York: John Wiley and Sons.

Wehlage, G., Rutter, R., Smith, G., Lesko, N., and Fernandez, R. (1989). *Reducing the risk: Schools as communities of support.* Philadelphia: Falmer.

Willis, P. (1977). *Learning to labor: How working class kids get working class jobs.* New York: Columbia University Press.

1

Community: An Alternative School Accomplishment

Mary Anne Raywid

Introduction

One of my first impressions of alternative schools—and surely one of the reasons they have fascinated me—is the strong sense of community that prevails within them. The effective schools literature familiarized us with the importance of school community, and attempts to generate it are not uncommon now. But when I first began looking at alternative schools, in the 1970s, such a notion was alien to conventional school preoccupations and would probably have been dismissed as irrelevant, if not inappropriate. Yet a sense of something akin to community was one of the first things that struck me about alternative schools—and it became a central feature of what I was soon calling the "magic" of alternatives. It often seemed palpable from the moment one stepped inside the school door—reflected in the sounds and appearance of the place and expressed even more directly in the words and behavior of students and teachers.

I recall my astonishment on one of my first encounters with an alternative school, when a boy stepped up to me in an otherwise empty hall, smiled a greeting, and asked, "Can I help you?" Adults can't always expect such friendliness from adolescents, and certainly not in schools, and I was amazed. It took me some time to understand such a display of the sort of hospitality with which an adult might greet a

Mary Anne Raywid

guest. I had first to come to know the genre well enough to be able to say to myself, "Well, why not? He *owns* the place."

Words such as *ownership* and *commitment, caring, respect, trust,* and *family* have all been linked with the idea of community, as have *culture* and *climate* and *ethos*. There have now been several attempts to explore the concept of community directly in its application to schools (Lehman, 1991; Raywid, 1988) and to identify related attributes of schools (Bryk and Driscoll, 1988; Gregory and Smith, 1987). I want, in this chapter, to extend both of those discussions, supplementing the meaning of community as it applies to schools and identifying it in various types of alternative schools.

We might begin by noting that unlike *culture* or *climate*, as these terms have been applied to schools, *community* is not evident in all schools. It can be said that every school has a culture and a climate, be these positive or negative, strong or weak. But not every school has (or is a) community. Thus, *community* is a term denoting an accomplishment, rather than exclusively a descriptive term—and with the exceptions of *culture* and *climate*, all the other terms cited above as frequently associated with community *(caring, ownership, commitment, respect, trust)* are also achievement terms: To apply them is to assert that some schools have managed to arrive at them even though others have not.

And just what is the accomplishment? To assert that a school is a community is to suggest that within it one finds genuine interest in and acknowledgment of all the individuals involved by other individuals—students as well as teachers, administrators, and staff. Awareness of and responsiveness to others' happiness or sorrow, growth, accomplishments, and misfortunes is an integral part of daily life in the school that is a community. Such a school is a place where those involved bring their psyches, a place they can be and express themselves and find companionship, understanding, and support. It is thus a place they find attractive: It is *theirs*, not just an institution, but a place in which to live and find meaning. What is more, those involved in such a school community share an awareness and self-consciousness of these characteristics.

But community is not a "seen one, seen 'em all" matter, nor an all-or-nothing proposition. Communities come in varying degrees of expansion, development, and strength, and they can be as varied as the alternative schools that have been so successful in spawning them. The particular type of community a school generates reflects that school's "personality" and culture. Some foster a sense of closeness and interdependence and mutual support, while others pursue that direction more tentatively, and yet others seem bound extensively by a commitment to the right of each to march to a different drummer. Some alternatives appear to be communities dedicated to the larger public interest—to alleviating sociopolitical ills and transforming their local community—while others are more explicitly attuned to developing the group's immediate members and attending to their situations.

Alternative school communities differ also as to predominant traits, in ways quite parallel to those in which individuals differ: In some, for instance, humor appears a continuing central feature, while compassion has more prominence within another alternative school community, and yet another seems more occupied with individual or civic responsibility.

Alternative School Types

Alternative schools are not, of course, all of a piece. In fact, many of them are explicitly committed to ideas obligating their uniqueness, e.g., ideas like responsiveness to the immediate student population and a commitment to school-to-school diversity. Yet it is possible to discern types. Several years ago I identified three, on the basis of differences in how their students come to be there, what they expect of the alternative, what their teachers expect of them, and the kind of school ambiances that result.

Type I alternatives appear to be the heirs of many of the 1960s and 1970s alternatives, established in response to demands that education be rendered "more humane, more responsive, more challenging, and more compelling for all involved" (Raywid, 1990). Such programs sometimes enroll able and highly accomplished students, distinguished perhaps by a determination to make their schooling a meaningful experience. Sometimes the youngsters attracted are among the highest achievers, with strong leadership ability. For other students, dissatisfaction with previous school experience has limited prior accomplishment. In either event, Type I alternatives are likely to be educationally demanding programs, drawing students across ability and accomplishment levels, biased perhaps in the direction of a willingness among their students to assume more responsibility for their own education.

In contrast, Type II alternatives are programs openly and explicitly designed for the worst of students. They have aptly been called "soft jails" since their students typically are "sentenced" to them, often as one final opportunity before expulsion. In a number of places, it is

25

understood that those sent to Type II alternatives may be permitted to return to the regular program as a reward for good behavior.

Type III alternative schools are quite different in that they are nonpunitive, but designed for youngsters presenting special needs—for example, students requiring remediation, or in emotional difficulty, or who are pregnant or substance abusers. Given the current interest in preventing the at-risk population from dropping out, Type III alternative programs are today probably multiplying faster than either of the other two varieties.

Now one might reasonably expect the ambiances or general climates among the three types of alternative schools to differ considerably, with the punitive orientation of Type II programs contrasting strongly with the other two. Such differences might in turn be expected to yield and sustain quite different sorts of communities. No one arrives by choice at a Type II alternative program, and to be sent there is something of a disgrace. The expectations as to ambiance following from such circumstances would be completely fulfilled in many Type II alternatives, where one finds a stern, relentless imposition of highly structured behavioral demands. Yet other Type II programs appear rather different. What one often finds is that within them the punitive orientation defining the Type II alternative has given way to a considerably more positive and compassionate stance on the part of its staff. The result is that it becomes in effect a Type III program.

This is sometimes a matter of evolutionary change and sometimes just a matter of the difference between the authorities who have mandated a program and the sorts of people chosen to implement it. In some such programs (though certainly not in all Type II alternatives), a staff may deliberately incline toward a rehabilitation approach in preference to a punitive one. Under such circumstances, the experience of students does not resemble that of prison inmates. Rather, many feel they have been "expelled to a friendlier place," as one study of such programs expressed it (Gold and Mann, 1984).

In such a situation, the general climate of a Type II alternative may bear a lot of resemblance to that of a Type III program, with a fair amount of support and nurturance extended by the faculty in both situations. The two also share other important features. First, both Type II and Type III alternatives enroll youngsters seen by the regular school as losers. Whether for moral reasons, reasons of limited capacity, or other handicap (personal, financial, familial, or ethnic), these are students whose past performance makes subsequent school success unlikely. Often the youngsters involved have accepted the perception that they are losers and internalized the message. Thus, low self-esteem and low estimates of their own ability to succeed are shared by a number of the youngsters enrolled in both Type II and Type III alternative schools. This may actually stimulate the forging of strong bonds between them—but it also disposes them to see themselves as a community of losers and one denigrated by others. What is more, like their students, Type III as well as Type II alternative school faculties are inclined to see their charges this way too.

Such an orientation on the part of the teachers involved is likely to assure several far-reaching effects. First, it will very probably depress teacher expectations and hence, student accomplishment. Moreover, it virtually guarantees that teachers will locate the reasons for failure within the students rather than within the school. The consequence of such a premise—often deeply buried and taken for granted—is not only a tolerance of failure but an avoidance of exploring school changes of the only sort of magnitude that could matter: If it is assumed that the problems lie within the students, then changes in school organization and program and practice are not the solution and probably can't matter very much. An evaluation of a massive, multi–million dollar effort to restructure schools for at-risk youngsters—a *failed* effort—recently summarized the result of such an assumption this way: "The most serious limitations of the [failed] interventions was their implicit assumption that the problem was to find ways of altering students rather than the institution" (Wehlage et al., 1992:91).

A final commonality between Type II and Type III alternatives tends to yield similar ambiances and communities in the two. It is perhaps the most crucial difference between Type I communities on the one hand, and Type III on the other. Teachers in the latter are likely to see their charges as weaker than other students in some important way and as needing more help and direction than other youngsters—an orientation disposing them toward a *clinical* posture in the way they treat their charges. However sympathetic and compassionate they may be, their gestalt tends to be professional, rather than communal. It assumes that they, the teachers, remain primarily the professionals engineering the development of their students, rather than first and foremost human beings accompanying and guiding the young in their progress toward competent maturity.

The difference is sufficiently fundamental and pervasive in our society to warrant a bit more detail. Perhaps it can better be displayed in an analogy, shifting the scene from school settings for at-risk youngsters to professional preparation programs. Two sets of recommendations for preparing teachers were identified by one analyst as the contrast between people who saw themselves as "colonizers" of prospective teachers, and those who saw their role instead as one of inviting would-be teachers into "conversation" (Johnson, 1990). The first orientation calls for imposition justified on the basis of some presumed superiority (power, competence, knowledge), the second for joint examination, discussion, and illumination. The first orientation is a carryover from conventional schools where teachers see themselves as professionals responsible for the enlightenment and development of the immature. The second orientation is more communal in its downplaying of status and power differences in favor of an invitational and collaborative stance.

One crucial difference in the results of the two is that the first approach perpetuates two cultures in the school, adult and student, or professional and client. Even though the adult professionals are kindly and benevolent, they are nevertheless a separate group. The persistence of the two cultures is likely to produce an adversarial situation or at least conflictual occasions. The communitarian orientation, by contrast, does not heavily emphasize generational and knowledge contrasts and is thus less generative of subcultures organized around these differences.

In sum, then, there are likely to be several key differences in the ambiance and communities of the three types of alternative schools: Since the Type II alternative is modeled on jail or reform school, it stands in striking contrast to Types I and III. The student subculture in a Type II alternative may reflect some sort of community, but the adult or official culture is stern and punitive. Both Type I and Type III ambiances appear positive and invitational by contrast. The therapeutic model reflected in Type III programs is considerably more positive than a reform school model, but it is still impositional and leaves intact a dominant adult or "official" school culture on the one hand, and a separate student subculture on the other. Type I alternatives often display a single culture linking the adult and student groups within the schools. When such an accomplishment occurs, it seems to emerge within a context that is invitational, as opposed to clinical and impositional.

Since it is the Type I alternatives, then, that are most likely to arrive at the accomplishment that community represents, much of what follows pertains more to Type I alternatives than to Type II or Type III.

Community

Sociologist Ferdinand Tönnies long ago contrasted the two kinds of social groupings observable in modern society, identifying them as

28

gemeinschaft communities and gesellschaft, which are not really communities at all (Loomis, 1963). The members of gemeinschaft communities have emotional ties to one another and are linked by shared values and beliefs, recurring interaction with one another, mutual dependence, and a shared commitment to a particular place—a neighborhood or town or area. What is more, they are conscious of a spiritual bond between.

Gesellschaft groupings, by contrast, have no such feelings of kinship. Tönníes associated gesellschaft groupings with the world of business and government, the public world, as opposed to the community groupings of family and friends, and he correctly predicted their dominance in urban society. Gesellschaft pseudocommunities are assemblages brought into existence by contract rather than feelings of kinship—for example, the people employed by a corporation or who go to the same resort.

The interactions of gesellschaft members are far more superficial and fleeting, and they are largely instrumental—occurring, that is, in order to accomplish particular purposes and essentially limited to such purposes. The separate and individual interests of the parties involved continue to dominate gesellschaft interactions, and in the absence of loyalties or sentiments to determine social patterns, rules and contracts and conventions are adopted to maintain the peace.

Charles Cooley, another early sociologist, drew a related distinction in contrasting what he called "primary" and "secondary" associations: primary associations are relationships where the parties' interest in each other is broad, extending across multiple lines of activity (Cooley, 1937). A friend or family member, for example, is interested in an individual as a person—in her past and future, in her work and hobbies and worries and pleasures. Secondary associations, on the other hand, are marked by their limited purposes, and in such relationships—presumed to be temporary—interest is confined to the instrumental purposes bringing the parties together. Thus, the connection between two people who work in the same office, or between shoppers and checkout counter clerks, are secondary associations.

Tönnies and Cooley correctly foresaw that the lives of individuals in industrial societies would consist increasingly of the secondary associations of gesellschaft noncommunities. Both thinkers reacted wistfully to the passing of community and its primary associations. At the same time, however, a parallel development was being welcomed and recommended for adoption as the way to organize our burgeoning public life in the interest of both fairness and effectiveness. It was a system designed to assure that individuals were employed by virtue of what they knew, not whom they knew or who their fathers were, and that those most knowledgeable made the decisions that workers were held accountable for executing. The name of the system was bureaucracy, and it was urged by reformers of the early twentieth century as the best way to end the corrupting influences of political patronage as well as the best way to assure effective performance and productivity.

It was not long before these developments began to influence schools. During the early years of the current century, there was an extensive effort, particularly within cities, to install the new organizational pattern as the way to operate education. Thus, many reform-minded, forward-looking school officials moved toward bureaucracy. The move had consequences that today are very apparent. For our purposes several of them are crucial. First, the bureaucratic emphasis on appointment by competence brought impersonality as well as fairness. Its insistence on narrow, highly specific role definitions and restrictions brought stability by assuring that school wouldn't fall apart when a key staff member left. But it also brought fragmentation as the educational task was divided up, assigning teachers to different grade levels and subjects, and it reduced the role of individual talent and interest and personality in determining a particular teacher's work. And finally, the recommended shift from a social order determined by loyalty and sentiments and shared assumptions to one controlled by explicit, written rules and regulations was of enormous consequence.

As bureaucracy gradually became the standard organizational structure for schools—in suburban and rural areas that wanted to be part of the reform as well as in urban districts—it determined the way in which teachers would relate to one another. The pattern became that of secondary associations in gesellschaft settings. In some places, attempts to apply scientific management to school administration brought similar effects to classrooms and the way they operated.

By and large, however, the transformation of *classrooms* to secondary associations and gesellschaft noncommunities occurred indirectly and as a by-product of organizing school employees according to such a pattern. At least initially, bureaucracy was seen as a way of organizing employees—the producers—not the recipients of the services being delivered. Gradually, however, bureaucracy's norms, and the norms of professionalism that began to influence teachers' aspirations and behavior, began to affect the ways teachers related to students and students were expected to relate to one another. It was recognized that young children need personalized environments and nurturance, but it was evidently assumed that they outgrew that fairly quickly. By the time they were twelve and ready for the seventh grade, we put them into institutions that virtually guaranteed the depersonalization and essential disconnectedness that are the hallmarks of secondary associations and gesellschaft. By assigning each youngster to seven or eight different classrooms each day, each with a different teacher and possibly with different classmates as well, and by assigning each teacher 150 or even more students a day, it was virtually guaranteed that primary associations could not be cultivated and gemeinschaft could not develop.

From the vantage point of hindsight, it appears that youngsters were able to tolerate daytimes of gesellschaft because there were afternoons and evenings and weekends and holidays of gemeinschaft. Human beings, it is widely held, need close association and connection with other human beings (Bronfenbrenner, 1980; Wachtel, 1989). So long as such connection was provided outside of school, youngsters could do without it inside. Mid-century and the changes tied to World War II and its aftermath are generally thought to mark the turning point in that regard. The concentration of the nation's population in metropolitan areas, the decline of the extended family, employment patterns, mobility patterns—all of these conditions led to the decline and disappearance of gemeinschaft from the lives of many youngsters. This, say many, makes it doubly important that students experience it in schools.

Now much of this development was evident and being discussed in the 1960s and early 1970s when alternative schools began. Indeed, some who were directly associated with alternative education made it quite explicit. Social commentator and philosopher Paul Goodman produced several books reflecting the themes expressed here. One that he titled *People or Personnel* (1963) focuses precisely on the human effects of bureaucracy, secondary associations, and gesellschaft. And he was not alone. The protest against bureaucracy, so familiar a part of the current scene, really began in the 1960s, when a lot of social criticism began to focus on what were called its dehumanizing tendencies. A considerable amount of that criticism was directed explicitly at schools, and one prominent theme of the student protest of the 1960s was precisely the impersonality of large schools and universities. One of the banners of the era, in fact, sarcastically mimicked the message borne on computer cards and proclaimed, "I am a human being. Please do not bend, fold, spindle, or mutilate."

Not surprisingly, then, community became a prominent theme in a number of early alternative schools. Outsiders were sometimes critical of such a preoccupation, and there were charges of a "touchy-feely" ambiance which was both saccharine and wasteful of school time. Whether it was alternatives or critics' minds that changed, such criti-

31

cisms have become far more infrequent since the effective schools literature began to emerge.

Beginning in 1979 with the publication of *Fifteen Thousand Hours* (Rutter et al., 1979), research began to indicate that school climate and shared values and consensus as to fundamental direction are centrally important to school effectiveness. As Rutter and his colleagues concluded, "the style and quality of life at school was having a relatively pervasive effect on children's behavior" (Rutter et al., 1979: 183), and hence on their performance and achievement. Such questions led quite naturally to the matter of whether, and what kind of, communities obtained in schools.

Qualities of Alternative School Communities

The communities that seem to thrive in alternative schools appear strikingly different from those of other schools (Erickson, 1989; Erickson et al., 1982). This seems particularly evident in those we have identified as Type I alternatives. Though clearly differing one from another, most seem to share a number of qualities. The following pages attempt to identify those qualities. Subsequently, there is a brief attempt to identify the conditions that produce them.

Respect

One of the most noticeable qualities of the gemeinschaft community in alternative schools is that of respect. The degree of respect shown alternative school teachers by their students is not usually found in other schools. It appears based, however, not on respect for the office but for the individual. A teacher, then, must earn the respect of students. A major requirement for doing so appears to be treating *them* with respect.

Alternative school students frequently respond to questions about what is special about their schools by saying that they are treated with respect there—a situation they then often contrast with their previous schools.

Adolescents identify the word *respect* with the word *caring*, explaining a noncaring school as one lacking in respect for its students.

The two are not synonymous, but respect may be the foundation of caring. As manifested in alternatives, it seems to consist in a willingness (1) to take an individual seriously, and (2) to sustain authentic courtesy in exchanges.

To take another human being seriously is to be willing to hear what she has to say, even if her position and agenda are at odds with one's own. It is also to reflect some degree of concern with that individual's current psychological state—how she perceives her current situation and how she feels about it. This calls for an openness to what is presently on a youngster's mind and a receptivity to hearing her present understanding of a problem or situation that are not always present in teacher interactions with students. Respect does not require that a youngster's wishes prevail. It does mean that her wishes must be held germane, important, and deserving to be heard.

Respect also demands sustained and authentic courtesy, which is more than a matter of superficial civility. It requires foregoing that sort of rank-pulling that enables teachers, however subtly, to convey doubts about a student's integrity, capacity, goodwill, or essential decency. When adults interact this way with their own peers, they recognize that they are acting discourteously. To do so with students is to take advantage of an unequal power distribution: the student's situation is such that a response in kind represents impertinence and insubordination. Thus, he is put in a position where he must choose between punishable behavior and his own dignity. Authentic courtesy would never demand such a choice. The acknowledgment and preservation intact of a student's dignity, under all circumstances, is what youngsters appear to mean by respect.

Joe Nathan, a longtime alternative school teacher before becoming a national spokesman for school choice, dramatizes the message with a story he tells frequently about a youngster named David who responded to a teacher's collaring and shouted, nose-to-nose demands that he remove his hat by leveling the teacher. According to Joe, once enrolled in an alternative school where he was treated differently, David became a model citizen.

Caring

The quality of caring is also ubiquitous in alternative schools. It is related to but differs from respect. Whereas no teacher who denies students respect is ever likely to be known as a caring teacher, caring goes further and requires more. Respect is something extended to everybody, as due all, and it is passive, a quality of the response made to youngsters' words and behavior. Caring differs: it is both particularistic and proactive. It is particularistic in that it is deliberately extended *differentially* to people, specifically acknowledging and addressing their uniqueness, and it is proactive rather than expressed only as a response. To care is to reach out, to initiate positive interaction rather than waiting for the other to move. This kind of recognition of children as individuals and reaching out to their particularity are prominent in what youngsters seem to mean as they speak of teachers who care. It goes without saying, of course, that the message conveyed in reaching out is of positive affect—support, approval, appreciation, regard, admiration, concern, fondness. Personal interactions that convey caring are abundant in alternative schools.

One sort of manifestation can be seen in a recent issue of one alternative school's newsletter. The author—the school's director—describes a set of skills taught to students and recommends them for parents also. They relate to what he calls "active listening," which consists of several components: focusing, as to eye contact, body language, responses; drawing out, which consists of showing we are tuned in by encouraging, questioning, restating; and acceptance, or "trying to show the speaker that we really want to understand even if we don't agree. . . . We want to walk in his or her shoes, feel what the person feels, experience the world that the speaker inhabits" (Abbott, 1992). The message details quite a sound implementation plan for what Nel Noddings calls "engagement" and identifies as a hallmark of caring in her well-known work (1984).

Caring also manifests itself in the extent to which alternative schools manage to personalize learning and other activities that are often handled in quite impersonal ways. For instance, at the graduation ceremonies of one alternative school, each candidate is presented individually by his or her advisor, who describes something of the talents and accomplishments of that individual. At another school, each graduate is presented by a fellow student, who offers a brief statement about the student before presenting a diploma. Atypical as they may appear, such practices are not unusual in schools where caring is valued as something to be taught and learned. Alternative schools, remember, are gemeinschaft communities that have deliberately rejected the impersonality of large bureaucratic institutions. The result is that they have built in the practices and arrangements which make possible the nurturance and expression of caring.

Inclusiveness

A third quality of alternative school communities is inclusiveness. Alternatives are not cliquish, and in fact there are continual attempts to make sure each participant is drawn into the circle and none are allowed to remain outsiders. It is difficult for any individual to remain on the fringes, either physically or psychically, since invitations will be proffered and concern expressed about hangers back. The carefully nurtured sense of responsibility for one another makes it not only permissible but obligatory for each individual to reach out to fellow members of the community if any appear in difficulty.

Such bonds are not too extraordinary among youngsters, especially among teenagers. And research suggests that among some groups of teachers, the ties of primary associations are evident—particularly in private schools, and more often in small public elementary schools than in high schools. But given the chasm typically separating adults and adolescents, what is somewhat unique is a communal inclusiveness that incorporates both staff and students. James Coleman noted some years ago that schools typically have at least two cultures: the adult culture of the staff that is the school's official culture, and the student subculture which usually consists of beliefs and values quite foreign to those of the official school culture (Coleman, 1961). In fact, the subculture typically stands in adversarial relation to the adult culture and can oppose it at virtually every turn. The unusual thing about alternative schools is not that the adult and student cultures are harmonious and compatible but that there appears to be only a single culture. That is, the adults have managed to persuade the youngsters of the veracity of their assumptions and the worth of their values. Thus, fundamental disagreements are fewer, and conflicts rarely find the teachers pitted against the students. When struggles occur, the alignments are otherwise and hence less likely to endure than adult-student splits might prove.

Such coherence is no accident, and it emerges from a variety of arrangements and practices. For instance, the usual physical divisions between staff and students are not part of most alternative schools. There is typically no separate teachers' lunchroom nor teachers' lounge, and teachers and students relax together and eat together as well as work together. There is often no separate teachers' meeting room and no prohibition against students sitting in on teachers' meetings. Although it may be rare for any students to endure a full meeting, being in the room for parts of one—or moving in and out of the room while the meeting is taking place—is a common occurrence. There is, in short, a pervasive tendency toward inclusion in preference to the exclusion of anyone, extending to groups as well as to individuals and manifested in alternative schools through various arrangements and practices.

Trust

Yet another prominent quality of alternative school communities is trust. Members of the community trust one another and are thus willing to disclose themselves and their work to their colleagues to a degree that appears extraordinary. The trust walks and rappelling that organizational developers use with adults as a means of team building are activities that many alternatives sponsor for their students. They are both symbol of and metaphor for the kind of mutual trust that is engendered as one individual quite explicitly places his or her physical safety in the hands of another.

To cite two examples from Urban Academy, an alternative school in New York: Not long ago, I watched two teachers vie with one another in a faculty meeting to describe the new courses they were teaching (time preventing both of them from doing so on that afternoon). The contest appeared entirely friendly and ended quickly when one deferred to the other, but the remarkable thing was that this was something both really wanted to do. Elsewhere, the presentations would have occurred only if required, or perhaps have been perfunctory or truncated in response to the political risk involved or the criticism that could ensue or the narrowed prerogatives that could come from exposure. But when questioned separately afterward, both of the teachers who had wanted to describe their work reported that they wanted to do so because they fully expected the occasion to yield them important, highly valuable feedback. Such an expectation suggests several kinds of trust: certainly in the goodwill and general supportiveness of colleagues and also in their professional competence and capacity to be of assistance. But it also suggests a different sort of trust: in the use of power and authority in such fashion as to attach minimal risks to personal exposure. Thus, exposure is far more likely to yield benefits than high costs.

A second example suggests how a somewhat different kind of trust is sustained, and why students come to understand that the school is a place where they and their interests will be protected if need be. I was surprised one day at Urban Academy to hear Herb, the director, summon a student from the hall in uncharacteristically angry tones. There followed a brief exchange in which Herb was obviously heated and issuing orders. Afterward, he told me that the boy had passed another calling him a "Goddam faggot," not heatedly or in anger, but with the casual contempt adolescents sometimes display. Herb was not disturbed by the swearing—accepted as a fairly standard feature of adolescent speech—but the "faggot" incensed him. He told the boy, "Look, this is a small group and all of us are aware of others' sexual preferences—and you are not going to taunt him with that any more than we would let you sneer at him for being fat or slow or Jewish or anything else that may happen to bug you." The taunter had walked away without responding, and it was impossible to assess the effect of Herb's obviously angry statement. The boy could have no doubts, however, about the school's commitment to maintaining an environment in which one person could trust another.

Empowerment

A fifth quality common to the community found in Type I alternative schools is a sense of empowerment or potency within the school. Interestingly, even in alternatives that their teachers describe as rather highly structured, students sometimes report a strong sense of efficacy and empowerment. Students feel that they will be taken seriously and that their feelings count, since there will be a serious attempt to come to grips with their concerns. Given the widely shared conviction in many schools that student desires are considered irrelevant, this is a considerable accomplishment. How does it happen?

Many of the early alternatives sought to empower students by fashioning themselves as participatory democracies in which all members of the school community had a direct voice in decision making and voted on issues. This town meeting form of empowerment proved time-consuming, and it sometimes failed when particular youngsters consistently proved influential by virtue of fluency, sheer tenacity, or otherwise, while others did not. Larger schools sometimes attempted empowerment through the machinery of representative democracy instead, but this arrangement inevitably leaves the bulk of the student body as noninvolved nonparticipants. Both political models satisfied some people that enfranchisement does not assure empowerment, because to have a vote is not necessarily to command very much influence.

Thus, some alternatives abandoned a political model of decision making altogether, in favor of one that is more reflective of gemeinschaft. The result was to look less to formal machinery as a guarantee for empowering each member of the community and more to other ways of doing so. One such way is to seek genuine agreement on major issues to be resolved. This is often pursued by examining such an issue in groupings of various sizes and compositions before the matter comes up for all-school consideration. This is the procedure at University Heights High School, Bronx, New York, where all parties agree there has been only one instance in the school's six-year history when the principal has overridden a consensual decision reached by students and staff.

Another way is to simply invite decision making by those who care enough to remain involved. This is the pattern of the Village School in Great Neck, New York, where decisions are made in weekly lunchtime sessions attended by all members of the community who wish to come, teachers as well as students. Those entitled to vote consist of all who attended the immediately previous meeting. Over the years, the school has found that individual patterns of participation shift according to the issues being discussed. It is an arrangement less conducive to the emergence of a continuing group of influentials than are participatory or representative governments. An arrangement favoring a fluid and self-determining group of decision makers is one way of respecting the concerns of community members, who may very well feel strongly about one issue and want to be heard and to vote on it, while not being as moved to do so on another set of issues.

A positive feature of this and other empowerment measures that appear more gemeinschaft than gesellschaft is that they provide a way to respond to the intensity of feelings on an issue. In allotting one vote per person, a democratic voting system ignores whether a vote is registered with strong or weak conviction or whether one is cast casually or even in ignorance. Gemeinschaft systems are likely in one way or another to register that.

In other programs, it is not specific decision-making procedures at all that seem to account for the sense of empowerment on the part of students, teachers, and even parents: it is the conviction that the nature of the community assures everyone a hearing and the ability to affect school events and arrangements. Such a situation obviously depends on assumptions as to the goodwill of other community members. It reflects confidence that if one cares enough to speak, one will be heard, and that if one's caring is intense, that will somehow be reflected or accommodated in the decisions which ensue.

Commitment

One of the most immediately evident qualities of alternative schools is the commitment of their constituents. Students in alternatives identify strongly with other members of the school community. They are bonded both to teachers and schoolmates. Students commonly liken their schools to "family" in describing relationship patterns. Some analysts have suggested that a "membership" metaphor better captures the intensity of the ties (Graham, 1980). They find it the sort of attachment ordinarily reserved for a group enthusiastically chosen and held a prized association.

A number of the people who have written about alternative schools have found this sort of attachment to be one of their most striking features. It is first an attachment to people, to teachers and friends, and it is an attachment to this particular school. It is also an attachment to what their school stands for. Thus, when the program stresses the value of knowledge and learning, this is likely to be internalized. Quite commonly, youngsters who have previously been doubtful prospects for high school graduation commit themselves to college as well. It is the quality of commitment that may explain why alternatives students thus often have college attendance rates surpassing those of their districts.

Both students and teachers are expected to genuinely invest themselves in the school. While conventional schools focus on behavioral conformity, alternatives seem far more concerned with internalization of their norms and values. They are also more actively concerned about the involvement and engagement of all. Thus "in-school dropouts"— the disengaged who are physically present but absent in mind and heart—are a relatively rare phenomenon in alternative schools.

"Commitment is experienced," asserts one analysis, "'as a partisan, affective attachment to the goals and values of an organization, to one's role in relation to goals and values, and to the organization for its own sake, apart from its purely instrumental worth'" (Buchanan, quoted in Firestone and Rosenblum, 1988: 3). This sort of response from staff and students describes the situation of a surprising number of alternatives: members of the entire school community personally take on the school's mission and values, see themselves not only as pursuers of those values but as obligated to help others reach them as well, and are strongly attached to the school as valuable in itself, not just as a means to a diploma or a job.

Why are youngsters so drawn to alternative schools? What is it they find so attractive about them? My guess as to the most magnetic feature is that a certain people-centeredness looms large in alternatives. This accords with the interests of youngsters of all ages—particularly adolescents—and it has the effect of enabling them to come to know and accept themselves. The person-centeredness is manifested in various ways. In the first place, teachers focus on it. A national survey of alternative school staff found that sixty-three percent identify the nature of the personal relationships generated to be the single most distinctive feature of their schools—more important than teaching strategies or curriculum or activities (Raywid, 1982). It is this emphasis and the way it is played out that account, I suspect, for a number of the other qualities identified here (caring, respect, inclusiveness, trust, empowerment). The person-centeredness of the school not only emphasizes the value of each and every individual—something most schools rarely, if ever, undertake to do with any explicitness—but it helps each one to recognize worth and potential within herself. Alternatives are likely to make self-study an explicit part of the curriculum. So self-preoccupation is not only encouraged in alternative schools, the self becomes an object of inquiry. And the development of self is pursued in such direct ways as leadership training or human relations skills acquisition, along with more conventional fare.

Building Community

These six qualities—respect, caring, inclusiveness, trust, empowerment, and commitment—appear to be the major qualities defining the communities so apparent in alternative schools. There are numerous ways in which alternatives seek to build and sustain such community. One has just been mentioned: the inclusion of self-study as part of the curriculum. It is not always a separate course—many alternatives make it part of advisory or family group discussions—but the deliberate study of oneself, one's problems and attitudes and capacities and values and assumptions is undertaken in one school setting or another, alongside, and in interaction with, peers who are simultaneously studying *themselves*.

Early in my study of alternative schools, I asked a teacher at one of them whether the self-study materials his group was working on were primarily a matter of individual self-development or of community building. He replied thoughtfully that it would be hard to serve one purpose without the other. Actually, it is not hard to envision circumstances that would attempt to do so, since such circumstances are not uncommon in conventional schools. But it was accurately reflective of his school that the two purposes were always conjoined.

The advisories or family groups mentioned above are important parts of virtually all alternatives large enough for them to be relevant. Such groups place youngsters with a particular teacher in a group where the individual will remain throughout her years in the school. The group becomes the home base or primary point of identification for the student, and the only permanent one, since class membership is short-term. The advisor, who in many schools is selected by the student, functions as teacher, parent, confidant, liaison between child and school and school and home, and if needed as an advocate for the youngster in either setting. The advisor is also, as someone has said, "The Expert" on each of his advisees. Such knowledge, and the ability to function in these several capacities in relation to a student, cannot emerge from minimal contact or formal association alone. Advisories cannot be mere homerooms. In some alternatives they meet daily, for as long as an hour. Not uncommonly, in order to permit small advisory groupings, administrators and staff, as well as teachers, serve as advisors.

The size of these groups, their longevity, and the way they are composed and function all make for a tightly knit community among advisory members. But genuine community is also sought *across* advisories to unify the whole school. If the total student body is large enough for advisories (e.g., beyond forty or fifty), then schoolwide community cannot be pursued in the same way that community is built within the advisory. In many alternatives, it is created through weekly all-school town meetings or exchange sessions. Retreats are used by many alternatives, often with a two- or three-day weekend retreat occurring soon after school opening in the fall, and another in the spring.

A number of alternatives have created ritual celebrations that also serve as community builders, for example, the annual Egg Drop at the Metropolitan Learning Center in Portland, Oregon, where students attempt to devise containers and devices enabling them to drop a raw egg undamaged from the school roof to the playground. Some alternatives have annual events requiring schoolwide assistance and collaboration, such as the Children's Day sponsored annually by the Village School in Great Neck, New York, for all the young children of the town. Virtually all of the alternative school's students contribute to the occasion as mimes or clowns or booth operators or game directors or activity operators.

The director of one well-known alternative says that in addition to such annual events, alternative schools need a really major all-school project about every third year (Lehman, 1991). His school, the Alternative Community School in Ithaca, New York, recently constructed a "Yurt Retreat Center," a twenty-four-foot structure. Teachers, students, and parents spent many hours together working on the project. It was a venture Lehman describes as "building community by building a community building" (Lehman, 1991: 4).

A rather different kind of way in which community is maintained in alternative schools is through the deliberate cultivation of a social order built more on norms and values than on formal rules and regulations. This, of course, is a lot more demanding and time-consuming than simply announcing rules or disseminating written copies. It requires a lot more contact for inducting newcomers and enabling them to learn the school's customs and traditions. It is a move away from formal organization and in the direction of social control through less formal means, and thus it is a move toward gemeinschaft regulation in preference to the legal and contractual control mechanisms of gesellschaft. The informality does not signal a shift from rules to no rules, but rather a difference in the sources of social control. For adolescents, the norms of a gemeinschaft community can prove far more binding than the regulations imposed by a gesellschaft organization. The gemeinschaft approach also has the advantage of stimulating the internalization of behavioral rules. Since this is what adult self-control and self-direction are presumably about, the advantage is not minor.

As all of this attests, the strong communities found in alternative schools are no accident. The attempt to build and sustain them is reflected in the school's organizational structure, in its curriculum, in the way time is allocated within the school, and in the way teachers and students encounter and interact with one another and the array of settings in which they do so. But it is not just in these or other particular structures and arrangements that community is built and sustained in alternative schools. Perhaps most fundamentally, what has been called a humane and collaborative orientation, as opposed to a custodial and impositional one, pervades everything that goes on in the school. There is a sustained effort to make education a conjoint undertaking, rather than something one party forces on the other.

Even disciplinary situations reflect such commitment and priorities. At Central Park East Secondary School, where the overarching school theme is the cultivation of five "habits of mind," youngsters sent to the office for disciplinary reasons are treated first as learners rather than as candidates for punishment.

When those "naughty" kids appear in our office the first thing we ask them to do is sit down and write for us. We ask them to tell us what happened from two different viewpoints, to give us some information (evidence), and then explain what they could have . . . done differently. The latter request is an effort to help students see patterns and connections between their behavior and the things that happen to them. It's using our "third" Habit of Mind. (Meier, 1991: 2)

In this way, perpetrators must bring to bear three of the habits of mind the school seeks to inculcate in trying to understand and explain their difficulties. This is the first consideration, not punishing an offender. Thus, the quest for genuine community—and the sustaining of the conditions that make it possible—remain a pervasive consideration in virtually all that occurs.

References

Abbott, M. (1992). Focusing. *Alpha* 14 (3). (Alpha is an alternative high school in Livonia, Michigan.)

Bronfenbrenner, U. (1980). On making human beings human. *Character* 2 (2): 1–7.

Bryk, A., and Driscoll, M. E. (1988). *The high school as community: Contextual influences and consequences for students and teachers*. Madison, Wis.: National Center on Effective Secondary Schools.

Coleman, J. (1961). *The adolescent society: The social life of the teenager and its impact on education*. New York: Free Press.

Cooley, C. H. (1937). *Social organization*. New York: Scribner.

Erickson, D. A. (1989). The communal ethos, privatization, and the dilemma of being public. In S. Cohen and L. C. Solomon (eds.), *From the campus: Perspectives on the school reform movement*. New York: Praeger. 136–53.

Erickson, D. et al. (1982). *The British Columbia story: Antecedents and consequences of aid to private schools*. Los Angeles: Institute for the Study of Private Schools.

Firestone, W., and Rosenblum, S. (1988). *The alienation and commitment of students and teachers in urban high schools*. Washington, D.C.: Office of Educational Research and Improvement.

Gold, M., and Mann, D. W. (1984). *Expelled to a friendlier place: A study of effective alternative schools.* Ann Arbor: University of Michigan Press.

Goodman. P. (1963). *People or personnel: Decentralizing and the mixed system.* New York: Random House.

Graham, R. A. (1980). Practical alternatives for educating the poor: Education remedies for youth unemployment. In *A review of youth employment problems, programs, and policies*, vol. 3. Washington, D.C.: Vice President's Task Force on Youth Employment, U.S. Department of Labor Employment and Training Administration.

Gregory, T., and Smith, G. (1987). *High schools as communities: The small school reconsidered.* Bloomington, Ind.: Phi Delta Kappa.

Johnson, W. R. (1990). Inviting conversations: The Holmes Group and tomorrow's schools. *American Educational Research Journal* 27 (4): 581–88.

Lehman, D. (1991). Building community in an alternative secondary school. *Changing Schools* 19 (3): 1–5.

Loomis, C. P. (trans. and ed.) (1963). *Community and society*, by Frederick Tönnies. New York: Harper and Row.

Meier, D. W. (1991). Letter to students, parents, and staff. *Newsletter 9.* (Central Park East Secondary School): 2.

Noddings, N. (1984). *Caring: A feminine approach to ethics and moral education.* Berkeley: University of California Press.

Raywid, M. A. (1982). *The current status of schools of choice in public secondary education.* Hempstead, N.Y.: Project on Alternatives in Education, Hofstra University.

Raywid, M. A. (1988). Community and schools: A prolegomenon. *Teachers College Record* 90 (2): 16–28.

Raywid, M. A. (1990). Alternative education: The definition problem. In S. Williams (ed.), *Alternative school choice.* Bloomington, Ind.: Phi Delta Kappa. 25–33.

Rutter, M., Maughan, B., Mortimore, P., and Ouston, J. (1979). *Fifteen thousand hours: Secondary schools and their effects on children.* Cambridge, Mass.: Harvard University Press.

Wachtel, P. L. (1989). *The poverty of affluence: A psychological portrait of the American way of life.* Philadelphia: New Society Publishers.

Wehlage, G., Smith, G., and Lipman, P. (1992). Restructuring urban schools: The New Futures experience. *American Educational Research Journal* 29 (1): 51–93.

Creating a School That Honors the Traditions of a Culturally Diverse Student Body: La Escuela Fratney

Robert Peterson

Introduction

In the midst of a cold January in 1992, the staff, parents, and students of La Escuela Fratney began a "No-TV Week" for the second year in a row. As in the first year, controversial questions arose. Should we ask for a complete ban on watching TV? Should the parents, brothers, and sisters of Fratney students also be asked to stop watching TV? How could we schedule the week so it wouldn't lose out to Super Bowl competition? How could we make sure to condemn television's misuse in society rather than the technology itself? Finally, was it worth all the time and effort it would take to ask families to forego one of their favorite pastimes?

Discussions raged on the parent/staff Curriculum Committee and on the Site-based Management Council. Despite questions, the Fratney staff and parents plowed ahead, scheduled the week, and proceeded with the no-TV campaign.

Two parent meetings were held to discuss the campaign's details, one daytime meeting and one at night. At the meetings, parents resoundingly supported No-TV Week.

At the meetings and in flyers sent home to parents, the parent and teacher organizers of the campaign explained that we wanted the No-TV Week to be more than a gimmick or novelty. Rather, it was to be a serious approach to questions nagging many parents and teachers:

How can one control a childhood pastime that, according to the American Academy of Pediatrics, consumes more time than any other childhood activity except sleeping? How can one counter an activity that fosters mental and physical passivity and that undermines creativity? That perpetuates sexual and racial stereotypes, promotes violence, and encourages the buying of useless and expensive products and unhealthy food? That presents a distorted view of reality? That often robs children of the sleep needed to do the best possible work in schools? That too often replaces conversation and social interaction?

Based on questionnaires returned by parents and students after No-TV Week, we succeeded in raising many of these questions. One parent, for example, explained that before No-TV Week her family always watched TV during dinner; afterward, she told the children that the TV would be banned during dinner so that family members could talk to each other.

Another parent decided to institute no-TV days three times a week. Another put the family's television in an attic room to discourage TV use. A fourth said her two children now ask for a no-TV night so they can play games with Mom and Dad.

About fifty percent of the school's 350 students took part in the No-TV week. They signed No-TV contracts, kept logs of their TV-viewing habits, wrote diaries of how they survived a No-TV Week, interviewed family members about the impact of TV on their lives, and examined stereotypes and advertisements on TV.

I mention the No-TV Week because it is a concrete example of how La Escuela Fratney not only tries to analyze problems facing our children and our society, but tries to do something to help solve those problems. It is a philosophy that is at the core of La Escuela Fratney, whether we are discussing the environment, racism, television, fighting on the playground, or the ever-present tendency in schools to track students along race, class, and gender lines.

La Escuela Fratney was established in 1988 by a group of parents, teachers, and community members in the Riverwest neighborhood of Milwaukee, one of the city's few integrated neighborhoods. It is hard to encapsulate in a few words anything as complex as an urban kindergarten-through-fifth-grade public school with 350 students (65% Latino, 20% African-American, 13% white), most of them eligible for the federal free lunch program. But in essence, La Escuela Fratney is a bilingual school with a multicultural, antiracist curriculum in which all students learn both English and Spanish. The school's educational philosophy incorporates broad progressive values of cooperation and respect and a whole-language approach to reading and writing. It is governed by a council of parents and teachers, within the parameters of the Milwaukee Public Schools.

The school began when a small, multiracial neighborhood organization mobilized the community and in just a few months won control of an inner-city elementary school building. Its success, in fact, was so swift and unexpected that even those of us who had organized the effort were taken aback. What we found, actually, is that winning is harder than losing. This fact would continue to haunt us through our first five years as we struggled to take responsibility for creating this new school.

In this chapter, I would like to outline three key stages in the history of La Escuela Fratney, and the lessons we have learned from each stage. First, there was the struggle with the school board to establish Fratney School, which lasted for a few brief but stormy months in 1988. Then there was the struggle over developing the school's curriculum and program, which lasted six months. Finally, there is the ongoing struggle to run a quality school in a low-income urban area with an antiracist philosophy based on respect and cooperation—a philosophy at odds with many of society's dominant values.

Stage One: The Struggle to Establish Fratney School

In late 1987, La Escuela Fratney was only a dream—a hope—of a group of parents and teachers who gathered in each others homes on the northeast side of Milwaukee, a city of 700,000. The central administration of Milwaukee's public schools had announced the closing of a ninety-year-old school building in the neighborhood. It meant little to the district bureaucracy that the neighborhood around the school was one of the few racially integrated, working-class neighborhoods in the city.

In response, some parents, teachers, and community activists organized a group called Neighbors for a New Fratney. The group wanted to start a quality school in an integrated neighborhood governed by a council of parents and teachers, a school that children would want to attend, where youngsters would be taught progressive, antiracist values in a bilingual, Spanish/English setting and where they would learn through cooperative and innovative methods. In a few short weeks we developed a comprehensive proposal for a two-way bilingual, whole-language, multicultural, site-managed, neighborhood, specialty school—called La Escuela Fratney for short.

The school administration had other dreams, however, which came to be viewed as nightmares by some community activists. The administration wanted to turn the empty building into an "Exemplary Teaching Center." The staff was to be comprised of "master teachers" defined as those with masters' degrees and at least ten years' teaching experience using the techniques of Madeline Hunter, an educator who has extensively marketed a "teacher-proof" instructional method. Their job would have been to work with Milwaukee Public Schools (MPS) teachers who were having classroom difficulties and who would have been brought in for two-and-one-half-week training sessions. In response, parents questioned whether they wanted their kids taught by a series of bad teachers. They also argued that such a center could be established anywhere, while the New Fratney proposal could only unfold as envisioned at its present site in a multicultural neighborhood.

Our posters went out on New Year's Day, 1988. We called for community meetings and a public hearing. The public hearing coincided with a bitter snowstorm that forced all schools to close the next day. Still, the turnout for the meeting was so large that it convinced the school board of the need to give our proposal serious consideration. They directed the district's school administration to meet with us and to try to come back with a revised recommendation.

From the beginning, the leadership at the central office did not appear to understand our project. The administration put forth a "compromise" proposal to combine their Madeline Hunter–type teacher training program with our project. What we had proposed was in fact opposite to their plan. They wanted a top-down model for a teacher training school organized and run by the central office. We wanted one run by a council of parents and teachers. As members of Neighbors for New Fratney sat negotiating with the top administrators in the superintendent's conference room, the absurdity of the situation became evident. One teacher pointed out that the proposals couldn't be combined, that either a school was to be run by the staff development academy or by a group of teachers and parents. Moreover, the teacher continued, the central office's proposal for the teacher center had not mentioned the word "parents" once. "Wait!" responded one top administrator. "While it's true we didn't mention 'parents' once in our proposal, your proposal didn't mention 'Central Office.'"

The representatives of Neighbors for a New Fratney left that meeting almost in shock. There was a failure to understand the proposal, but worse yet an atmosphere of fear pervaded the meeting. The administrators only spoke after raising their hand and being recognized by the superintendent and then only in tentative fashion. More frightening was that in the hall after the meeting three staff members came up to members of Neighbors for a New Fratney and, while glancing over their shoulders, urged them not to compromise—they thought that the proposal was sound and should be left intact. They said, however, that they couldn't say anything out of fear of repercussions.

We stuck to our position and continued to mobilize our community. We did this in the midst of favorable political conditions. The school board had a few months earlier gone on record in favor of site-based management. Members of the African-American community led by Howard Fuller (who became Milwaukee superintendent of schools in June of 1991) were demanding an independent school district, charging among other things that the bureaucracy was incapable of listening to parents. School board members had become aware of the benefits of a whole language teaching approach, in part due to the previous efforts of *Rethinking Schools*, a quarterly newspaper whose editorial board included a number of members of Neighbors for a New Fratney. The long and short of it was that the school board not only passed our proposal and established the first city-wide specialty school with neighborhood preference—which meant giving children who lived in the neighborhood first choice in enrollment—but the board also directed the central office to cooperate with Neighbors for a New Fratney.

School board members were also influenced by the quality of the teaching of individual teachers. One member later remarked that during a key school board meeting he found himself in the back room discussing the Fratney proposal with a top MPS administrator and realized that the man hadn't the slightest idea of what our proposal involved. "Quite honestly," the board member stated, "I didn't really know what you were talking about either, but I knew this much. My son had started first grade in a classroom of a teacher who used what she called whole language techniques. By Thanksgiving my kid was coming home and writing and publishing his own books, excited about reading and writing, loving to read and to be read to. I knew I had to support the Fratney proposal."

Lessons from the Struggle to Establish the School

- A small group of people can change reality.
- Concisely written, quality position papers are instrumental in changing schools.

- Antiracism and equality are key factors in building multiracial unity.
- Winning is often harder than losing.

An important lesson from the initial stage of our struggle to win a school can best be summed up in the words of Margaret Mead, who said, "Never doubt that a small group of thoughtful committed citizens can change the world; indeed it's the only thing that ever has." Both the "progressive" political community in Milwaukee and the educational community were shocked at our initial victory. People have become so used to losing social struggles—on behalf of civil rights, labor, women, etc.—in the last fifteen years that a clear victory was very unexpected. When people asked, "How did you do it?" the simple response was hard work, being well organized, and acting quickly when opportunities presented themselves. Teachers and parents, having been inculcated during their own years of schooling with notions that the rich and famous are the makers of history, have rarely understood the importance and power of organized grass-roots movements in changing society.

This is not to say such success is easy, particularly in a big-city school bureaucracy. But we knew what we wanted, we researched what was necessary, and we used all the resources, connections, and energy that we had to make it possible.

A second lesson is that concisely written, quality position papers are instrumental in specific school struggles. The Neighbors for a New Fratney circulated a twelve-page document that summarized the entire proposal, ranging from the pedagogical rationale to enrollment statistics in the neighborhood. Especially in the educational arena, and if widely circulated as a part of an overall organizing strategy, such a document can have a huge impact.

A third lesson is that antiracism and equality are key factors in building multiracial unity. The organizing effort would have failed if African Americans, Latinos of various nationalities, and whites hadn't worked closely together. Working in multiracial groupings in a racially divided society is difficult, with the success of such efforts often dependent on the underlying politics of the project and the individuals involved. We looked at "equality" in three different ways: first, as a value that we wanted to teach the students; second, as a way to define the relationship between parents and teachers as we strived to become true partners in raising children and running a school; and third, as a way to structure the balance of power between the two languages at our school, English and Spanish.

In addition, the proposal explicitly called for antiracism to be taught as a value. Some activists of color saw this as a further indication that this project was serious about building multiracial unity.

The final lesson from this stage of the struggle was that winning is often harder than losing. Having won the control of an entire school, we found ourselves in a qualitatively new position. We now actually had power to do something about problems that in the past we as teachers and parents could really only complain about. In addition we faced a whole new set of problems that teachers and parents out of power don't have to deal with, from school security to staff who didn't fit with the program.

In most schools teachers and parents don't have much power to influence policy, which often leads to isolationist or cynical attitudes toward any problem that extends beyond the immediate classroom, for the teacher, or beyond their own children's needs, for the parent.

A victory for parent and teacher power on the school level therefore redefines many problems, allowing them to be approached in a fresh and broader manner. This is not to say that all or even most educational problems can be solved at the school level—for they cannot—but in fact it refocuses the problems to where they should be addressed—collectively at the school. Then when it is apparent either district, state, or federal policy guidelines must come into play, parents and teachers will be in a much better position to influence such policies.

Stage Two: The Struggle Over Planning the School

The school board's approval essentially concluded the first stage of the struggle—the struggle for political power. It lasted only eight weeks. The next stage was struggling over the program—from staffing, to selection of the principal, to renovation of the facility, to curriculum and materials. Unfortunately, what the district administrators failed to do politically at the board level, they attempted to do administratively.

For example, despite the explicit order by the school board to cooperate with our group, a couple of weeks passed with no meeting or contact between the central office and Neighbors for a New Fratney. Finally, by chance, we learned about an important meeting to plan Fratney that was to take place the following day. Although uninvited, we asked a parent to attend. Because the parent had no idea of where the meeting was to be held, she waited until five minutes after the meeting was scheduled to begin. She then approached the secretary of the administrator in charge and asked to be taken to the meeting. The secretary, who did not know this parent had *not* been invited, escorted her into a room of open-mouthed, surprised administrators. At that time a joint meeting was set up to start the planning.

This was not the end of our struggle with central office administrators. Between March and September the administration tried to undo our effort in a dozen ways. They continued to stall, ignore, and even sabotage the efforts of our group. For example, to deal with the problem of recruiting faculty who wanted to be in this particular program we proposed that when staff openings were announced, all teachers be given a one-page explanation of our program. The Milwaukee Teachers' Education Association agreed, as did lower-level administrators. But the higher authorities thought otherwise and the proposal was never acted upon.

Another example occurred when the community called for a nationwide search for a principal. The administration refused and then proceeded to stall in hiring someone. Finally, a month before the school was to open, and in opposition to what a parent committee had recommended, the administration recommended the appointment of a woman with only suburban experience. She was bilingual—but in English and German, not English and Spanish. This was seen as a direct affront to the community, particularly the Hispanic community, and once again the Neighbors for a New Fratney mobilized. Holding picket signs bearing slogans such as "Remember Goulart"—in reference to a similar struggle at the College for the Deaf in Washington, D.C.—dozens of parents came to school board meetings. Bowing to pressure and publicity, newly hired Superintendent Robert S. Peterkin recognized the mistake made by his predecessor and rejected the recommendation. Peterkin hired an interim principal acceptable to the community.

Then there was the question of developing the curriculum. Five teachers wrote a draft curriculum at the central office in late June and in July. There are 240 administrators at central office and it was difficult working among people who had bitterly opposed our plan. Budgetary information was given only if we asked exactly the right question. Secretarial help seemed in extremely short supply when it came to our needs. One of the Fratney teachers remarked at the time that working on the Fratney project at central office was like being a peace activist with a job in the Pentagon.

Even minor issues became a source of antagonism for some central office personnel. For example, there were old desks at our school—called bicycle desks because the chair is attached to the desk. Needless to say such pieces of furniture are not particularly conducive to cooperative groups which require chairs placed together in a circle. Despite repeated requests, the administrator in charge refused to change the desks for newer ones, until one day when a Fratney teacher announced to him that we had changed our minds. We wanted the old desks to stay because on the first day of school all the parents, teachers, and students were going to pile them up on the playground, call a press conference, and expose the administration for failing to support our project. The next morning, two truckloads of new desks arrived at our school.

As a consequence of such administrative resistance, our whole planning process was too rushed. Even more important, the administration refused to appoint anyone to work on the project full-time, so we went from approval by the board in February to an opening in September, with no one working full-time or even part-time on the matter during the entire period. Since this experience, the administration has seen fit to put someone in charge—usually an administrator—of the opening of any new school, at least a semester in advance.

When we returned in mid-August to make what we thought were to be final preparations for an opening a few weeks later, we found that necessary renovation had only just begun and that the school still needed to be cleaned from the previous spring. Curiously, nothing we had ordered in July had yet arrived. We called vendors, and they told us they had no record of our orders. Much to our horror we discovered that, although the requisition forms had been signed on July 18 or before by an associate superintendent, the forms had sat in the purchasing division for a month because the department did not have an authorization card with the associate superintendent's signature. We learned that the forms had not been sent out until August 15—a full month after we had completed them. The error was particularly annoying because most classrooms had been emptied when the school closed, our two-way bilingual program needed new materials, and the few library books that remained at Fratney were in boxes because of the delayed renovation of the library. We started school with virtually no materials. "Well, at least we ordered a decent Xerox machine," one of my colleagues said hopefully. "We can rely on that for the first few weeks of school." But of course when we called up to check on that order, somehow it had been lost.

That was the last straw. We pondered, "Was this all happening because of sabotage or incompetence?" To this day, we do not know. We prefer to believe it was sabotage, because the alternative is even more frightening.

Robert Peterson

Needless to say we did not sit back and wait. To make a long story a bit shorter, we stormed back up to the central office. Fortunately, this time we had actually gained two allies, the new superintendent and his assistant, Dr. Deborah McGriff, now superintendent of Detroit Public Schools. McGriff was flabbergasted by our story. She listened intensely as we hinted that our next step would be a round-the-clock occupation of the school. She took immediate steps to get the administrators in line.

The next day parents and teachers met again in the superintendent's conference room, but this time the atmosphere had changed. Word had come down from the top that we should be helped in any way possible. Representatives from Neighbors for a New Fratney spoke openly and were in charge of the agenda. We agreed on how to overcome a host of problems.

A couple of days later, after visiting on the first day of school, Superintendent Peterkin called Fratney a "model" of his version of school reform, referring both to the need for heavy parental involvement and for a unified vision of what a school should be. Finally the tide had turned.

Lessons from the Struggle over Planning the School

- School districts must allocate sufficient resources and time to plan new schools.
- New structures need to be created to encourage parent and teacher participation.
- Lines of authority and decision-making processes must be clear to all.
- Training of staff and parents must take place early in the process if they are going to have genuine power.
- Parents and teachers must not be afraid of playing hardball.

School districts that are planning new schools or programs within schools must allocate enough time and resources to do a decent job. The money invested up front, before a school opens, is well invested, eliminating confusion and problems. Specifically the lead time to start a new program should be at least a year. Money should be allocated so that staff and parents can spend extended time over a period of several months to plan and revise the new program.

New structures—task forces, committees, and so forth—have to be created to allow parental and teacher involvement. At the insistence

54

of Neighbors for a New Fratney, joint committees were established between central office administrators and parents and teachers. This was something new for many administrators, and it meant meeting after regular work hours.

Internally, we patterned ourselves after a typical community organization with subcommittees and a steering committee. Unfortunately, because of our truncated time line, things had to occur so quickly that the steering committee did more work than was originally anticipated.

Lines of authority within the school administration should be made clear, from the superintendent and school board on down. In the final six months of planning for a new program this "line of authority" should include one person, preferably on a full-time, paid basis as the coordinator of the project. As indicated earlier, the Milwaukee Public Schools now appoints a principal or program coordinator to a new school a semester in advance; however, such appointments should not compromise the power of the broader planning body of parents and teachers.

School districts must assume the responsibility for training teachers, parents, and principals to run an entire school. This should include training in budgets, purchasing procedures, personnel policies, labor contracts, physical plant maintenance and repair, and a host of state and federal guidelines. Without such knowledge, even the most dedicated group of parents and teachers can have their efforts thwarted by administrators who can use obscure guidelines and policies as obstacles to change. A tactic of bureaucrats that is all too common is omission. If the right question isn't asked by the parents or teachers, they are kept in ignorance until it is too late. Parent and teacher groups should demand training and designate among themselves who will become an "expert" in certain areas so that as a group, their collective knowledge will be equal to or even deeper than that of their possible opponents.

Finally, through a number of incidents during the planning stage, we learned that at times it is necessary to play hardball with recalcitrant school officials. At times, public demonstrations and the judicious use of the press are necessary tactics in winning these kinds of struggles.

Stage Three: Running the School

The first day of school, in August of 1988, brought us to the third stage of struggle, the implementation of our program. We could now finally direct our energies and attention to the business of creating a new program at La Escuela Fratney.

Unfortunately, the consequence of months of inaction and poor planning were acutely felt throughout the first year. But the problems had a positive effect, too: they brought parents and teachers together. The steady opposition from the administration forced constant meetings of people in homes, community centers, and even public parks to plan strategy and mobilizations. It taught us that a successful urban school needs an active parent/teacher/community alliance to sustain it as well as a common vision of what is meant by a quality school. Differences, at times sharp, arose between parents and teachers during this early stage, but the common goal of creating a multicultural school run by parents and teachers held us together.

For example, one difference emerged over what should be the composition of a council that would run the school. From February through September the steering committee of Neighbors for a New Fratney was essentially making all decisions for the school. Power had to be transferred from that group to the teachers who would work there and to the parents whose children had enrolled. Members of the steering committee put forth different ideas on the composition of the council, ranging from having two parents elected from each of the eleven classrooms with only two teacher representatives, to a proposal for equal parent and teacher representation. The matter was partially resolved when we learned of a new agreement between the school board and the teachers' union, prescribing that all such councils needed fifty percent plus one teacher representation. After much discussion Neighbors for a New Fratney decided that to fight the school board and the union would be futile and that instead, we should adhere to the agreement, but include in our council's procedure a provision for parent alternates that would essentially ensure equal voice at site-based council meetings.

Now in our fifth year of operation, we are on a much stronger footing than when we started, but we continue to struggle with the hard questions of how to provide a quality, antiracist, humane education to an urban student population. Several problems have confronted our project that make our success more difficult than we had anticipated:

1. Fundamentally negative features of school life in public elementary schools—such as overcrowded classrooms, inadequate physical facilities, lack of resources, and lack of time for teacher preparation, joint planning, parent/teacher con-

ferences, and parent and teacher in-services—impede reform efforts.

2. Moving from a traditional text-centered, teacher-talk paradigm to a whole-language, activity-based paradigm, and from a Eurocentric tradition of teaching, to an antiracist, multicultural approach to teaching is difficult even for the most experienced teachers, given the problems mentioned in number 1. It is even more difficult for veteran teachers who transfer in and for newly hired teachers who might be resistant to or at best unfamiliar with our innovative practices.

3. The natural flow of people in and out of the program—parents, students, and teachers—has created a situation where several people with the original vision who helped start the school have left. In addition, despite the written explanations of our school in a variety of media, new parents enroll their children in our school for a range of reasons, and some are unclear about our methodologies. Also, new students regularly transfer into our school (the only criterion is that after first grade the student needs previous Spanish experience—so most of our transfers are Spanish-speaking immigrant children), and they have not had the same experience with student-centered approaches and sometimes have difficulty in adjusting.

4. Providing truly bilingual services is challenging in a society that is so English-dominant/chauvinist. There exists a natural "English pull" in our country, and placing Spanish on an equal level with English in our school has not been easy.

5. We had underestimated the negative influences that our violent class- and race-stratified society has had on children and how much it takes to overcome such influences.

6. Maintaining a high level of parental involvement, particularly among those people who have been traditionally alienated from school, people of color and poor people, is difficult.

7. There is a contradiction between needing teachers and parents to be involved at the district level to change policies which could directly affect conditions at Fratney and needing the same committed teachers and parents to put their full effort into running and improving Fratney school.

Robert Peterson

As I describe the main features of our program I will show how we have attempted to deal with the above set of problems.

Two-Way Bilingual Program

Several members of Neighbors for a New Fratney had experience with second-language acquisition in the developmental bilingual program in the Milwaukee Public Schools. Building on the strengths of the MPS program, we decided to start the first two-way bilingual program in Wisconsin. Native Spanish and English speakers are in the same classrooms in order to avoid separating language groups and to give meaning and purpose to the acquisition of two languages. This enhances students' self-esteem, because no matter what social class they come from, they bring something of value to the classroom: their language. We have learned that for successful bilingual learning there has to be a strict separation of the two languages and language environments, so that children are forced to use their second language. If classes are always conducted bilingually (i.e., a teacher explains the material first in one language and then another), the students may rely only on their native tongue and not be motivated to learn the second language.

By the end of our second year we realized that English was still too dominant in our school. We looked at the experience of other two-way bilingual schools in other cities and critically examined the first two years of our practice. Discussions were held among staff, at the site-based council, and at a special meeting of parents of kindergarten students who were in two classrooms that had been organized differently. At the beginning of our third year we adopted for the whole school, the method that had been used in our kindergarten. Two teachers of the same grade team teach between 54 and 60 children (27–30 children per class). The children are in two groups. One day they go to the Spanish room and receive instruction in Spanish; the next day they go to the English room and receive instruction in English. The teachers are bilingual, but one teaches in English and one in Spanish. This approach has increased the use of Spanish in our school and encouraged team teaching. At the same time, it has exacerbated the problem of a lack of common planning time and complicated other matters such as report cards and parent/teacher conferences.

Despite the problems, a key strength of our program is its two-way bilingual nature. It sends a strong message to the students and their families about the equivalent value of Spanish and English and the people who speak them. This has in turn made Spanish-speaking parents more comfortable in visiting and volunteering at our school and has sent a signal to the larger Latino community that staff and parents of La Escuela Fratney are strongly committed to broader equality issues.

A Multicultural, Antiracist Curriculum

Our vision of multiculturalism goes beyond what we call the 3-*F*'s—facts, foods, and faces. While we incorporate human relations–type activities, we also attempt to address issues of race and power. We highlight the experiences of people of color in our school-wide themes and attempt to draw on music, history, art, stories, poetry, and literature from various geopolitical groups such as African Americans, Hispanics, Native Americans, and Asian Americans. We also believe children should be *taught* to be antiracist, that is, that racism is unscientific, immoral, and that it has been a damaging social disease throughout our nation's history.

Given that the student and family population is diverse at our school, such a multicultural, antiracist policy is important for not only our long-term educational goals but for short-term survival and community building within our school. One way we attempted to deal with the problem of people being at different levels and points of view on this issue was to develop a year-long process by which we as staff and parents defined what we meant by multicultural, antiracist education. Working through our curriculum committee, the site-based management council, and staff meetings, parents and staff went through five drafts to come up with a joint statement that outlines the philosophy and implementation of multicultural, antiracist education at our school. Now, efforts in this area are directed toward broadening our staff's own knowledge about race and different cultures and improving methods of assessing how well children are doing in this area.

This policy has also brought us closer to groups in the broader community. Because we are guided by this philosophy, we pay special attention to which community artists and presenters are invited into our classrooms and school events. Such involvement on the part of individual members of the community has strengthened our ties with our community as a whole.

Robert Peterson

The Whole-language and a Natural Approach to Learning First and Second Languages

We believe children learn to listen, speak, read, and write by listening, speaking, reading, and writing. Our classrooms are student-centered, experience-based, and language-rich. What does this mean? For example, our children write in their journals daily. We use big books, shared reading, book clubs, storytelling, the writing process, daily interactive journals, drama, and puppetry. Many classrooms publish books written by children, and the books are in turn cataloged and put in our school library. A fundamental reason why this approach is used at Fratney is our belief that education should be based on the experience of the children and be relevant to their lives, families, and communities. By thinking, investigating, and writing about our community, children reconfirm the worthwhileness of themselves and their families and simultaneously think about the problems that they and our society as a whole must confront. Many teachers use homework assignments that encourage children to survey their community and interview family members and neighbors. This validates the importance of what "common" people think and also forges stronger ties between family, school, and community.

A Thematic Approach in the School Curricula

We try to integrate as much of the curriculum as possible through our school-wide themes, which teachers and parents develop on an annual basis. We stress social responsibility and action. For example, in recent years our themes have been: "We Respect Ourselves and the World," "We Send Messages When We Communicate," "We Can Make a Difference on Planet Earth," "We Tell Stories of the World." Within the context of each theme, we also try to choose a school-wide project. In exploring the theme "We Send Messages When We Communicate," one of the subthemes was "TV Can Be Dangerous to Your Health." We organized the No-TV Week described earlier. After the first year we did this, both the parent curriculum committee and the site-based management council had extensive discussions summing up the project. They concluded that while in some cases TV watching was moderated on a long-term basis, the school needed to help teach children to view media critically, because the reality is that most children will continue to watch lots of television. Recognizing the validity of these criticisms, the following year teachers focused more on developing the critical

60

skills of children as they watch TV shows and advertisements. Some students and teachers examine violence on television, as well as race and gender stereotypes.

One year, during the theme "We Can Make a Difference on Planet Earth," each class chose a project that would show they can make a difference. The nine-week theme culminated in a presentation during which children shared what they had done. Projects included recycling, raising money for homeless children in El Salvador, treating each other better in the classroom, and testifying at a public hearing in favor of creating a nature preserve adjacent to the nearby Milwaukee River.

Our use of school-wide themes has helped teachers new to Fratney more quickly understand some of our underlying philosophies and methods. It has also helped to bring the students and staff together in common projects that have served to underscore the things we all have in common.

Parents and Teachers Run Our School

The school-based management council of parents and staff members meets monthly and makes the major decisions. We chose our principal; rewrote our report card; developed polices around homework, parent involvement, and multicultural education; redirected parts of our school budget and developed a policy that encouraged critical discussion of issues such as the Gulf War. We also have a curriculum committee, a fund-raising committee, and a building committee—the latter being a group of staff that meets regularly to deal with immediate school issues.

Significant parent involvement is one of two or three key characteristics of a successful school. We had substantial participation in the first two stages of struggling for the school, but once Fratney opened, the initial euphoria diminished and parent involvement declined. What we found was that those parents who continued to come were mostly white and middle-class even though the number of white children in our school is a small percentage. We did three things to try to counter that imbalance. First, we established quotas for our site-based management council, so that African-American and Latino parents were ensured seats. Second, we decided to redirect money from our budget to hire two part-time parent organizers—a Mexican American and an African American. Eventually those positions became a full-time position for one person. Finally, with the help of the Wisconsin Writing Project, which is part of the National Writing Project, we developed

61

a "Parent Project." We paid fifteen parents to participate in a six-week evening workshop in which they discussed school issues and wrote about their children. Parents who didn't usually participate in school activities were encouraged to participate. One result was that several of the parents who did participate in the parent project have decided to remain active in other aspects of our school.

La Escuela Fratney is also committed to community involvement. Last year this involved working with community activists to demand a new playground (for young children) at our school. Our "tot lot" was dominated by a jungle gym in the shape of a tank. When we took over the school, we refused to follow the easy route to have it removed, as some in the peace movement recommended. Instead we involved parents and students in the process and set our goal in the larger context of peace education. Our preparation paid off as we demanded from the city that they give us $70,000 to get a new tot lot. The mayor's office opposed our demand at first, saying the city only replaced two tot lots a year and that we were number 60 on the list. The thought of waiting thirty years didn't hold much appeal for us. Their second argument was that if they gave in to the Fratney parents and students, then, "Who knows, maybe other school communities would demand the same?" "That's exactly what should happen," we said, as we proceeded with our organizing and won the new tot lot.

Lessons from the Struggle to Run the School

- Sufficient time needs to be allocated on an ongoing basis to assess progress and govern the school.
- School-level leadership needs to have both a vision for the future and the competence to conduct daily affairs efficiently.
- Parent involvement needs to be substantive and far-reaching.
- System-wide change needs to occur if innovative schools are going to be institutionalized.

After five years at building a school with roots in the community we have learned enough lessons to fill several volumes. I will focus on just a few, and go into detail in the area of parental involvement.

Just as sufficient time needs to be allocated to plan a new school or program, time also needs to be allocated on an ongoing basis for parents and teachers to assess progress and govern the school. Through creative scheduling we were able to gain some additional time for teachers. This included shifting the afternoon recess to follow lunch recess, thus giving teachers a little more time during lunch to plan for afternoon classes; arranging art, music, and physical education classes so teams of teachers have time together; and starting school ten minutes earlier in order to "bank" time so that once a month the children leave early, giving the staff a half day for planning.

While getting enough time for staff to plan is difficult, getting sufficient time for parents and teachers to work together is even more problematic. We have found no easy solution, but have managed by making sure that our site-based council meetings are held regularly and run efficiently, so that maximum benefits come from them.

A second important lesson is to have quality leadership at the local school level. This leadership may come from the principal, a nonclassroom teacher such as an implementor, classroom teachers, or the site-based management council, or a combination of the above. But such leadership must have the commitment and the ability to completely provide day-to-day management while not losing sight of the original vision of the school. This is particularly challenging given outside bureaucratic pressures on public schools and the constant influx of new staff and parents. School leadership on the one hand must respect and listen to ideas of new people, but at the same time educate them about the importance of a common vision. Without leadership that thinks boldly and strategically about promoting the vision of a school, that vision will wither with time and changes in staff.

A third key lesson is that parent involvement needs to be substantive and far-reaching. It must extend beyond the pizza fund-raisers and volunteering for field trips. The central issues are power, resources, and presence. Do parents exert real power during their time spent in the school? Is there an ongoing, daily presence of parents in the school and in the classrooms? Are sufficient resources allocated to schools so that parent involvement can be adequately organized? The Fratney experience shows that parents are more likely to come out if they are able to exercise genuine power in decisions that directly affect the future of the school and their children's lives. At Fratney this has meant having parents and teachers deal with issues such as curriculum, budget, facility renovation, and personnel.

Empowering parents in this regard is full of contradictions, however. Just because a perspective comes from parents doesn't mean it is progressive. In fact, throughout history parents have played contradictory roles—at times fighting for the rights of oppressed peoples, at other times supporting book banning and school prayer and opposing equality and desegregation and the teaching of evolution. The bottom-line question is, what kind of politics are being promoted by the parents? How can a school community hear the voices of all parents and yet remain true to its vision?

Similarly, just because teachers are pushing something, doesn't mean that their proposals necessarily reflect sound educational policy. In urban centers, especially, where teaching staffs are predominantly white and children are mainly of color, the perspectives of some teachers and their organizations may be racist and class-biased. Teachers have a lot to learn from economically impoverished parents, many of whom have cultural experiences different from those of the teachers.

The key to creating a school that honors the diversity of its student population is to maintain a healthy relationship between the staff and the parents. Such a relationship is by definition tension-filled. Given the race and class divisions in our society, and the fact that they manifest themselves sharply between teachers and students' families at most urban schools, conflicts will arise. In fact, the very existence of such conflict or tension implies a substantive level of parent involvement. Whether a school can creatively manage and put such tension to good use, however, is a completely different question. Key to any such success is a common commitment on the part of parents and staff to a vision of a multicultural, antiracist school and, at the same time, a commitment to struggle as equal partners for its implementation.

There are several factors that go into ensuring that there is significant parental involvement at a school such as Fratney. First, the staff has a perspective that holds parents in respect and understands the importance of their participation at virtually all levels of the school operation. Parents must feel welcome through the words and actions of all staff—from the secretary who greets them to the classroom teachers and assistants who care for their children. At Fratney this perspective was contained in the very first documents presented to the board by Neighbors for a New Fratney and later codified in the parent-involvement statement approved by the site-based management council two years later.

A second factor is that the structures set up at the school must allow for substantive parental influence on school policy. Without such power, the likelihood of parents putting in long-term time commitments is nil. Fratney has assured this through a site-based management council that meets monthly. Other institutionalized forms of parental decision making include the curriculum committee and general parent meetings. The curriculum committee, which has met monthly for the last four years, consists predominantly of parents; its members thoroughly discuss issues of curriculum such as policies around homework, whole language, math, multiculturalism, and report cards. General meetings are held occasionally throughout the year, the most important one being in October when representatives to the site-based management council are elected.

A third factor is the devotion of adequate resources and time to ensure the organization and involvement of parents. At Fratney this has meant the hiring of a parent organizer whose priority is to recruit parents to become involved in the school at all levels. Our parent organizer acts as host, translator, advocate, and troubleshooter.

Another example of Fratney's school support of parent involvement is the previously mentioned Parent Project. The Parent Project is led by two teachers and includes fifteen parents who meet weekly for six weeks to discuss school and family issues and to do some writing. The parents are provided a stipend for their participation as well as child care and transportation. Each year the project ends with the publishing of a book of the parents' writings about their children. Many of the parents who have been involved in the Parent Project have become further involved at Fratney.

A fourth factor in involving parents is the quality of communication between the school and parents. For many schools such communication goes only in one direction—from school to parents. Certainly parents need to be kept informed, and many schools don't even do that. However, the flood of papers sent home are often written in incomprehensible ways or in a language not spoken by the parents. Such written documents at Fratney are always written in Spanish and English and laid out in a way that is easy to read. But oral communication through phone calls and face-to-face discussions has proven even more important, both because it is two-way and because the interaction of a dialogue ensures better understanding. Our full-time parent organizer, working with classroom teachers, organized two room-parents for each classroom (one English and one Spanish speaker) to help facilitate increased communication and assist the teacher.

A final factor in successfully involving parents is logistical. At Fratney, quality child care is provided at all parent meetings. A phone bank is organized once a year so that all families are called and personally invited to our annual Family Fun Day. When major policy statements are under consideration—such as homework policy, changes in report cards, multicultural policy, and so forth, we have circulated several written drafts over a period of months between staff meetings and parent meetings.

Robert Peterson

Conclusion: Reflections on School/Community Building

The absurdity of the city of Milwaukee's recommendation that we wait thirty years to fix up a run-down playground in a working-class neighborhood reflects the even more absurd priorities of the larger society. For the price of just two of the tanks used in the Persian Gulf War, or four Patriot missiles, we could rebuild all sixty playgrounds that need renovation in Milwaukee.

Just as Fratney's tot lot depended on demanding a reprioritization of public funds, so too does the success of the entire Fratney experiment. Large class sizes, a lack of teacher planning time, and the broader problems of poverty, child abuse, and unemployment all reflect the misguided priorities of putting private profit ahead of human needs.

For our efforts to bear fruit we must have not just a local vision, but a national vision as well. We must pursue education reform in the context in which it is embedded. Our schools cannot be saved in isolation from saving our cities, our families, and our children. An educational reform movement can not succeed without being part of a broader and more powerful movement to reform the basic structures of our society.

On a small scale we have seen this happen in the very origin of the Fratney project. By having parents, particularly those in the African American and Latino communities, demand greater control and participation in schools, an opening was created for Neighbors for a New Fratney. Similarly, our ability to train new teachers in progressive teaching techniques and train all our staff in multicultural, antiracist education is greatly enhanced by new district-wide policies that allocate monies for such matters.

The larger question, however, remains unanswered. How can our school community work within the context of broader struggles to make our city and nation a safer, healthier place to live? Our successful organizing campaign to rebuild our school playground was a small example of how a broader neighborhood coalition could obtain non–school board funds for a project that benefited both the school and the neighborhood. A similar effort succeeded in closing down a neighborhood bar that was having a negative effect on the community. These small efforts contain the seed through which broader community coalitions and projects can be built to link the parents of inner-city school children to activities and movements that will ultimately improve urban schools and communities alike.

Just as educational reform must be placed in the broader societal context, the Fratney experience has shown us that the reformation of

66

any particular school is strongly influenced by district-wide curricular reform and structural change. Of course the renaissance of any particular school—whether it be Fratney, the Bronx New School, or Central Park East—must be defended. These schools deserve more power and resources in the hands of the local councils of parents and educators who are running them. They serve as models for other educators. At the same time we must admit the limitations of school-by-school reform. Most of the fine alternative schools of the 1960s died as their originators moved on. The success of many of these schools, Fratney included, depends on the expenditure of ridiculous amounts of time and energy, something that is rarely reproducible.

We must institutionalize structures that allow and foster these kinds of change within the public schools and within the teaching profession itself. Specifically, time for staff development and collaborative curriculum planning must be structured into the school day and school year. Paid parent organizers, based at the school level, would substantively strengthen parent involvement. Assessment procedures that are not dependent on standardized achievement tests should be adopted at district, state, and national levels (i.e., for federal Chapter I programming).

Ultimately, the success of Fratney and other similar school projects is bound up tightly with the success of the broader social movements for justice and equality in our society. A school is not an island that can flourish unassisted if it is being hammered daily by waves of poverty, inequality, and violence.

3

The Denali Project

David Hagstrom

Introduction: The Loss of Homeland

If our children are to have bright and promising futures, we need to modify the way we think about school, family, and community. Our society has gone through some extraordinary changes over the past four decades. All across America, long-term patterns of family life have been markedly altered, if not completely transformed. The two-parent family is no longer the bedrock standard around which this society is oriented. Instead, we now have a multidimensional understanding of the family that is in a state of flux and transition. At the same time, because of increased mobility, many Americans have lost their ties with a particular geographic place; no specific land or region invites personal allegiance. The once-clear knowing about a homeland has been muddied.

Despite these social transformations, schools haven't changed all that much. Most certainly, they have not attempted to appreciate or adopt changed family mores, values, or practices. At best, they have attempted to belatedly cope with these changes. About ten years ago, I wrote a column for the *Chicago Tribune* entitled "Schools for a People Far from Home" (Hagstrom, 1981). In that piece, I reviewed a report of the work of Daniel Yankelovich, from the April 1981 issue of *Psychology Today*. His study presented a chilling view of an alienated people lacking a sense of community. I argued then that schools preoccupied with the basics were missing an opportunity to help children reclaim a sense of being at home. What I yearned for was something that might help us and our children move through our uncertainties and confusion to a clearer sense of where and who we are.

Since writing that column, I've moved to Alaska, developed an Alaskan orientation, and seen even more extreme examples of family deterioration. Here, schools *have* made modest adaptations to changing family patterns and give indications of even greater response and responsibility in the days ahead. As a result of my work in Alaska, I have come to believe that if Alaskan schools were to collectively develop and nurture a new concept of *extended family*—to include everyone who lives within a school neighborhood—we would be amazed at the richness and depth of personal development that would result. A school-birthed notion of extended family might in turn contribute to the vitality of the neighborhood at large—bringing comfort to the lonely, strength to the oppressed, and a sense of well-being to the entire community. Within such a context, schools could grow and children would thrive as learners.

This vision informs the Denali Project. An age-old African saying (also well known by Alaska Native peoples) declares, "It takes an entire village to raise a child." Rather than focus on absences or problems (single parents, dysfunctional family characteristics, etc.), the Denali Project celebrates the presence of everyone in the school community and encourages each person to do whatever is necessary to express his or her particular talent or ability. At the same time, each person shares responsibility for all the community's children.

This concept of creating an extended family is one of two major philosophical underpinnings of Alaska's Denali Project. The other is the creation of a rich understanding of a sense of place within the minds and hearts of the Denali people. Tony Hiss (1991) has said that understanding where you are in place and time may be almost as important as understanding who you are. Hiss shares the observation that our regional landscapes, our cities and countrysides, hold the key to our leading meaningful, satisfying lives. If we can unlock some of the mysteries within our natural surroundings, if we can learn to appreciate the flora and fauna of those natural settings where we live out our lives, if we can begin to understand the land around us—then our social and personal existence will take on new meaning.

David Hagstrom

Creating Community: The Denali Project

The Setting

Denali Elementary School is a downtown school in Fairbanks, Alaska. Once a proud centerpiece of the community, the school lost much of its sense of purpose as the community grew, built new schools, and left Denali to simply pick up and take care of those children who remained in the city's slowly deteriorating inner core. When I came to the school in 1988, teachers were leaving, parents were unhappy, and the children wanted something more from their school experience.

The Denali school community consists of a rich mix of ethnic groups, people from many different socioeconomic levels, and an interesting blend of longtime Alaskans and those new to the city. About twenty-five percent of the children are Alaska Native, another ten percent are African-American, and approximately fifteen percent are children from a wide variety of other minority backgrounds (Chinese, Korean, Filipino, Icelandic, etc.). The remaining fifty-percent Caucasian population consists of children born in twenty-eight states or other nations. The mothers and fathers of Denali children are in the military, or have a subsistence life-style, or are C.P.A.s, bank presidents, and C.E.O.s, or are artists, or are on welfare, or are engaged in fifty-two other forms of work activity. Denali children live in modern apartments, shacks, trailer homes, tenement houses, and $200,000 showplaces along the river. The Denali community is "the world in miniature," says the superintendent of schools. And, as in the world, every kind of misery and joy imaginable can be found there.

I came to Denali from the University of Alaska-Fairbanks. I was a professor in the Department of Education at the time, specializing in school leadership. The work was interesting and I enjoyed my teaching, but I longed to try out some of the approaches I preached in university classes in the day-to-day world of a public school. I was asked to come to Denali "until they could find a real principal . . . maybe in about six weeks." It was all the challenge I needed. Although the invitation was issued only three days before the beginning of the school year, I was there on day one, bright with hope and expectation but without a plan to meet the needs of at-risk kids. Little did I know it at that time, but over the next three years teachers, parents, and the children themselves would give me the ways to really make a difference in the lives of the Denali community.

Change from the Inside Out

Sometimes it is necessary to seize the moment. That's how we came to examine the mission of Denali School. At the close of school one day, five of us—two teachers, two parents, and I—stood by the office and discussed ways of linking curricula to student's experience. In a school like ours, we said, we've got to build on children's natural curiosity. They are such explorers outside of school. Why can't we help them discover more inside the school?

We decided the time was right to involve ourselves in serious conversations about this. "Who should be involved in such discussions?" one parent asked. "Oh, probably all the teachers and all the parents," said a teacher, "but let's just start with the five of us." "When should we start?" "Next Tuesday morning before school," was the answer. "Six in the morning at my house. Come for breakfast," one parent suggested. This is how we made our start at what turned out to be re-forming our school community as an extended family interested in finding our place.

As it turned out, the manner of our beginning ensured our success. School reform often is unsuccessful because it attempts to bring change to an institution from outside. We have all heard stories about top-down, mandated change: school district central-office personnel deciding all schools will initiate team teaching practices, state departments of education declaring all districts will use a new math curriculum, a national commission pushing parents to become involved in the work of their local schools. Sustained change doesn't occur in these ways. No matter how well-intentioned, outsiders cannot bring meaningful, long-lasting change to schools.

Change mandated from outside does not succeed because it does not involve the people who will be affected. Those who will live with the consequences are not involved in determining what needs to be changed, why it needs to be changed, and how it is to be changed. Top-down, mandated change means having to follow someone else's agenda according to someone else's timetable. It is easy to understand why such attempts fail. Just consider how resistant we are to doing anything not a part of our own personal value system. We make the time to do those things we feel are important. Those things considered important to others that we have not yet accepted or considered important have to wait their turn. We may or may not get around to them. This resistance is so simple to understand. Why haven't school reformers come to realize this commonsense truth?

Mandated change is doomed from the start because it attempts to

David Hagstrom

alter the culture of an organization without the permission of those at the culture's core. The Denali Project, however, began near the school's heart. Change was initiated from the inside. As a result, basic ways of doing school business were revised, major program changes occurred, and the very nature of the organization was altered. Reform at Denali School began with a breakfast meeting attended by only five persons.

At that meeting, I was told that parents and teachers aren't often asked their opinions about schools. They talk among themselves, of course, and there's much "if only" talk—if only strong values were taught at home, if only teachers were better paid—but conversations about the mission of the school do not occur. The parents and teachers at our breakfast meeting found discussion about what we wanted for Denali's children to be extraordinarily satisfying. Yes, we should connect our school program to the experiences our children were having outside the school. As a result of the Valdez oil spill, our children had been questioning the ways Alaskans care for the land and sea. Why not have an environmental focus for the school? From the earliest discussions at that initial meeting, it became clear that parents and teachers felt discovery and the environment were themes worth exploring as a curricular focus for the school. It was at this point that I knew we were really onto something.

The group decided to meet again the following Tuesday. Wasn't it a bit outrageous to be meeting at six o'clock in the morning for a school discussion like this? "Not at all," said one of the parents. "This is the only time I've got. Besides, I feel fresh at this hour." The others agreed and each vowed to bring an additional person the next week. We also agreed to see to it that the makeup of the Tuesday morning meetings always reflected the ethnic and socioeconomic makeup of the community as a whole. As a result, Alaska Native, Asian, and African American participation was strong from the start. From the very beginning, members of the group were quite clear: they did not want this conversation to be exclusive.

I volunteered to ask our students how they felt about Denali becoming a discovery school, where they could discover the excitement of inquiry—especially in the areas of science and math—and where they also could discover their own full potential. Here are a few samples of their written responses:

> I think the discovery school idea is a good idea because science and math are fun. I hope to make a career out of science. I know that a lot of the kids in my class love to explore and so

72

do I. I think the teachers should learn more about science so they can share more about that subject. I also think we should learn how to help the environment.

—*Stephanie Sandberg*

I'd like the teachers to learn more about science so they can tell the students more about the earth and sea. I like to discover things so I think the discovery school idea is good.

—*Jimmy Biddle*

I think the discovery school idea is a great idea because it gives the kids a chance to learn what they're interested in. With a discovery school you can go further than the textbook and do things like planting and growing a garden. It would be neat for the teachers to learn more things to teach us.

—*Kyla Cleworth*

At our next meeting, I read a couple of student responses to the group that now numbered ten. The notion of our becoming Alaska's Discovery School was now fueled by the positive reactions of the children. Parents and teachers attending that second meeting soon found themselves deeply involved in conversations about the nature of our children (what they're like and how they learn) and about the ways we could, in fact, become a discovery school. Our children really are curious, we affirmed. "They're very interested in animals," said one teacher. "They love to figure out how things work," said another. Parents began to talk about the connections we could make with the science departments at the high schools and at the university. "We have a world-famous science institute just three miles from here," a parent announced emphatically. "Let's find out if anyone over there wants to help us." So our second meeting ended with our reaching out for help.

This was the beginning of what was to become a predominant characteristic of the Denali Project: We declared what we didn't know and what we wanted to know. We asked who could help us obtain the needed information. In this case, we knew the university had the resources. We began making calls to science professors at the University of Alaska Fairbanks. Somewhat to our surprise, they welcomed our inquiries and gave us their enthusiastic support.

Beginning the next Tuesday, three university science professors and a high school biology teacher joined our discussions. By now it was clear we were accomplishing much more than simply identifying the characteristics of the school and determining the kind of schooling we wanted for our children. We were developing a new understanding about the interests of our children and how they learn. We were beginning to realize the importance of our simple idea of connecting the curriculum to our children's interests. Perhaps of greatest importance, parents, teachers, and other community members were beginning to feel a sense of ownership in the school. Everyone in the Tuesday meeting felt we were really onto something significant. We decided it was time to begin involving Denali's entire teaching staff.

As the teachers were invited to the expanded Tuesday sessions, their responses were recorded. "I've been wondering what you've been up to and now I'll be able to find out for myself." "You know, folks have been saying Denali is the best-kept secret in Fairbanks. Maybe the secret has something to do with Tuesday mornings." "It's awfully early, but if you're figuring out ways to help the kids, I'll be there." And so they were. From this time on, there were always thirty-five or more teachers and parents at our six o'clock meetings.

Now there was no turning back. We'd stumbled on the way to turn our school around, and that way was to involve the parents, teachers, and members of our wider community in meaningful conversations about our children, how they learn, and what they want to learn. Our desires became strongly influenced by those of our children. As a school community we'd grown a lot. Eventually, the membership of our Tuesday Morning Club (the name that began to be used for the discussion group) decided the time was right to begin involving the school district central office. The superintendent, Rick Cross, had been talking about the availability of funds for the older schools to make physical changes and order new equipment. Because Denali was the oldest elementary school in Fairbanks, we felt it deserved a portion of those monies. Tuesday Club members had visited the newer schools, had seen the modern computer labs and the up-to-date science facilities. They couldn't understand why their school shouldn't have similar supplies and equipment.

Superintendent Rick Cross and the members of the school board were also beginning to talk about the possibility that schools might apply for special "focus program" grants. Denali's Tuesday Morning Club saw these focus-grant possibilities as inviting and intriguing. Why couldn't Denali School be the first focus school in Fairbanks? How could we access such funds? I was instructed to confer with central office personnel to find answers to these questions.

The superintendent informed me that a representative group of parents and teachers from Denali should make a presentation to the school board to request status as a science-math focus school. But first we'd need to practice before the superintendent's cabinet (a group of central-office administrators). The central office staff would let us know if our presentation was ready to be given to the board. We agreed on a time and a place for the practice presentation. And then Rick said, "You'll only have twelve minutes to get your idea across. School board agendas are very full and that's all the time you'll be given."

"Twelve minutes is all we've got?" was the response I received when I told Tuesday Morning Club members of my success. "Yes, that's what we've got," I said. "How can we get our vision across within that time frame?" Gary Laursen, a high school science teacher, stood up and proclaimed, "Our only hope is to make it almost totally pictorial. These board members will need to see what it is that we have in mind." The club decided to make six or seven posters, with a different person holding each poster and giving just two or three minutes of explanation. The message would be the visuals.

These were the words we determined best expressed our vision for the school:

- Denali Elementary Wants to Be Alaska's Discovery School
- Total Community Effort
- Teachers as Learners
- A New Partnership with the University
- A Curriculum Based on the Characteristics of Our Children and the Needs of Alaska
- Bringing About Change from Within
- Shared Leadership

Because our Denali family is such a rich mix of ethnic/racial and socioeconomic origins, we decided to have the seven posters held by seven children who represented Denali's special cross section of the world. Our seven speakers should represent the makeup of our Tuesday morning discussion group, so we selected a high school teacher, a university professor, a member of the Fairbanks business community, the principal, a Denali teacher, and two parents to tell our story and to plead our case for focus school status. We truly wanted Denali to become Alaska's Discovery School, and we viewed the board presentation as the critically important first step toward the realization of our dream.

On the appointed day, when we made our first practice run in front of Rick's cabinet, only the superintendent responded.

"Twenty minutes long," Rick said. "I told you twelve minutes and I'm holding you to that. Give it again and cut out eight minutes. Also,

David Hagstrom

I told you when you gave me the overview that we'd consider this idea only if it was guaranteed to be a long-term effort. I don't want to see you focusing on something else in a couple of years. Let me know the number of years you're going to commit to this idea."

We cut those eight minutes by dropping one point from each person's presentation and talking faster. More important, I told the group, "Okay, folks, from this point forward we've got a seven-year plan." We gave the presentation again. Exactly twelve minutes. When we got to the end, Rick stood up, moved toward the door, and told us, "See you at the board meeting." That was it. And we cheered.

As it has turned out, the superintendent's demand that our plan be worked out over a period of years has accounted for much of the success of the endeavor. Rick's insistence that we commit ourselves year after year, without yielding to other inviting projects or interests that might tempt us, has made an important difference between our project and other innovations that flit in and out of schoolhouse doors. In an exhausting three-week period between the rehearsal and the school board presentation, the members of our presentation team did in fact work out a timetable for staff development, curriculum revision, student development, and community activities over a seven-year period.

Our actual board presentation was, at one and the same time, anticlimactic and marvelously celebrative. An interesting phenomenon occurred at that meeting: more than one hundred Denali parents crowded into the board room. It was standing room only, and according to one board member, more parents and teachers attended our presentation than had attended any other noncontroversial, noncrisis school board activity. I heard one mom exclaim as she left the room, "I'm so proud of Denali tonight." I think that's how we all felt. We'd accomplished something very special in a time period that had spanned no more than six months. As one Tuesday Morning Club member said later on, "We're such ordinary people, but we've actually accomplished some rather extraordinary things." What these ordinary people did was indeed extraordinary. They turned a school around. And they did it from the inside out.

Building on Success

Our ideas were eventually recorded in a little green booklet that we now refer to on a regular basis. It's our mission statement: *The Denali Discovery School Plan*. In it, we describe the curiosity we see in our children and the hopes we have for Alaska—the need we feel for having a better balance between giving and taking in our state. We describe our vision of an elementary school that captures the natural curiosity of children and creates a discovery-school focus. We list the expectations we have for changes teachers will make in the ways they teach and the expectations that teachers and parents have for new learning for the children. We describe what is meant by community effort, how teachers are to become learners again, and how the community's vision is linked to the need for a massive staff development effort. The plan outlines these efforts, provides science course descriptions, contains ways to revise and align the curriculum, and lists improvements expected in student achievement and attitude. The little booklet also notes goals for each of the seven years and provides ways to evaluate progress being made with the project. It provides an outline, a time line, and the incentive that children, teachers, and parents need to keep the school moving forward.

The massive staff development effort outlined in our plan now operates full force at Denali School. As a result of money received from First Funds and an Eisenhower Grant for the Improvement of Elementary Education, Denali teachers became engaged in a weekly effort to develop their own knowledge of and skills in teaching science, skills which would be used in turn to develop science knowledge, skills, and abilities in the children. Denali is no different from elementary schools across the nation: our teachers are primarily trained in language arts; they have had few courses in science and math. The parent and teacher members of the Tuesday Morning Club believed that an understanding of science and math would give Denali kids an edge on the future. On Fridays during the first two years of the project, science professors from the University of Alaska-Fairbanks came to Denali to work with the teachers. Along with them came twenty or more substitute teachers to take teachers' classrooms, thus enabling the regular staff to work on their own education. Those in-service sessions are more modest now, but the university-Denali tie is as close as ever; professors continue their strong commitment to make the project work. They believe strongly that they are true members of this school community.

This course work led to spin-offs: an award-winning gardening program, science connections with our sister school in Japan, a schoolwide computer network, and recycling efforts. One of our most popular programs is a community garden, just sixty feet from the school. Three years ago, a parent with a 4-H background came up with this wonderful idea. Agreeing that all kids could benefit from an understanding of how things grow, parents and community members pitched in to help.

David Hagstrom

Every child in the school has a personal plot in the garden. We take advantage of this hands-on science opportunity by coordinating our school-wide science curriculum appropriately by grade level with what's occurring in the community garden. When school isn't in session, the 4-H Club and interested neighbors water and tend the garden. With summer temperatures in Fairbanks reaching the 80s and 90s, and with twenty-two to twenty-three hours of sunlight daily in June and July, we've been able to grow some beautiful flowers and lush vegetables: giant cabbages, carrots, beans, peas, potatoes, pumpkins, melons. At state fair competitions, we've won numerous first places. The community garden is a source of pride.

As pleased as we were with our communal efforts and a rise in students' achievement test scores, we knew we still were not doing enough to meet the needs of our at-risk children. Because of the project's success and our continuing concerns, Denali's parents and teachers elected to apply for the private support of the RJR Nabisco Foundation. Of the approximately 1600 applications that were received by the foundation, Denali Elementary and fourteen other schools nationwide were chosen as "Next Century Schools."

With this three-year influx of $750,000 Denali has been able to embark on a number of unique projects tied to the school's overall vision. Teachers have begun the time-consuming and intellectually demanding process of rethinking the science curriculum. They have developed a curricular matrix composed of scientific themes and processes that is now used as a vehicle for structuring the course work they present to students. Themes include such topics as rain forests and endangered species, plant growth and development, and magnets and motions. For each topic, students apply scientific processes such as the following: observing; questioning; predicting; hypothesizing; measuring; collecting, organizing, interpreting, and presenting data; and applying findings. Teachers are currently developing kits composed of curriculum guides and the material needed for appropriate hands-on activities for the different themes that are part of the overall curriculum.

In addition, Denali sponsored a science camp for elementary school children throughout Fairbanks during the summer of 1992. This camp focused primarily on natural history. A comparable camp for the summer of 1993 is also planned, although teachers are committed to extending their focus to topics such as space, chemistry, and technology. Building upon the school's concern about nurturing a sense of place, students also have the opportunity to participate in an exchange program with an Athabaskan village in the Alaskan Interior. Denali hosts students from this village during a week-long stay in Fairbanks and sends a contingent of its own children to spend a week living among Alaska Native families. There, they will feed sled dog teams, go dog mushing, learn how to set rabbit snares and a marten trapline, and participate in dances and songfests. Members of the Denali Advisory Board are sensitive to the fact that the Nabisco funding will end in 1994 and are now anticipating ways that they might sustain these educational opportunities through other fund-raising activities.

Evaluation activities associated with the "Next Century School" grant have demonstrated that the Denali Project is having an impact on both students and teachers. Although the initial improvement in Iowa Test of Basic Skills scores (attributed by some to improved morale) has remained steady, most teachers and parents associated with the school are convinced that current assessment procedures are not sophisticated enough to measure the real growth Denali students are achieving in science. Therefore, the staff has been very involved in the statewide movement to develop alternative assessment measures. Denali teachers have pioneered a variety of observation and project-type assessment strategies; using these measures, Denali students demonstrate significant gains.

Members of the school community, parents as well as teachers, are quick to point out that there are other measures of the school's success. They note, for example, that the number of students participating in district and state science fairs has increased dramatically over the past few years—from a handful in 1987 to 126 in 1992. Anecdotal records transmitted from middle schools that enroll students who have graduated from Denali also indicate that Denali students understand the curriculum they encounter in the seventh and eighth grades better than students from other schools. They are commonly viewed as among the most outstanding students in their science classrooms.

Finally, and perhaps most significant, is the impact the reform effort has had on the professional lives of Denali's teachers. As a group, they have attempted to "unpack" what it means to integrate a discovery-science approach into their own instructional practice. In their conversations regarding this topic, they have entered a reflective teaching mode seldom visited by elementary classroom teachers, considering such issues as the relationship between children's exploratory activities and conceptual development. Teachers' self-report forms furthermore indicate that they are teaching more science using the discovery-science approach. These developments have been documented in "Belief into Practice: An Exploration of the Linkage between Elementary Teachers'

Beliefs about the Nature of Science and Their Classroom Practices," a doctoral dissertation prepared by Deborah Pomeroy (1993) for the Harvard Graduate School of Education.

Reflections

Looking back on the initial work of the Denali Project after four years, I share the following observations. First and foremost, the experience illustrates how the interactive and collective process of developing a mission for our school served as a vehicle for creating a Denali community. The building of our "extended family" began with our efforts to articulate our wishes for our children and our beliefs about who our children are. Just as members of an actual extended family come from different walks of life and carry particular roles through which they contribute to the group, so did members of the Tuesday Morning Club. Some came from teacher and parent groups, others from the university, and still others from the business community. They ranged from the well-to-do to those on welfare. Alaska Natives, African Americans, Asian Americans, and Caucasians all brought their special perspectives and skills to the effort.

The project is an example of shared vision building. As a principal new to the school, I really didn't know what I was doing at the time and in fact was just following my leadership instincts. It now seems to me that I acted to facilitate the creation of a sense of family within a school community and to establish a deep understanding of the place that is home to the school family. I felt the first question I needed to ask teachers and parents was, What are your hopes and dreams for our children, and how can the school make these hopes and dreams into reality? When I asked this question at our first Tuesday morning meeting, I truly had not a clue to the possible answers this group of people would provide.

It was fascinating to me, and a bit scary as well, to later hear folks articulate science and mathematics as the program areas they wished to develop. It was fascinating in that I said to myself, "Well, of course this is the way an Alaskan school should prepare children for full and productive lives. Why didn't I think of this?" It was scary in that I knew very little about science and math. I had been an English and social studies teacher, and I was a sociology and psychology major in college. "I would have been quite the resource," I thought to myself, "if they'd said, 'We want Denali to be a social studies school.'"

But they didn't say that. They said, "We want Denali to become Alaska's Discovery School, rich in opportunities to explore mathematics and science." Although none of us were experts who could quickly and easily create a Discovery School, this turned out to be an advantage. None of us were granted power by the group by virtue of possessing certain knowledge. In fact, the one teacher who did consider herself to be an "expert" found it difficult to locate her niche within the project. Our general, collective lack of knowledge and our inexperience in science and math gave everyone a place in the emerging school community concerns. We were able to figure out collectively who could help us with needed resource information or skills, or we had some interests we could personally develop. Although the approach to science education at Denali is *not* extraordinary in terms of current trends in science education, what is extraordinary is the total school commitment to it and to the rethinking of practices and learning and exploration which it necessitates.

In the development of our own interests and talents, and in the collective search for resource assistance, *we became a family*. We tapped into long-ignored science-related hobby areas; mine was amateur radio and gardening, one parent's interest was mining and minerals, another's was astronomy. A group of parents and teachers worked together to develop science kits—a series of boxes containing readings, experiments, and other materials related to a given subject—that could be checked out by children and their parents; now, at any one time, scores of these kits are checked out from school and are being used at home. We became ad hoc personnel resource recruitment teams. We even formed teacher-parent research groups to check out math and science teaching techniques in Japan. (We actually went to Japan, as ethnically balanced teams of Denali teachers, parents, and children, seeking answers that would work for us.) We began to understand and care for each other as individuals while working toward common goals. We became an extended family in the process of making the school what we wanted it to be for the children.

Two examples of the way we created this sense of family seem especially worth sharing: the creation of "talking circles" within the staff, and the establishment of the Native elders project within the school. Both activities are central to the care we provided for one another.

At the conclusion of our first year together, the Denali teachers accepted an invitation to attend a summer in-service session in Sitka, Alaska. At this meeting, the teachers asked themselves how they could better support one another in the difficult business of transforming the school into a true community. While parent-teacher activities were worthwhile and important, the teachers felt they had to have some form of support group just for themselves. One of the Alaska Native teachers suggested that the faculty adopt the Native process of gathering in "talking circles" to express individual concerns and create group cohesiveness. So, within a circle format, on a regular basis, the teachers went around the group, each time introducing themselves (in terms of their family upbringing) and sharing joys and concerns (uninterrupted) for as long as they wanted. This practice brought the staff together and created an extended family.

At the beginning of the second year, the project was clearly focused on "resources available to us." As we brainstormed these resources, a parent urged us to consider the opportunity that was almost uniquely ours: to explore the talent and knowledge available to us from our Alaska Native elders. We had already initiated an Alaska Native Education Program within our school, whereby all students were introduced to Alaska Native practices and ways of knowing. Why not establish a teaching format that would allow elders to be present within the school to share Native science practices and special Native teaching techniques—storytelling in particular? And so we did! On a regular basis, Alaska Native elders have "lived" in the school, have learned to love the school, and have taught the children to appreciate their unique talents and abilities.

In ways such as these, we also created a sense of place. We didn't start out saying, "This meeting is called for the purpose of creating a sense of place." Instead, as we went about the work of making Denali a fine science-math school, we realized that for the children to have the kinds of science experiences they needed, they would have to develop an intimate understanding of the natural world they lived in—in Fairbanks, Alaska. They needed that knowledge to be able to decide what changes they wanted to make in their world. In Denali's case, the children decided we needed to give more to Alaska. Now it was time to add to the beauty and richness of Alaska with wise environmental practices and a careful nurturing of the land.

The Denali Project was, and is, a family affair rooted in place. But I didn't start out thinking that's what I wanted. I didn't start out with a vision for the school. I simply asked the people, "What do you want for your children?" In truth, I was committed to help make into reality whatever the people answered. But I had no grand scheme for the school. What I did have (and still have) is a strong love for the children and a deep respect for the teachers and parents.

Recommendations

If I were to make just one recommendation as a result of my participation in the Denali Project, it is this: On a regional basis, set up special leadership institutes offering principals the opportunity to think through their own attitudes about school-community relationships and to develop skills to help their school communities assess strengths and weaknesses, determine the characteristics of the children they serve, and plan the unique and particular programs that truly suit the people who inhabit that place. In this way, we'd help aspiring and practicing principals develop the attitudes and skills necessary to facilitate change from the inside out.

Transforming schools into true communities (that is, thinking about a school as a community, instead of an organization) is *very difficult work*. The Denali community experienced firsthand some of the ironies about school improvement described by Carl Glickman (1990):

- The more an empowered school improves, the more apparent it is that there's more to improve.
- The more an empowered school works collectively, the more individual differences and tensions become obvious.
- The more an empowered school becomes a model for success, the less the school becomes a practical model for other schools to follow.

I am convinced that the only way to transform schools—and to sustain that transformation—is for the individual school initiators, the principals, to come together on a regular basis and to support one another in this endeavor. Without a support-group network, I am convinced that the individual efforts of changing schools—one school at a time—will fail. The work is simply too frustrating and exhausting. As the saying goes, "we need each other." That goes especially for principals attempting to create schools that are true communities! As another saying goes, "Everyone wants to go to heaven, but no one wants to die" (Memphis Slim, as quoted in Glickman, 1990).

Denali is an example of a school that has made basic changes from the inside out, changes that are making a difference in the lives of children. This has come about as a result of widespread community effort and facilitation on the part of the school leadership. The Denali Project may not fit every school and, as Glickman points out, the specifics of what is being done at Denali are not meant to be duplicated across the country. Each school and every community is different.

David Hagstrom

However, the broad concepts of community involvement, a proactive attitude, and the notion that our schools need drastic reform could apply to all schools everywhere. I hope this story of the Denali Project gives you the encouragement to become involved in turning a school around and, as a result, turning around the lives of children that you care about.

Conclusion: Schools for a People Far from Home

It is critical that the people of a particular geographical location cultivate a deep understanding of their sense of place. In fact, it is in the discovery of place that one achieves identity and truly begins to understand oneself. This is especially true in Alaska, where so many recently transplanted residents feel dislocated and misplaced. I am no different. A transplant from the Midwest, I had to make all of the adjustments people make as they find their way in a new land. In some ways, I adjusted successfully. In other ways, the adjustment was a disaster. I yearned for my home place, wishing to be miraculously whisked away and carried back to my Wisconsin farm. When the opportunity came to be at Denali, something deep inside recognized that this assignment held an important reward for me. As I helped the Denali people discover who and where they were, I found myself "at home" as well.

In the *Chicago Tribune* column I wrote a decade ago, I argued for neighborhood involvement in local schools as a way to bring meaning to people's lives: "Let's put our people to the task of determining what schools should be, support the work in ways that count, and watch the best ideas grow" (Hagstrom, 1981). I argued for local control in determining goals of good schooling in neighborhoods and in shaping programs. By getting involved in our local school, we would create a sense of community which, in turn, would allow us to feel more at home in our world. I believed then, and am more convinced now than ever, that "given the chance to seek out solutions, people in the neighborhoods will dream the big dreams. They will make no little plans" (Hagstrom, 1981). I concluded, "Strange as it may seem, as we take measures to improve schooling in our local school, as we become involved neighborhood by neighborhood, we may achieve much more than we set out to do" (Hagstrom, 1981).

Participation, involvement, and commitment may give us not just the schools we need, but also feelings of satisfaction and contentment—

feelings that signal having arrived home. Alaska's Denali Project was, and is, an initiative designed to erase the boundary between school and community. By creating community, we can become engaged in a homecoming of the spirit.

AUTHOR'S NOTE: In November 1991, I left the Denali principalship to begin my new work as director of the Alaska Center for Educational Leadership, an organization whose mission is to create a sense of school renewal and revitalization in all schools across Alaska. The Denali experience had encouraged me to try out the kind of leadership institute I have recommended. Although I am no longer a part of Denali's day-to-day effort, I continue to feel a part of this community.

References

Glickman, C. (1990). Speech at Meeting of International Network of Principal Centers, April 28, Breckenridge, Colo.

Hagstrom, D. (1981). Schools for a people far from home. *Chicago Tribune*, September 26.

Hiss, T. (1991). *The experience of place.* New York: Knopf.

Pomeroy, D. (1993). Belief into practice: An exploration of the link between elementary teachers' beliefs about the nature of science and their classroom practice. Ed. diss., Harvard Graduate School of Education, Cambridge, Mass.

4

Building Community in an Alternative Secondary School

Dave Lehman

"In and through community lies the salvation of the world." Thus psychologist M. Scott Peck begins the introduction to his book *The Different Drum: Community Making and Peace* (1987: 17). This may be overstated, yet building community is increasingly becoming a major concern in all kinds of groups from business and industry to social agencies and schools. Our need for community seems to be a basic component of who we are as human beings. Something in us yearns for connectedness to others and the transcendence of loneliness and separation. As McLaughlin and Davidson (1986: 10) note, "The word community contains the word unity and, on the deepest level, community is the experience of unity or oneness with all people and with all life."

In contemporary America, however, our need for the experience of community has been obscured by our desire for material comfort and security. Affluence and possessions have usurped the attention we once devoted to relationships. Wealth and goods, however, have not brought us the happiness we anticipated. Instead, our society has become increasingly fragmented, and loneliness, according to some sociologists and mental health experts, has achieved epidemic proportions (Wachtel, 1989: 166–68).

Some educators have argued that schools may provide a way out of this impasse. Because of the absence of community in other domains of contemporary life, schools may be one of the few modern institutions capable of helping the young mature in ways that will contribute to the well-being of the broader social environments in which they live (Raywid, 1988). Others have suggested that moving in this direction could be an antidote to many of the ills that currently plague our schools. Gregory and Smith (1987), for example, have observed that schools that cultivate a sense of community are characterized by increased commitment among students and teachers, less alienation, improved motivation, and greater autonomy for teachers. After reviewing data from the *High School and Beyond* study of 357 U.S. secondary schools, Bryk and Driscoll (1988) concluded that schools demonstrating a "communal organization" displayed less social misbehavior, lower dropout rates, higher student interest, and greater gains in mathematics achievement between sophomore and senior years. Teachers in these schools were also positively affected by the schools' greater sense of community. They "were much more likely to report satisfaction with their work, to be seen by students as enjoying their teaching, and to share a high level of staff morale. Teacher absenteeism was also lower" (Bryk and Driscoll, 1988: i).

If such conclusions are indeed as significant and as important as these studies seem to indicate, then what are the essential elements of a genuine school community? How might these be developed in a secondary school?

Essential Elements of Community

Bryk and Driscoll describe three "core concepts" found in schools that exhibit a communal school organization. First, such institutions are characterized by a set of common beliefs about what students should learn, how people in the school should behave, and the kind of adults students could become. Second, their teachers and administrators had developed activities capable of linking all school members to one another and the school's traditions. Third, social relations throughout the school were infused with an ethos of caring and collegiality. All of these concepts need to be present before a school can be characterized as a community.

Peck (1987) also outlines a set of factors that need to be kept in mind when people seek to create communitarian social environments. Learning how to communicate with one another is primary. Although many of us know how to establish positive social relations in some instances, the rules of this process, such as the need to acknowledge

Dave Lehman

rather than suppress interpersonal conflict, are generally unconscious and easily forgotten from one situation to the next. Making these rules explicit and practicing them can help people remember what works. Peck believes that the majority of people are capable of internalizing these rules and are generally willing to follow them, although the process of community building—with its stages of pseudocommunity, chaos, emptiness, and finally, community—will demand persistence and commitment.[1]

Our experience in building community at the Alternative Community School seems only to confirm these general ideas and to indicate that the "core concepts" and "stages" identified by others function in a cyclical series of changes due to the continual influx of new staff and students and the constant forming and re-forming of various groups within the overall school community.

Ways of Building a School Community

The Alternative Community School in Ithaca, New York, is a public, open-enrollment, self-selection school of choice for some 260 middle school and high school students whose backgrounds reflect the diversity of the Ithaca school district. Here we have developed a multifaceted approach through which we strive to create and continually build a sense of genuine community among our staff, students, and parents. Over the past eighteen years of our existence, we have discovered at least three general principles:

1. Community building is a continuous process of creating and re-creating and requires a school-wide project approximately every three years.
2. Community building needs to be worked on throughout the school year and in a wide variety of ways in order to involve all staff and students in meaningful activities.
3. Community building needs to include not only activities, but ongoing structures and process as well.

Following are the major ways, at present, that we are using to build community among our students and staff at the Alternative Community School.

88

Special All-School Projects or Activities

We have had to physically relocate our school twice in our eighteen years, and with each move came total school involvement in developing major input to our local board of education about where we should move, what kind of space we needed, what kind of new equipment should be bought, and what renovations would be needed. This was followed by summer work parties to clean up the outside grounds, to paint and organize the rooms, to construct shelves, to move furniture, to paint new murals on the corridor walls and a new sign over the front entrance, and finally to hold a grand opening ceremony. In the not too distant future, we hope the board approves the opening of a second satellite site to allow us to accommodate the large number of students on our waiting list, and this will, once again, provide an opportunity for community building.

Our most recent whole-school community project or activity has been the construction of a "Yurt Retreat Center"—an exercise in building community by building a community building! The original idea to build something came in part from the construction of a geodesic dome in the Catskills Mountains by a group of junior high school students in the Dome Project, an alternative school program in New York City. In his poignant and insightful book *To Become Somebody: Growing Up against the Grain of Society* (1982), Dome Project director John Simon describes their hopes for that project:

> The finished product, the dome structure, would embody the self-respect our program aimed to foster. The process of constructing it, however, would be at least equally important, giving cognitive and affective substance to our efforts. Our adolescent dome-builders would have to learn to measure, calculate, read plans, follow written instructions, perform tasks in proper sequence, and keep accurate records of their progress. They would also have to learn to cooperate, tolerate some frustration, delay gratification, cope with responsibility, make individual and group decisions, and develop self-discipline. (Simon, 1982: 71)

Our hopes for our yurt were no less grandiose. The yurt program began some two years ago on the initiative of the parents of three of our graduates who wanted to do something of lasting importance in appreciation to the Alternative Community School. With the direction and hands-on support of Bill Copperwaithe and the Yurt Foundation, this experiential learning activity began with the building of a "play yurt." During this two-day project we constructed a working model of a yurt out of Masonite board and ropes. The play yurt was designed to be transportable and used by youngsters in the prekindergarten program housed in our building.

We then moved on to the "real thing." To date, virtually all of the staff, numerous former students, and approximately seventy-five percent of the school's current students have been involved in constructing this wooden structure, which is twenty-four feet in diameter. An extended project group of students (those who had learned the most about the measuring, calculating, and reading of plans) met every Thursday morning with one of our teachers to work on the yurt. On weekends, work parties of staff, students, parents, and friends of the school devoted their energies to the project. In 1992, our annual fall retreat (see below) was turned into a five-day "Yurt Raising." Now that the yurt is completed, it is available for small groups of students in special classes or projects as well as staff for overnight, weekend, or longer "retreats" or study groups. Thus, it will continue to be used by our school to build community.

There is a particular authenticity in the contact made between teachers and students on the construction of the yurt, whether it be a matter of measuring the placement of boards for the "inner yurt" with a student classified as learning disabled, or working with two female high school students who were skeptical of their carpentry skills, or stepping back to let a ninth grader direct a group of other students in the design and construction of an elaborate scaffold for the nailing of cedar shakes to the roof. Staff and students all come to know each other more fully as total human beings, with strengths and weaknesses, points of discouragement, and times of great satisfaction at our accomplishments, when sharing the experience of building something together, in community.

Beginning-of-the-Year Student Orientation

We begin each school year with a three-day orientation, planned during the summer by an ad hoc group of students and staff. The orientation begins after Labor Day with a separate day just for new students. This is followed by two more days with the whole student population and includes a variety of small- and large-group activities for students to get to know each other, to make decisions about any key issues for beginning the new year, to do some writing, and to work individually with a staff member as an advisor in setting goals for the year and to develop a schedule for our first nine-week cycle.

Annual Fall Retreat

In about mid-October, the whole school, staff and students alike, leaves Ithaca for a nearby outdoor education nature center retreat facility for two days. The middle school students attend for one day, then they have a second day of special activities at school. Meanwhile, the high school students and staff stay overnight, spending the second day without the middle schoolers. Our student trips committee plans the retreat, and it typically includes opportunities for individual and group challenges on a "Project Adventure" ropes course, a game of "Survival," lots of sports, the preparation of meals together, an evening talent show, group singing, and time simply for everyone to hang out together.

During this retreat, there is something special about watching our middle school staff and students on the ropes course as they encourage and cheer each other on with each new challenge. Creativity and cooperation are developed as unusual mixes of students attempt the group physical challenges. Climbing a twenty-foot pole and then standing on the top and jumping to grab the bar of a rope swing—whether you are large or small, student or staff member, male or female, well coordinated or not—never fails to bring forth words of encouragement from those watching, calls of suggestions, then moments of deep respectful quiet. Finally, the boisterous cheering, even if the bar is missed, makes everyone feel closer.

Daily Morning Meetings of the Whole School Community

Rather than utilize the cold and impersonal public address system for morning announcements, we gather our whole school at midmorning in our small gym. For about ten minutes individual staff and students make announcements, acknowledge birthdays, ask for personal and family support at times of crisis, celebrate special accomplishments, and take our daily attendance by "family groups," with each staff teacher/counselor having a few moments to at least check in with his or her student advisees.

The week the Persian Gulf War broke out, emotions ran high with mixed feelings. It was natural for us to take some extended time to talk together at the morning meeting the day after the bombing began. There were tears shed for loved ones who had been called to serve, suggestions of things that could be sent to the troops, plans to organize efforts to end the war, anger and frustration expressed that the war was actually occurring, an offer to acquire information about resisting draft registration. It was a genuine time to let all of us speak about what was in our hearts and on our minds, and to listen respectfully to one another. Members of a community need to take time to listen to each other, and not just about school business.

Twice Per Week Family Group Meetings

Virtually every staff member serves as a teacher/counselor/ advisor for a small group of ten to fifteen family group members or advisees. These staff act as advocates for students, as liaisons to their parents, as advisors with respect to the school curriculum and each student's schedule, and as facilitators of small-group discussions regarding school and/or personal issues. They are organizers of special family group fund-raising events and other special occasions such as family group luncheons, long afternoons, overnights, weekend retreats (now being held at our new Yurt Retreat Center!), or special trips. These groups serve as small communities within our larger total school community and function as laboratories in human relations, helping students build communication and mediation skills similar to those outlined by Peck (1987) as essential to the development of a genuine community.

It is not uncommon for family groups to use their meeting time (and often lunchtime as well) to touch base with each other. This is simply a process where members of the group have a chance to say what is going on in their lives. Such sharing often brings these groups close together, for it is tremendously important that we build in time to listen to each other in striving to create a genuinely caring community. Family groups provide one such structure to help us accomplish this goal.

Student Committees and All-School Town Meetings

We run our school community democratically. Two of the key structures for organizing such democratic work are our student committees and our weekly all-school town meetings (or sometimes "half-school" or "quarter-school" meetings). Staff serve as facilitators of our student committees, which meet twice per week for the equivalent of a class period. A student Agenda Committee plans and runs the all-school town meeting based on proposals that have come to them. These meetings are used to make school-wide decisions and to have bimonthly special entertainment or fun events. Students select different committees to serve on each cycle or remain with their current committee.

Having both the all-school town meeting process and the family group structure provides us with the means for dealing with a crisis or tragedy in our school community. This past year we began the third week of school with the tragic death of one of our eighth-grade boys, who was killed while riding his bicycle home down the hill behind our school. Our all-school town meeting and family groups gave us the opportunity to begin the difficult healing process. We initially met in an all-school town meeting the morning after the accident to hear briefly about the tragedy. The rest of the morning was then devoted to meeting in pairs of family groups, each with its staff leaders and a professional social worker, counselor, or psychologist for an extended period of time. Abbreviated classes were followed by an early dismissal to allow all who so wished to attend the funeral. Without these structures and processes already available, we would have had to create something like them from scratch at a most difficult time of emotional strain. A community needs to create such structures and processes if it is to act on a value of caring.

Special Community-Wide Events

We have several annual school-wide, special, primarily evening events. In November, we sponsor a spaghetti dinner followed the next day with the Oxfam-America Fast for a World Harvest. We have at least one middle school and one high school drama production, a spring brunch, and an evening arts festival with art, music, and poetry. Recently, we have added basketball and volleyball competition with other alternative high schools in our area.

There is a special sense of belonging that comes whenever we cook food with one another. Cooking and eating together, with time to talk, play, and be entertained, produces a particularly powerful community-building feeling. This is another leveler, a common experience in which distinctions between old and young become subsumed in the activity and the camaraderie.

Dave Lehman

Annual Week-long Spring Trips

Students take on the task in their family groups to raise a portion of the money needed for spring trips. These experiential alternative learning activities recently have included local camping and rock climbing in the Finger Lakes region, short and long biking trips, camping and wilderness trips, horseback riding, fishing, and working and camping on a Mohawk Reservation. Some groups have traveled to foreign countries such as Mexico and the Virgin Islands. These groups meet weekly for at least one whole afternoon for an entire quarter planning and organizing their trips, training and learning special skills needed for their trip, and raising additional funds if necessary. They all have common goals such as tent camping and living close to the earth for the week, learning to work together as a small community, meeting a physical or other personal challenge, and having fun!

Year in and year out these trips result in powerful and personally transforming experiences for many of our students and staff. There are many examples of students who never thought they could do what was called for, who lacked personal confidence and self-esteem, and yet with the support of the group pulled through and rose to new levels of personal strength and understanding. There is something particularly important about being on the road for a week with a common goal, away from home, away from the familiar, coupled with a physical challenge like riding a bicycle with thirty or forty pounds for fifty to eighty miles a day, where you only have your companions to depend on for whatever happens. It calls on the deepest of personal strengths and the highest of human qualities. Time and again, life-changing stories convince us that all the time and energy put into planning and fund-raising is more than worth it.

Community-Service Requirement for High School Graduation

Our high school students must all complete a minimum of thirty hours of community service, either service in school, such as tutoring younger students or teaching one of our special extended projects, or in the greater Ithaca community, where students might assist with voter registration, volunteer in a local soup kitchen, or work with the homeless or the physically challenged. For as Mary Anne Raywid points out, we can't ". . . count on the somewhat mystical hopes of ever-widening circles, or on the automatic extension of fairly particular and immediate bonds to people and institutions at increasing remove. The school must

94

deliberately seek to bond youngsters to people and institutions outside the school" (Raywid, 1988: 24–25).

Recently, one of our African-American young men who registered voters in our downtown neighborhood as his community service had the profound experience of coming to understand the importance of being able to read and write, an experience which led him to want to return after college to his community to help others to learn and prepare themselves for higher education. A senior girl, who spent her entire last year at the school volunteering in a home for the aged because of her interest in the field of geriatrics, decided to pursue another occupational direction because of her experience. Another young man spent his senior year in Washington, D.C., volunteering with the homeless. He decided that he wanted to pursue a career of service to others. Beginning to care in the more confined (perhaps even safe) environment of the school community can indeed be the preparation for caring participation in the greater outside community during adulthood.

Middle School Promotion and High School Graduation

In June, on two consecutive nights, the whole school community (staff, students, and parents, as well as extended family members, former graduates, and friends) gathers for very special celebrations to promote and graduate our eighth graders and seniors. The middle school promotion is typically held outdoors at a local state park (with a large pavilion available in case of inclement weather). Each eighth grader is presented individually by his or her family group leader, who describes the unique qualities of each student that are to be highlighted and celebrated. Likewise, the high school graduation ceremony is held in a special location (selected by the senior class) with outdoor and indoor facilities. The celebration includes a presentation of senior projects (some of which are performed and others of which are displayed), a potluck dessert, and a similar presentation of each individual senior by a staff member close to that graduate. Each graduating senior receives not only his or her own diploma, but a rose, and a book individually selected by the staff.

There have been many wonderful senior projects at our high school graduation ceremony. The young man who completely rebuilt a Camaro and drove it to graduation, the lovely shawl and sweater that had been made starting from raw wool, a series of photographs of each senior done by a classmate that were of such high quality people couldn't believe they were the work of a student, original music, original dance, original sculpture, original computer programs—all demonstrate in concrete ways the special gifts of each of our graduating seniors.

Of even more importance is the process of having eighth graders or seniors come forward individually to be presented for promotion or graduation with poignant and humorous recountings of accomplishments and struggles by a staff member particularly close to them. For example, one of our graduates had received a serious head injury in late grade school that took away much of his memory. He had waged a heroic personal struggle to rebuild that memory and to accomplish the academic tasks needed to earn a full high school diploma. A young woman who had tried to take her life as a sophomore returned from an adolescent psychiatric ward to successfully complete high school and enter college. On and on the personal stories go. A school community needs to build its own rituals and to recognize its young people with special, genuinely meaningful celebrations.

Staff Community Building

In addition to the primarily student-centered community-building activities, structures, and processes described above, our staff have adopted several activities to help them, as well, become a small working community within our larger school community. For as Bryk and Driscoll note, ". . . if the adult school members do not see personal ties and cooperative behavior as central to organizational life and embrace 'the ethic of caring,' communal relationships will not occur even if there are many shared activities" (Bryk and Driscoll, 1988: 7). These activities, structures, and processes for staff include weekly staff meetings prepared and run by a small staff Agenda Committee, and bimonthly whole-staff Support Meetings with no business agenda. These latter meetings provide an opportunity to check in with each other and to do some ongoing team building. Here it was particularly helpful for staff to have a chance to work on their own processes of healing after the death of the student mentioned above. We adults, also, need to be able to work through such tragedies and need to create meaningful ways to support one another at such times.

In addition, we begin the new year with a four-day staff workshop at the end of August, planned by an ad hoc committee. These summer workshop times have been tremendously important over the years, not only to work on developing particular skills as teachers, but as times to be together as a staff, to cook, eat, play, and labor together before meeting with our students the following week. Staff need quality time together, just as do students, if they are to build community.

In these various ways, we have developed a multifaceted approach to building community at the Alternative Community School, an approach continually being revised, added to, or subtracted from as new ideas proposed by staff, students, and parents are integrated into traditions we wish to retain. We hope that as a result of this kind of experience during their secondary school years, students who spend time with us will take this experience of being part of a community and extend it into their future existence, thereby furthering what has classically been called "civic education," and helping to create a truly democratic "community of communities" in the broader society (Raywid, 1988).

School Community Building and the Global Community

It is crucial for students to learn to be part of a community in their school experience and do so in that life-transforming, experiential way that goes beyond mere academic learning. Since the 1960s, the world has irreversibly changed to such an extent that the transmission of culture from one generation to the next is no longer what it once was. Margaret Mead, in her provocative and useful book *Culture and Commitment: The New Relationships between the Generations in the 1970s*, states:

> Today, nowhere in the world are there elders who know what the children know, no matter how remote and simple the societies in which the children live. In the past there were always some elders who knew more than any children in terms of their experience of having grown up within a cultural system. Today there are none. It is not only that parents are no longer guides, but that there are no guides. . . . There are no elders who know what those who have been reared within the last twenty years know about the world into which they were born.
>
> We elders are separated from them by the fact that we, too, are a strangely isolated generation. No generation has ever known, experienced, and incorporated such rapid changes, watched the sources of power, the means of communication, the definition of humanity, the limits of the explorable uni-

verse, the certainties of a known and limited world, the fundamental imperatives of life and death—all change before our
eyes. We know more about change than any generation has
ever known, but we also stand over against and vastly alienated from the young who, by the very nature of their position,
have had to reject their elders' past. (Mead, 1978: 75)

It is this generation that is already having to deal with such pressing
new issues as land use and development in the creation of new communities. Charles Holzbog, a landscape architect in Wisconsin, pointed
out how such decisions involve crucial values and a need for change.
In a study prepared for the city and community planners of Mahoning
County in Ohio, he noted how the present pattern of land use and
construction of new housing developments ". . . is devouring the land
like an animal gone mad" (Holzbog, 1970). This study was done some
twenty years ago. He went on to state that "the city cannot now amass
enough land for the facilities it needs, to say nothing of upgrading the
old" (Holzbog, 1970). He then proceeded to describe an approach to
the creation of a new housing development, a new community, that
would be of mixed density, with private dwellings and commercial
buildings, combining people of mixed age groups and varying interests,
incomes, and backgrounds in areas with significant green space and
recreational facilities, without having a devastating impact on the natural environment. He concluded his study of this community as follows:

An environment should be more than useful. An artless environment is an inhumane one. Animals are capable of survival in
specific environments but man is capable of more than just survival in a multitude of environments. He is capable of giving
great meaning and form to the place where he lives and of
breathing a magnificence into his reason for being. Of what
value is an environment if it provides survival without satisfaction or fulfillment? (Holzbog, 1970)

I suspect this will become an even more crucial issue for the young
people presently in our secondary schools who will be making similar
decisions and living their adult lives in the twenty-first century.

Of what importance will education be in this thrust toward the
building of community in the great society? Margaret Mead states that
"we must create new models for adults who can teach their children
not *what* to learn but *how* to learn, not *what* they should be committed
to but the *value* of commitment" (Mead, 1978: 87). I suggest that this

is what we are trying to do at the Alternative Community School as we develop and experiment with structures and processes aimed at drawing students and adults into the experience of community.

Notes

This chapter is based on an article by the author with the same title which originally appeared in the October 1991 issue of *Changing Schools*.

1. These terms refer to what Peck has identified as four critical stages in the evolution of community. "Pseudocommunity" refers to the point at which people first gather together to create a new community. It is characterized by the avoidance of disagreement. As people interact with one another over time, however, disagreements generally become inescapable. Peck labels this stage of community development as "chaos." During this period, people try to convince others to adopt their own normative position; resistance and conflict become dominant elements in their dealings with one another. Peck argues that the only way out of chaos is organization or "emptiness." He suggests, however, that the alternative of organization is not community. Community can only develop as people are willing to accept the limitations of their own belief systems and look to the formation of something new that emerges from what all individuals bring to the group. From this new value, through consensus, "community" arises.

References

Bryk, A., and Driscoll, M. (1988). *The high school as community: Contextual influences, and consequences for students and teachers.* Madison, Wis.: National Center on Effective Secondary Schools.

Gregory, T., and Smith, G. (1987). *High schools as communities: The small school reconsidered.* Bloomington, Ind.: Phi Delta Kappa.

Holzbog, C. (1970). *An approach to a humane environment.* Milwaukee, Wis.: City Planning Associates.

McLaughlin, C., and Davidson, G. (1986). *Builders of the dawn: Community lifestyles in a changing world.* Shutesbury, Mass.: Sirius.

Mead, M. (1978). *Culture and commitment: The new relationships between the generations in the 1970s.* Rev. ed. Garden City, N.Y.: Anchor Press/ Doubleday.

Dave Lehman

Peck, M. S. (1987). *The different drum: Community making and peace.* New York: Simon and Schuster.

Raywid, M. A. (1988). Community and schools: A prolegomenon. *Teachers College Record* 90 (2): 16–28.

Simon, J. (1982). *To become somebody: Growing up against the grain of society.* Boston: Houghton Mifflin.

Wachtel, P. (1989). *The poverty of affluence: A psychological portrait of the American way of life.* Philadelphia: New Society Publishers.

5

Building a Community by Involving Students in the Governance of the School

Tom Gregory and Mary Ellen Sweeney

In this chapter, we attempt to demonstrate, through the portrayal of four events drawn from one public alternative school, how the authentic involvement of students in the running of this school contributes to the goal of building a strong school community.[1] The school from which we have drawn our examples is the Jefferson County Open School in Lakewood, Colorado, a school we have watched with much interest for the past decade. The events illustrate the Open School community's ethos of involvement of both students and staff in all aspects of the school's program. Although the Open School became a prekindergarten-through-twelve school in 1989, this chapter will focus on how governance functions in the school at the high school level, that segment of it with which we are most familiar.[2] We do not mean to imply, however, that it is only at the high school level that students are trusted to participate in the running of this school.

A Program That *Requires* Student Input

Many small, informal public alternative schools share at least some of the Open School's democratic values and practices. These schools are living illustrations of what is possible *within* the public sector. In the Open School, these practices take many forms, operate at many levels, and are highly interrelated. It would, therefore, be misleading to try to separate school governance from at least some description of how various programmatic elements function in the school. For example, the school community clearly sees the running of the school as educational; students' leadership skills are cultivated in joint student-faculty committees which often are treated as classes in which students can enroll.[3] A brief description of the most important of these separate elements of the program and of the school's governance structure may help readers better understand how each functions. The place of each in the life of the school, on the other hand, may best be described through the four events that we will portray.

Directing One's Own Education

The Open School's desire to empower students is most fundamentally manifested in the control it gives them over their own education. During their first weeks in the school, students begin examining their strengths and weaknesses in relation to the school's twenty-eight Graduation Expectations, identifying experiences they have already had that might satisfy parts of these expectations and designing new experiences that will satisfy others.[4] All of these deliberations begin to take shape as the student's first attempt to define an Individual Education Plan (IEP).

Advising

Students do not attempt these activities in isolation. Upon entry into the school, each new student is assigned a temporary advisor. Students may find a permanent advisor after their first eight weeks in the school. The student also joins that staff member's Advising group. In 1987, when Tom studied the school, the average size of these groups was fourteen. Every Friday morning is set aside as meeting time for Advising groups. The groups are more than homerooms. They are support systems; they are forums for discussing issues critical to the operation of the school and in this sense are a critical arm of Governance (described below); they sometimes help a member overcome an impasse in his or her IEP; and they are social groups. Staff members keep some of their remaining time free to meet individually with their advisees; all told, they devote about a third of their week to Advising. It would be difficult to envision the school's highly personalized program functioning in the absence of its considerable commitment to Advising.

Walkabout

The school's graduation requirements also include the completion of six major experiences or "Passages" that have been described by Maurice Gibbons (1974) as the Walkabout Curriculum. These six steps to adulthood, as some of the students refer to them, fall in the areas of adventure, career exploration, creativity, global awareness/volunteer service, logical inquiry, and practical skills.[5] Advisors, through an elaborate network of committees, help students formulate their plans for satisfying their Passage experiences.

Futures

Students are invited to play an active role in the ongoing reshaping of the curriculum by volunteering to be a member of Futures, a student-staff committee that has this responsibility.

Hiring

No element of any school's program is more critical than the composition of its faculty. Both students and staff form a committee that reviews applications for vacant positions and selects new teachers for the school.

Governance

The school operates on the principle of one person, one vote. The school is small enough to permit weekly all-school meetings—simply called Governance—that are run by students. Governance is a continuing experience in democracy. Any student or staff member may request that an issue become a topic for Governance.

Leadership

To lead Governance, a student must be enrolled in Leadership, a class that helps students perform this function effectively. Leadership also functions as an agenda committee for Governance.

All of these programmatic elements are highly interrelated.

The Open School's Program

The school is very small, with a population (at the high school level) of about 320 students. It gives no grades and emphasizes self-evaluation. The Open School demonstrates the sort of rich, empowering program that can be delivered to *all* students with the funding currently available to most public schools. Students freely choose to attend the school, which accepts them on a first-come, first-served basis regardless of their motivation, ability, or past school history. The school currently has a waiting list for all grades of approximately 1,000 students.

The school's highly personalized program contains all the trappings of the most visionary gifted and talented program. While we claim no particularly wide knowledge of gifted and talented curricula, we know of *no* program that offers, even to the privileged few, what the Open School offers to all of its student body.[6] This unusual mix of high-powered program and mostly typical kids creates considerable confusion for those trying to place the school in some tidy niche. Those who know of the school's fascinating trips (the students traveled over 600,000 person miles during the 1987–88 school year) or who have seen the blue ribbons from district-wide competitions hanging on the art work sometimes presume that the school is only for the gifted and talented. Those who know of the many dis-kids (the disadvantaged, disruptive, disoriented, disgruntled, disenfranchised, discontented, disagreeable, or discombobulated) who have left other schools to attend the Open School view the school as something of a Devil's Island. The vignettes that follow make it clear that the school is neither Utopia nor Devil's Island. It *is* a school that has learned how to give its students what would, in other more familiar schools, be considered unimaginable levels of trust and responsibility. The school *expects* its students to be involved, in numerous ways, in the running of the school.

The Several Levels at Which Students Are Involved

One way to convey the many levels at which students play a role in governing the school is to describe several key events that have occurred in the school. We consider none of these vignettes to be out of the ordinary; our long experience with the school leads us to judge each to be typical of how the school governs itself. Each episode does demonstrate how students are involved, not only formally but also informally, in establishing the school's policies and the rules by which the school community abides. The first vignette describes a portion of an Open School Governance meeting. The second describes how the school responded to a lounge area that a small group of students created quite spontaneously in a hallway of the school. The third vignette describes a session of Futures, one the school's committees on which students participate as equals with the staff. The last vignette describes a meeting of Leadership.

The Personalization of Lockers

Governance is the school's forum for discussion and reconciling of issues of school-wide importance. In the spring of 1988, Tom watched an issue develop around the practice by some students of personalizing their lockers. The decoration ranged from posters of rock groups to bumper stickers and political statements scrawled in Magic Marker to artful murals rendered in colored pencil and chalk. No one in the school was particularly bothered by the practice; it was seen as one more way for students to make the school their own. The school district's supervisor of custodians *was* bothered by it, however, and he upbraided Kathy Woolery, the school's custodian, for permitting the school to be "defaced." And so the decoration of lockers became an item on the agenda of Governance. The problem was discussed at length in two sessions. One focused on defining and understanding the problem—none of the kids wanted Kathy taking heat for their actions, but they didn't want anyone, particularly a stranger to the school, censoring their speech either. A second session, several weeks later, was devoted to the presentation of facts that had been gathered by individuals and to the proposals that several people had formulated to address the problem. We joined that second meeting. Perhaps 100 of the school's 230 students, a dozen visitors (prospective students and their parents), and essentially the whole staff were in attendance, a fairly typical representation. The meeting was being led by Jenny

Pund, a second-year student. After dispensing with several unrelated items, the group turned to the locker issue.

Jenny asked several people to present the facts they had uncovered. Dustin DeMilt, a student, related the district policy, which was seen by the group as yet one more rule that didn't fit this unusual school. The problem seemed to be the *outside* of the lockers; students could put anything they wished, within the limits of propriety, on the inside of their lockers. "It seems to be an image thing," he said.

Ruth Steele, the school's principal, summarized her discussions with the supervisor and with the area superintendent: The school needed either to comply with existing district policy or work to have its language broadened to allow what students were doing. A student asked if they could "put stuff on the outside as long as it isn't permanently attached, stuff that can be removed and placed in the locker overnight." Ruth wasn't sure but indicated that it might be one way to try to broaden the current policy. Someone else had sketched up a design for a small bulletin board that could be easily affixed to locker doors and removed at the end of the year. "Making and selling them could even be a fund-raiser for some trip group." He passed several copies of sketches around the group, but no one seemed particularly interested in this sort of solution.

Keith Leander, whose graffiti-encrusted locker located in the school's foyer had been the one that first aroused the supervisor's ire, waxed philosophical. "Graffiti loses some of its impact when it loses its permanence," he said. Those who had watched him recently spend several hours trying various solvents in his efforts to remove the graffiti on his locker chuckled.

Carol Wonko, a gifted artist, was concerned about limiting personal expression. "We have to have the right to put up images," she said.

Margie Thayer, a first-year student, offered to frame a letter to the superintendent of schools, proposing broadening the current policy. In the end, the group decided that it was just easier to limit personal expression to the inside of the lockers; an altered policy didn't seem worth the hassles that would be involved and the issue died quietly.

Analysis

In 1983, Bert Horwood attended four weekly meetings of Governance and confirmed for himself that the program was controlled by its participants. He described a pattern that continues today:

106

By design, Governance developed corporate responsibility in students through making collective decisions to support or undertake particular activities. The activities included organizing social service ventures, like helping abused children, and planning special classes, like ones dealing with human sexuality, for example. Other events included requests for an audience, like an outside group who wished to speak to students about world peace, and the purely recreational, like arranging an all-school ski day as a break prior to the onslaught of a new intake of beginners in mid-January. The proposals for these things came equally from students and from staff. (Horwood, 1987: 32)

Only one or two issues a year ever came to a formal vote in this school that tended to operate by consensus. The locker issue was not one of these. Discussion did not solve this problem; it simply put it in perspective. The governance pattern of the school empowered students to take the problem on. Had the practice, widely taken for granted in conventional high schools, of dealing with a problem like this by administrative fiat been used here, it likely would have had a very different impact on the school's sense of community. Students might, perhaps justifiably, have felt powerless and imposed upon. What the Open School's practices had rendered reasonable would have remained arbitrary.

The Hall Lounge

In 1987, when Tom studied the school, the Open School had a corner classroom that was designated as a student lounge, but it was so inhospitable a space—dark, cold, and noisy, with a major traffic route running right through its diagonal—that the students' avoidance of it was understandable. The kids relaxed elsewhere, usually on the smoking porch or in the eddies of the school's carpeted corridors. At the beginning of the year, an impromptu lounge took firm hold of one of these small tracts of hallway. Several kids became steady squatters on a five-by-fifteen-foot area just outside Kurt Belknap's classroom.[7] A glass firewall—the sort with chicken wire embedded in it—and a row of bright orange lockers decorated with bumper stickers and photographs comprised two walls of the Hall Lounge. Only the demands of passing traffic and access to Kurt's classroom held in check the space's remaining two boundaries. The Hall Lounge became an example of the manner in which the community that was the Open School dealt with one of its subgroups whose behavior had become troublesome to other segments of the community.

The membership of the Hall Lounge shifted continuously. Inge Pedersen occasionally cuddled with someone there, among the oversized pillows that the group had amassed. Bert Lucas, perhaps the school's youngest student, wanted dearly to be accepted by these older kids. He hung out on the perimeter of the lounge, usually wearing his army issue raincoat. He'd be fiddling with something, maybe bouncing a ball off a nearby wall and catching it in his lacrosse stick, waiting for his presence to be acknowledged in some way. Whatever its makeup, the group always seemed to include Neuman Copenhaver and Daren TeSelle. As the Hall Lounge had grown in the consciousness of those in daily contact with it, Neuman and Daren's steady presence made many think that they were the ringleaders of this largely innocent undertaking. The group had committed only one official transgression: the occasional playing of a small boom box in not-so-quiet defiance of Governance's long-standing prohibition on playing music in the halls. The whole matter seemed harmless enough that, for a week or two, no staff member or student felt a need to take issue with the situation. But almost every staff member and a number of students became, at some level, disconcerted by the Hall Lounge as it came to be used to more and more of an excess. From Monday morning through Friday afternoon, Neuman and Daren never seemed to be anywhere but in their lounge.

Finally, several weeks into the school year, the Hall Lounge became a topic in Governance. Students and staff gathered as usual in the library first thing Monday morning. The debate took on the classic dimensions of the rights of the individual counterpoised against the needs of the community. Some kids pointed out that the lounge group pretty regularly violated the school's prohibition against playing music in the halls. General discontent with the situation was expressed and specific complaints were raised.

"We have people running around the hall dressed in costumes," an angry senior said, "people who aren't doing anything, people who just sit there or crawl all over their girlfriends or boyfriends. It's just not good. We get prospective students and their parents as visitors to this school! I would *never* send my kid here after seeing you guys."[8]

The discussion led the school community to ask the lounge users to cool it. They did, for a while, but the situation gradually disintegrated back to its familiar pattern and discontent continued to grow. The Hall Lounge—a hotbed of social experimentation—was not a situation to which one could easily acclimate. Just when the staff and students adjusted to some recently introduced ritual, a yet higher level of craziness was embarked upon. "What if?" was an oft-asked question in the group. It led Ryan Hunsucker, a sometimes member of the group, to come to school one day—and only one day—dressed in a faded chenille bathrobe and slippers, just to see how people would relate to him. The bathrobe was a warm-up for the day he dressed in drag. The group was—as someone pointed out in a staff meeting—majoring in weirdness.

The problem of the Hall Lounge finally came to a head a few weeks later. From his desk in an adjacent room, Tom overheard Linda, the preschool teacher, out in the hall, scolding the group. He peered out the door through the chicken wire and saw Linda, who is about five feet tall, standing over these big guys who were sitting cross-legged on the floor. Neuman had colorful scarves tied around his bare biceps. Daren was wearing his floor-length duster and derby hat. They looked, wide-eyed, up at Linda as she sternly explained that her four-year-old girls had to pass through the boys' lounge act to get to the restroom. "Look, you guys," she said, "my girls are afraid to come by here and one of them has just wet her pants." The guys sat, waist-deep in pillows, looking as innocent and as respectful of Linda as their black eye makeup (in homage to the rock group Kiss) allowed. "Now enough's enough."

The incident got back to Rick Posner (or Poz), Daren's advisor, and it prompted him to call a lunchtime meeting of the Hall Lounge's prime culprits and some of the complaining staff members. As they waited for the last of the group to arrive, Tom thought about his many interchanges with Neuman and Daren and Ryan. He had said things to the guys—a request that they keep at least a three-foot aisle for passers-by and an oblique reference to the no-music-in-the-hall rule—almost on a daily basis. But as the group began to talk, Tom realized that, for the first time, he was going to *discuss* the matter with the students, to listen to their views. It had never occurred to him, amid all the craziness, that rational discourse was a possibility.

As the meeting started, it became clear that Poz *had* talked about the lounge, at least with Daren, his advisee. Poz asked the guys to explain their situation. They described some of the unsupportive physical conditions in the school. Everyone agreed that the regular lounge was inhospitable. Where else were they to go? What harm were they doing? Tom acknowledged that if they'd been doing any real harm, they probably would have been asked to disband weeks earlier.

"The problem is a bit more subtle than whether or not you're violating any rules," Rick Lopez said. He described his embarrassment in exposing visitors to so condensed a dose of the Open School's chronic public relations problem: idleness. "It's a crummy first impression to give those who are trying to learn about the school," he said.

"The school exists for us students," Ryan Hunsucker countered, "not for visitors."

Kurt talked about feeling besieged in his own classroom. The guys understood his situation. There was a problem when too many kids used the lounge at once.

"But it wouldn't be getting such heavy use if the school had a decent lounge," Neuman pointed out.

In the end, the guys agreed to reduce the size of their storehouse of pillows, to try to limit the amount of time they were on public display, especially on visitors' day, and to no longer play music, no matter how softly. Tom offered to help them develop a workable design for rehabilitating the regular lounge space. The project could develop into creativity or practical skills Passages for some of them.[9] In about a half hour, the ill feelings were aired and most of the differences were resolved.

ANALYSIS

In a way, the Hall Lounge flourished because of a central tenet of the school's Advising system: the Open School did not view the establishment of lists of universal rules as a particularly effective way to solve problems or to govern a community.[10] Matters of conduct and deportment were left to individual discretion much more than they are in most schools. The linchpin that held the whole delicate apparatus together was the advisor's judgment. Whether or not a kid was making satisfactory progress boiled down to the professional judgment of her or his advisor. Not much happened until the *advisor* recognized that a problem existed. By accident or by design, Neuman and Daren had placed their lounge as far from Rick Posner and Joy Jensen, their two advisors, as was physically possible. Because neither advisor had cause to pass the Hall Lounge probably more than once a week, Poz and Joy were likely among the last in the school to know that the Hall Lounge even existed. Both were also probably more comfortable with the *appearance* of idleness than many staff members. More important, other staff members recognized that Poz and Joy knew Neuman and Daren far better than they.

Perhaps the most unusual element of this dilemma was how long it took for a productive discussion to occur. The school's many available forums encourage kids and adults to talk through problems. But self-governance is often a messy, inefficient process. Throughout this episode, however, two of Mary Anne Raywid's six qualities of alternative school communities (see chapter 1 of this volume) were clearly evident: respect and inclusiveness. The school community's honoring and respecting of individual rights were tempered only by the needs of the group, a group that included everyone in the school. It would be naive to say that staff members and students were equals in the school: the weight of age differences, district-sanctioned roles and policies, and everyone's past experiences with schooling tended to set staff members apart. But one person, one vote and a culture of consensus continuously mitigated these differences. The Hall Lounge continued to exist in one form or another throughout the year, but the discussion had served an important purpose: the *problem* of the Hall Lounge died quietly that day in Poz's classroom, when some students and staff members finally shared their views.

What Should We Do about the Retreat?

In 1987, the Open School had two openings to the school year. Only returning students reported on the first two days of school, which were devoted to an overnight retreat at a church camp. Beginning students didn't report until the third day of the school year, when returning students played an integral role in welcoming the newcomers into the school community. The Open School is the only school we know of that has developed such separate start-up procedures for new and old students. But the retreat had regularly been problematic. It served two functions: one was social, allowing everybody to reconnect after a long summer apart; the other was academic, preparing these returning students to spend the next week largely on their own, back at school under the supervision of only two staff members while all the beginning students and the rest of the staff were off on a four-day backpacking trip high in the mountains. The social function, working in combination with the lack of a curfew—students were expected to govern themselves—led some kids to stay up all night, rendering them pretty useless for the academic function. So the whole idea of the retreat was being reexamined by the school, particularly by Futures. Futures, whose membership was comprised of both students and staff members, was a major element of the school's governance structure. Its work was considered highly educational, so much so that students could take it just as they would any class. Futures's task was to formulate proposals for altering the school's future academic program. The group met in the library after lunch and, on the day described here, it included six staff members and five students. Several other students joined the group as they finished lunch. Tom was one of the staff members in attendance.

Andy Fentress, a graduating senior, led the discussion. The staff had already discussed the problem, and Andy suggested that we begin the session with its report. Bruce Andrews, one of the school's science teachers, described the staff's discussion.

"We explored the problem from a number of angles," he began. "Should we scrap the retreat because it sets the wrong mood for the school year? Is it doing just what we want it to do the way it is? What are some alternative ways to accomplish the retreat's goals?"

"I think we should try to come up with three or four proposals to take back to the staff," Kurt Belknap, a staff member, said. He pointed to the board. "The staff's suggested these three for starters. Futures needs to add to and subtract from that and decode which ones we're comfortable with. Then we can take those to Governance and let the students decide which one they want. We go with that plan."

"We could have a retreat later in the year, but with the whole school," Ruth suggests. Although Ruth Steele was the school's principal, she functioned more as a head teacher.

"We could have one in May, or maybe after SDL," Bruce added.[11]

"After SDL sounds good," Jeff Bogard said. Jeff was another teacher.

"Like a whole-school retreat," Bruce clarified.

"If we had one at the end of the year, it could be another way to say good-bye to the graduates, too," Jenny Thekat, a student, said.

"That would work if we had two retreats," Bill Johnson, another staff member, said.

"That came up, too, when we talked," Kurt said.

"Isn't graduation the way we say good-bye to the graduates?" Tom asked.

"The ceremony. Yeah," Kurt said.

Silence fell over the group. They looked at the blackboard where Bruce had been scribbling down our suggestions. Finally, Kurt spoke.

"I think the message is that we're so divided on the issue that anything is possible." Rick Lopez, another staff member, exploded in laughter. "That's why we've got three basic proposals," Kurt continued.

"You have a way with words, Kurt," Ruth said. "That got right to the heart of the problem."

"We also talked about students taking more control of the retreat, of making it happen," Rick said, "setting up the norms of behavior, addressing the issues . . ."

"Planning the agenda."

"Whatever we decide to do," Kurt said, looking at the students, "students have got to take more control of it."

"I agree," Jenny said.

"Write that down," Jeff said.

"I think we need some feedback from the students at this point," Kurt said. "The staff's talked about this *a lot* already."

Several staff members concurred.

"Well, I think that it would be good to have more student involvement," Raylynn Czapko said. "The staff shouldn't have to babysit us; that's not the way this school operates." Raylynn was a new student and she asked how many days long the retreat had been in the past.

"It's about twenty-eight hours," Kurt said.

"Is that all we can afford?" Raylynn asked. Bill and Tom, who were up most of the night of the retreat, looked at each other and chuckled at the unimaginable proposition that the retreat be *lengthened*.

Andy tried to get us back on track. "The idea of the retreat is to socialize, see everybody, tell everybody what you did over the summer, and try to get everybody off on a positive start for the new year," he said. "It's real intense to try to do that in twenty-four hours. Adding the overnight aspect to it makes it difficult to accomplish all that. It creates a strain unless everybody is doing what they should be. I would think that coming for a half day on the first day of school, we could accomplish some of that stuff. We could spend the afternoon in Advising groups: they could each plan a trip, maybe for overnight, maybe just for the day. They could get away from the school. Maybe two groups could stay at school if they wanted to. The individual meetings with advisors that we do could occur on the trips. But I don't think the overnight aspect of the retreat is necessary."

"So you're saying," Ruth asked Andy, "that we'd have everyone here in the morning for something like Governance where we could reconnect with everybody. And after that, advisory groups?"

"Yeah, this is the first day of school—Monday. And then Tuesday would be advisory day," Andy added, "like it is now. But we can't have ten groups stay here; it wouldn't work. They'd run into each other. It would work even if they just went to the Dairy Queen and sat there—or went to the park or whatever. It's away from school. It could also still be an overnight." Andy looked exasperated. "I've been on three retreats. We set out to do these three things and all of them got done half-assed at each retreat. We had to complete them back here, at school, anyway."

"I think your idea's pretty good," Jenny said, "because it automatically has the students doing most of the planning. It's also nice because it's not a big production; it's not something you have to worry a whole lot about."

"Basically, you see the overnight as a detriment to the job of starting the year?" Bruce asked Andy. "You're eliminating that so you must feel that it's a drawback to the retreat."

"Well, you can always find the positive in it," Andy said. "The staff skit every year is great, but that's about the only thing. There's just a lot of overkill on the socializing part of it."

"I really don't know how it's going to work," Kelly O'Neill, another student, said. "When you first get back together with everyone, you just want to be with people and go wild. You don't want people saying, 'Okay, it's nine o'clock, let's do this' or 'it's ten o'clock, now we do this.'"

"I don't think that's going to be a problem with Andy's plan," Jenny said. "The structured part of the first morning is not too long and then you've got Advising."

"Andy's idea seems to give us every facet of the old retreat minus a couple of its 'fringe benefits' like being exhausted the next day," Bruce said. "I can't remember a retreat where a lot was done the second day. We didn't even have good feelings about it. I remember tension, griping, and all that on the second day. I think Andy's proposal is a healthy option. It allows staff members to do what they need to do with their Advising groups and still maintains everything else."

After testing the idea further, Futures decided to forward three options to the staff: Andy's proposal, a proposal to discontinue the retreat, and a proposal to maintain the retreat as it operated this year. The proposals and staff's comments about them were then discussed and acted upon in Governance.

ANALYSIS

Systematically rotating leadership of the school's deliberative bodies was a familiar practice in the school. Even the staff's weekly meetings were led by individuals on a rotating basis. Ruth led staff meetings on only three occasions during Tom's year in the school: the two days of meetings prior to the opening of the school year and the last meeting of the year. The Futures session described here is another clear example of Raywid's quality of inclusion; the ethos of the school mirrored Seymour Sarason's (1990) axiom that those in a school who will be affected by decisions should play a proportionate role in making them. Staff members tended to dominate this particular Futures discussion, but much of their dialogue was filling students in on the staff's earlier discussion. All ideas, regardless of who offered them, were given a fair hearing. And perhaps the most interesting alternative plan that was suggested, the one that would eventually be shaped into the format that the school used the following year, was suggested by Andy, the student who was leading this session.

Adjusting to a New Home

Any student could lead Governance, the weekly all-school meeting, but those who wished to do so had to enroll in a class called Leadership. Leadership met once a week in the spring of 1992 when Mary Ellen attended the session described here. Seventeen students were present at the beginning of the class. Two student visitors, contemplating attendance at the Open School, two parent visitors, and Jane Blackstone, a part-time architect-in-residence who was sponsored by the Colorado Council of Arts and Humanities, were also present. Pat Sliemers, a staff member, took attendance and Judi Justus, another staff member, wrote the agenda on the board:

1. feedback and evaluation of the leadership provided by the two students who had led the previous Governance meeting;
2. further discussion of Lindsay Horn's Passage proposal for an all–high school Multicultural Day;
3. Jane Blackstone's presentation of her ideas for redesigning Munchie into a more usable space;[12] and
4. a follow-up discussion of the current direction and tone of the school that had first been raised at the last meeting of the group.

As Judi listed the agenda, students continued to straggle in. An additional nine joined the group in the next fifteen minutes.

The meeting began with everyone critiquing the performance of

Scott Guenther and Maurene Soshé, leaders of the last Governance meeting. Individuals assured the two that they had taken care of business; the session had had a good flow. Maurene volunteered that she had been bored with Governance; she felt that some people took too long to make their announcements or present their issues. Judi stated that she thought the meeting had gone very well because people hung around at its conclusion.

After the feedback for Scott and Maurene was completed, Lindsay explained her idea for a Multicultural Celebration that she proposed to satisfy her practical skills and global awareness Passages. The celebration would take the form of a series of concurrent workshops designed to heighten students' awareness of multicultural issues. She was concerned that the celebration would be perceived as coercive. She wanted kids to buy into the idea, and she asked the Leadership group for suggestions for accomplishing that goal. Pat suggested that Lindsay be more direct with her instructions. Pat appreciated Lindsay's concerns about students' acceptance of the idea but suggested that Lindsay offer dates and some possible workshop topics to aid the planning process. As the discussion proceeded, Lindsay was given other advice by students and staff members. This discussion, they said, had given them a clearer understanding of Lindsay's intentions. Advisory groups would discuss the idea before Governance decided whether to adopt Lindsay's proposal. Lindsay was satisfied with the discussion, stating that she had a clearer idea of what to suggest and that the group's enthusiasm was encouraging.

Jane Blackstone's item was next. She described her ideas for a project to redesign Munchie. She would present her drawings and models to the school community in a few weeks, but first hoped to collect people's ideas. She wanted to involve the whole school community through a survey. A group of students—all boys, as it turned out—had also volunteered to participate in a brainstorming session. The brainstorming would be followed by an implementation stage that developed the ideas offered by the school community. The group thought the proposed process was quite workable.

"How come all males?" Pat asked. "No blooming female architects? That's interesting!"

The final agenda item resumed a discussion—at times quite intense— that had erupted at the last meeting of Leadership. Pat led the group back into the topic by recalling how the last meeting had ended. "We'd just begun a good discussion about what this place is like and had shared some of our frustrations about it," she began, "when we were interrupted by the fire drill, and then it was time to go to our next classes. But it really felt scattered last Thursday. Judi and I thought it would be good to at least talk about where we are."

Tim Hunnicutt suggested that they refresh their memories. He began but then paused, looking embarrassed. "I can't remember much but maybe someone else can."

The group laughed and Marie Langley picked up Tim's suggestion. "It was turning into an argument at the end because everyone was so upset and frustrated. It was basically about the keys that were missing, bathrooms being vandalized, and other problems. Some of the students don't think that the teachers are being as equal as they could be to some of the students. I know that the students were really upset about the discussion because it was the kind that touches feelings a lot."

"Good summary, Marie," Pat said.

After an uncomfortably long pause, Maury Demitoulas said, "I didn't want to bring arguing up, but we do so much complaining here. It's all right to an extent, but it gets unproductive. That's what I saw happening last week. It was pretty cool, the way people started venting their feelings, but then we lost focus and really didn't come up with any solutions."

"I think other bad feelings came into it, too," Marie said. "I think the conversation got so heated because people were saying stuff that they were mad about. It didn't have anything to do with missing keys or vandalized bathrooms."

"I was wondering," Tim said, "if we *have* all these pent-up feelings, shouldn't we have a way to let them out? Something like the Friday meeting that we had that was for only students?"

Judi asked Tim to add the thoughts he had expressed to her after Leadership last week.

"What I'm thinking," he said, "is that we are finally getting to the point where we are getting hostile to each other. I think getting mad once in a while is good for this school." Making reference to what was for many students a "forced" move from the school's previous home in Evergreen and its merger with Tanglewood, he said, "I think we should release our feelings about having to come down here. Then, we need to open out again. We need to get the openness back."

"I was talking to Judi after Leadership," Lindsay said, "and she asked me, 'Are people really that angry? Are they really that hostile?' She was really surprised at how heated the discussion got. I heard some of the anger from the students, but I don't think it was necessarily communicated to the staff. Even the way we talk about ourselves as 'students' and 'staff.' I notice how we place each other in these categories, and we lump people together and talk about them. A lot's going on, a lot of procrastination, a lot of frustration, and not much of a feeling of power. But there's no dialogue about how we can change that situation. Or maybe there are many dialogues going on. We may be talking among ourselves and getting nowhere."

After a pause, Pat asked, "What are some of the rest of you thinking, both from this week's and last week's discussions?"

The long silence that followed was broken only occasionally by nervous laughter. Finally, Tim said, "We need another fire drill." The group's laughter broke the tension of the moment.

Lindsay asked Pat and Judi, "Did you guys talk to the teachers? Do they feel this tension?"

"I didn't specifically ask them," Judi said. "Actually, I was surprised by the number of people I talked to after the meeting who just took what happened in Leadership more in stride than I did. I was really surprised by the depth of the anger. Other people seemed to feel it was okay or they didn't want to deal with it. So they didn't let it bother them, or they agreed with Tim that it was 'necessary' or with Lindsay that 'that's just how people are feeling.' The anger was just stronger than I expected."

"Now I see why we had these students-only meetings," Maury said. "No staff was there to hear our feelings, and that was a good environment for it to happen in. And we couldn't hear your feelings on it either. But we lost touch in a way because you couldn't see how we were feeling. I don't mean to be putting 'you guys' in a category but it's hard not to. I think we should have a big meeting, maybe still run by Paul—he did a good job of running the student meeting—but we should have everyone come. I'm sure you guys have feelings on this as well as us. I'd like to hear you and I'd like you to hear us."

"We might need a lot of time for staff to talk about things first," Judi said. "But it might be the way to go for a future meeting. When is your next meeting?"

"I would hope that everyone in here would go to your meeting," Pat said. Judi nodded agreement. "You're an important link, because you hear these issues discussed in greater depth. Other links are the advisory groups and Governance. It's important for you to express these things in your own way."

The group was running out of time. "Well, here we are at eleven o'clock again, time to move on to our other classes," Pat said. "I hope you'll take Judi's suggestion and bring up some of these things." As students left, she added, "And be on time! You guys in the back, you're really coming in *late*!"

Tensions build up in all schools. Mary Ellen's visit to Leadership was during one of the school's most trying periods, after its move into a strange building almost twenty-five miles distant from its former home in the mountains and during its continuing effort to effectively transform two schools into one. Arnie Langberg, the Open School's first principal, once said, "Don't judge a school by the problems that it has; judge it by how it goes about solving those problems."[13] A repeatedly observed characteristic of the school's staff was its unwillingness to ignore discontent. The school, like numerous other small alternative schools, had established several forums for solving the problems that inevitably arise as it changes. In this sense, Lindsay's comment that "there's no dialogue about how we can change that situation" must be viewed in the context of a school where the normal practice was to rather naturally move from the sensing of a problem into a discussion of it, often simultaneously in several different deliberative bodies. That process had been going on for months in this case, but the dialogue finally seemed to be taking on a clearer focus at the time of this event.

Judi and Pat discussed the problem at the next staff meeting. Several of the students discussed the problem in their Advising groups the next morning and in the following weeks. But reestablishing an identity is one of the most difficult tasks a school can face. It will not be accomplished easily or quickly.

What Are the Limits to the Involvement of Students in a School's Governance?

Raywid (chapter 1, this volume) describes two types of communities. For our purposes we will call them school communities: Gesellschaft communities are rule-bound arrangements with the rules regularly being imposed from above, while gemeinschaft communities are governed by their members. Until the advent of the alternative schools movement, most American schools were pseudo (gesellschaft) communities; it is a heritage that continues to shape our habits and thinking and must be consciously confronted to be overcome. Teachers in all schools, for example, want to be recognized partners in decision-making processes (Sarason, 1982). They want to share in school governance matters with their building principals. Yet these very teachers, Sarason notes, typically treat their students in the same undemocratic manner for which they criticize their principals.

The comprehensive high school is an institution created for another generation that has been unable to adapt sufficiently to new demands. James Coleman, for example, points out that, when the modern American high school was conceived,

> ... a very different relationship existed between the old and the young. Authority then was much more inextricably linked with financial dependence than it now is. As long as a child lived at home he or she was expected to mind the head of the household. Accordingly, the schools that were created for the youth of that era expected youth to *mind*. ... Gradually over the past few decades that fundamental relationship between the older and the younger generations has changed. In most families in the United States today a shift in the relationship occurs around age 14, in some families, much earlier. As today's children mature, minding adults begins to be replaced in most families by a form of negotiation.[14] But our youth still attend high schools based on the idea that adolescents will mind. (Coleman, paraphrased in Gregory, 1992: 2; emphasis in original)

Teachers in gesellschaft schools, beleaguered by students who won't mind, do form treaties with their students (Powell et al., 1985; Sedlack et al., 1986; Sizer, 1984). But these pacts are hardly harbingers of budding democracies; rather, they are the survival mechanisms of people entrapped in an institution in the middle stages of environmental collapse. Constructive forms of individual negotiation seldom occur at the school level in gesellschaft schools because they violate a fundament of such institutions: They expect kids to *mind* adults.[15] A school designed in an era when adolescents were treated as children has great difficulty, today, treating them as adults.

Contrast this picture with that found at the elementary school level where children typically still do mind. Sarason (1982) informally observed teachers in six classrooms in suburban elementary schools for one month, watching how they functioned as governing bodies. From these teachers' actions, he inferred several premises of their policymaking behavior:

1. Teachers know best.
2. Children cannot participate constructively in the development of a classroom constitution.

120

3. Children want and expect the teacher to determine the rules of the game.
4. Children are not interested in constitutional issues.
5. Children should be governed by what a teacher thinks is right or wrong, but a teacher should not be governed by what children think is right or wrong.
6. The ethics of adults are obviously different from and superior to the ethics of children.
7. Children should not be given responsibility for something they cannot handle or for which they are not accountable.
8. If constitutional issues were handled differently, chaos might result. (Sarason,1982: 217)

Three things are reasonably deducible in this list: First, one reason that elementary school may still be seen to work well is that the premise that kids will mind still generally obtains at this level. Second, these very teachers who themselves craved more participation in administrative matters in their schools saw no need to involve their students similarly. Third, these teachers apparently do not see it as their responsibility to prepare children to engage in democratic processes; that task is being left to secondary teachers, usually in schools too big to accomplish it.

Daniel Greenberg, of the Sudbury Valley School in Sudbury, Massachusetts, contends that schools are the obvious place for students to experience group, moral, and social development and to take risks:

The chief non-family social setting of children in developed societies is the school. What better place to begin to give children the experience of democratic rule making, with all the trappings? Where better to learn the art of debate, the need of taking other people's views into account, the benefits of openmindedness, the balancing forces of personal and community interests, the nature of political power-blocs, the joy of victory and the anguish of defeat, the ability to recoup a loss and plan for future gain? (Greenberg, 1987: 46)

Several theorists and researchers agree with Raywid that we need to move toward gemeinschaft school communities, that students should participate more fully in the setting of school policy and in other matters which affect their learning. William Schubert (1991) suggests that the players most affected by curricular planning should be included in it; he sees it as a democratic right. Lewis Aptekur (1983) found that Mexican-American secondary students perceive their schooling experience more favorably if they think they are involved in decision making and the management of school policy. Involvement was defined as the ability to talk with administrators and to have things explained to them. These students did not ask to be part of the policymaking process, but they did want policies explained to them. Dennis Treslan (1983) contends that secondary students need practice making decisions—particularly, we think, if Sarason's observations about elementary practices are pervasive—and that the advantages of such involvement outweigh the disadvantages. Frank Riessman calls for the expansion of the role of students in governance matters so that the school may truly become their community; he warns of the prospects should we do otherwise:

> It is not that students have not been expressing themselves. They have: by tuning out, acting out, and dropping out. This is because there is not a channel through which they can be heard and where an open dialogue can take place. If the students are not really heard, the school will not be a community, but an alien zone where peer pressure functions as a negative obstacle, rather than a basic source of communal energy. (Riessman, 1988: 2)

Peter Senge (1990), in *The Fifth Discipline: The Art and Practice of the Learning Organization*, calls for schools to use systems analysis to examine their assumptions to execute meaningful change. Educators are baffled when curricular innovations realize only minimal results and no real change. Senge advises that we need to examine complex situations from multiple levels to identify the patterns behind diverse problems. Using such a systems approach and an application of his other four disciplines (personal mastery, mental models, team learning, and shared vision), a learning organization can provide an environment in positive tension, one in which all members of the community can develop and perform on a self-actualized level.

A public high school can provide an environment in positive tension, one that enables a Ryan Hunsucker, chenille bathrobe and all, to be more than a weird kid. He can be the thoughtful kid who offers a perceptive comment about school conditions. A public high school can develop a structure that enables even new students like Raylynn Czapko in Futures immediately to become active agents in the conduct of the school's affairs. A school's structure can enable an Andy Fentress to propose a plan that can ride on its own merits as it is discussed by the entire school community, a plan that can lead to a major alteration in the way in which the school welcomes back its students at the beginning of the year. The structure can be self-correcting by enabling a group of students to point out that stresses from a move that occurred two years earlier remain unreconciled and to devise a process for finally constructively airing students' pent-up hostility about what has happened to them and to their school. Proposals such as these do not have to be enacted by the school community to be important. The key point is that they are not proposals being brought by students to adults who then decide their merits; they are proposals that either students or adults, and often both, bring to the whole school community which then weighs their merit.

Getting from Here to There

John Dewey, contemplating the challenge posed by the social ferment of the industrial revolution, wrote in 1916 that "Democracy has to be born anew in each generation, and education is its midwife" (quoted in Wirth, 1993). The factory schools we conceived over the following decades and institutionalized in the 1960s have been poor midwives. The best of our public alternative schools, created in the information age and for a new generation, have shown us the path to more democratic schools. But few school people are yet willing to acknowledge their efficacy in this regard. Even for those visitors to the Open School who understand the power of its processes, the school is both exhilarating and demoralizing.[16] They marvel at its practices, including the way it involves its students in the governance of the school, but can't see how they could possibly install all of them in their own schools. They cannot, of course, at least not all at once. The Open School has taken almost two decades to get where it is, and the transformation has been more struggle than uneventful evolution. But saying that doesn't help those suddenly confronted with a functioning approximation of their ideal school to understand that they must blaze much of the same trail for themselves. The pitfalls they face are predictable:

School Size

The sheer size of many of our schools, particularly our high schools, negates the governance model of an Open School (Gregory, 1992). Many will not be able to accomplish the task until they drastically

123

reduce their size. Ostensibly, we create huge institutions in order to provide powerful academic programs. The reasoning is fallacious on a number of counts (Sizer, 1984; Gregory, 1992). The size of most of our schools is a major handicap, even a fatal flaw, in establishing strong communities based on democratic principles. Schools must be very small—the Open School probably pushes the upper limits in this regard—to support the governance practices that we have described.

Program

While space does not allow us to describe the sort of powerful program that even a very small high school can have at current levels of funding, we have tried to provide glimpses of it.[17] We think that the key tenets of the transformation are individualizing the program, allowing students to learn in the absence of teachers, and providing extensive opportunities to learn outside of formal classes and particularly outside of the school.

Relationships Between the Old and the Young

To develop democratic schools that promote authentic, participatory governance practices we must dramatically alter the power structure of the institution (Sarason, 1990). In an age of rapid change when no one has all the answers, teachers and students must become colleagues, and within reason equals (Benne, 1970). Enough working models of how we must change already exist. But as history has taught us, simply aping them is insufficient to the task. Each school must find its own way to democracy.

The Role of Governance in the Open School Community

Governance at the Open School is not *government* as we usually think of it, that is, the process of enacting laws. A list of the laws that have been passed in a session may be a useful measure of the productivity of a legislative body; it is not a good measure of school governance at the Open School. In a way, the opposite is the case; in the ethos of the school, passing a new rule feels a little like admitting defeat: "It's a bad sign that we have to resort to this." Governance—in all its manifestations—at the school is best understood as communication, the continuing response to the natural tensions that arise between the equally valued goals of honoring the individual and maintaining a healthy community.

Notes

1. This research was supported, in part, by the Maris and Mary Proffitt Endowment of the School of Education, Indiana University. Tom Gregory also would like to publicly thank the Lilly Endowment for the generous fellowship that enabled him to spend an entire school year at the Open School. Two of the events related here are adapted from *Making High Schools Work: Lessons from the Open School* Published by Teachers College Press. © 1993 Teachers College, Columbia University. One vignette was collected by Mary Ellen Sweeney.

2. In 1989, the Jefferson County Open High School, then known widely by its informal name, Mountain Open, merged with its philosophically similar prekindergarten-through-ninth-grade "feeder" school, then known as the Tanglewood Open Living School. The new, combined school is called the Jefferson County Open School, or the Open School for short.

3. The Open School is performance-based, not credit-based. Therefore, it would be inaccurate to say that students receive credit for such experiences. Rather, the experiences offer them opportunities to build evidence for their portfolios. They could lead meetings, work in groups, carry their share of the load, etc., all of which were elements of the school's graduation expectations.

4. The twenty-eight expectations fall into three domains. The intellectual domain contains the familiar content areas of reading, writing, history, foreign language, etc., but also humor. The personal domain contains concepts such as meeting one's commitments and taking risks. The social domain contains concepts such as confronting others in a constructive manner and the ability to function effectively in groups. Each expectation has two or three pages of guidelines that help students and their advisors design individual plans for satisfying that expectation.

5. See Gregory (1991) for a detailed description of how Passages work at the Open School.

6. About ten percent of the students would probably have been labeled gifted and talented in other schools; about another ten percent are identified as special education students. Since special education students were formally identified by law, this estimate is verifiable. About fifty percent bore those characteristics that would have led many to label them as "at-risk" in other

schools. These estimates are Tom's amalgam of several staff members' perceptions.

7. All students' names are pseudonyms. However, by unanimous consent, all staff members' actual names are used.

8. Words to this effect were said in Governance that day. These particular statements, however, were lifted from a March 1988 interview with a graduating senior.

9. Designs for refurbishing the student lounge never moved beyond preliminary sketches and discussions.

10. Indeed, the students' general perception was that the school had only three rules. Known collectively as the "Three No's," they were no drinking, no drugs, and no sex as a part of any school activity. The school had other rules such as no skateboarding on the front steps and no smoking anywhere but out back, on the smoking porch, but students did not think of these self-imposed prohibitions as "rules." It seemed as though only those restrictions imposed by adults were considered to be "rules." Horwood (1983, 1987) also noted this phenomenon during his study of the school.

11. SDL is short for self-directed learning, the generic name that the school applied to a number of different approaches it has used to orient beginning students to the rigors of the Open School's personalized program.

12. The school ran its own cafeteria service called Munchie. Under the guidance of Joy Jensen, who was both teacher and dietitian, volunteer students planned, prepared, and served lunch each day. The move into a new building, which included a conventional cafeteria service and staff, had required months of negotiation with the central administration and with the cafeteria staff as the school community worked to regain what it considered an integral part of its program and one of its key elements of community, the preparation and eating of food together.

13. Said in a private conversation with Tom in 1988.

14. Children also now mature physically at an earlier age than they did when the high school was conceived. The average age of the onset of puberty has been descending about one year in each recent generation.

15. The centrality of this concept is perhaps most evident in the degree to which control and disciplinary concerns often dominate the criteria by which the performances of secondary school administrators are reviewed.

16. Mary Ellen, who encourages many of her teacher education students to visit the school, has noted a general theme in their comments after seeing the school. They wish they could do high school over again—at the Open School.

17. The program has, however, been described in detail elsewhere. See for example, Mary Ellen Sweeney's doctoral dissertation, "An Exploratory

Structural-Functional Analysis of American Urban Traditional and Alternative Secondary Public Schools"; Bert Horwood's book *Experiential Education in High School: Life in the Walkabout Program*; Tom Gregory and Gerald R. Smith's book *High Schools as Communities: The Small School Reconsidered*; and Tom's recent book, *Making High Schools Work: Lessons from the Open School.*

References

Aptekur, L. (1983). Mexican-American high school students' perceptions of school. *Adolescence* 18 (70): 345–57.

Benne, K. D. (1970). Authority in education. *Harvard Educational Review* 40: 385–410.

Coleman, J. S. (1987). Families and schools. Address presented at the annual meeting of the American Educational Research Association, Washington, D.C.

Dewey, J. (1916). The need of an industrial education in an industrial democracy. *Manual Training and Vocational Education*, 17: 409–14.

Gibbons, M. (1974). Walkabout: Searching for the right passage from childhood and school. *Phi Delta Kappan 55* (8): 596–602.

Greenberg, D. (1987). Idea notebook: Teaching justice through experience. *Journal of Experiential Education* (Spring): 46–47.

Gregory, T. (1991). Walkabout day. *Changing Schools* (Spring/Summer): 1–5, 10.

Gregory, T. (1992). Small is too big: Achieving a critical anti-mass in the high school. Unpublished position paper prepared for the Hubert H. Humphrey Institute for Public Affairs and the North Central Regional Educational Laboratory.

Gregory, T. (1993). *Making High Schools Work: Lessons Learned from the Open School.* New York: Teachers College Press.

Gregory, T. B., and Smith, G. R. (1987). *High schools as communities: The small school reconsidered.* Bloomington, Ind.: Phi Delta Kappa.

Horwood, B. (1983). Draft account of Jefferson County Open High School. Unpublished manuscript, Queen's University, Kingston, Ont.

Horwood, B. (1987). *Experiential education in high school: Life in the walkabout program.* Boulder, CO: Association for Experiential Education.

Tom Gregory and Mary Ellen Sweeney

Powell, A. G., Farrar, E., and Cohen, D. K. (1985). *The shopping mall high school*. Boston: Houghton Mifflin.

Riessman, F. (1988). The next stage in education reform: The student as consumer. *Social Policy* 18 (4): 2.

Sarason, S. (1982). *The culture of the school and the problem of change*. Boston, Mass.: Allyn and Bacon.

Sarason, S. (1990). *The predictable failure of educational reform: Can we change course before it's too late?* San Francisco: Jossey-Bass.

Schubert, W. H. (1991). Ten curriculum questions for principals. *National Association of Secondary School Principals Bulletin* (February): 1–10.

Sedlack, M. W., Wheeler, C. W., Pullin, D. C., and Cusick, P. A. (1986). *Selling students short: Classroom bargains and academic reform in the American high school*. New York: Teachers College Press.

Senge, P. M. (1990). *The fifth discipline: The art and practice of the learning organization*. New York: Doubleday.

Sizer, T. R. (1984). *Horace's compromise: The dilemma of the American high school*. Boston: Houghton Mifflin.

Sweeney, M. E. (1983). An exploratory structural-functional analysis of American urban traditional and alternative secondary public schools. Ph.D. diss., Portland State University.

Treslan, D. L. (1983). A mechanism for involving students in decision making: A critical issue in educational planning and administration. *Clearing House* (November): 123–31.

Wirth, A. G. (1993). Education and work: The choices we face. *Phi Delta Kappan* 74 (5): 361–66.

6

Empowering Students to Shape Their Own Learning

Arnold Langberg

Conventional wisdom about the education of inner-city public school students who are primarily people of color and often on welfare or part of the working poor requires that they be kept in tightly controlled environments and drilled on the basics. This is justified by the assertion that such students both need and want structure and discipline because these elements are lacking in their home situations. The daily experience of most students and teachers demonstrates the futility of this model, but the conventional thinkers respond by just trying to tighten the screws even further.

In 1988, with seed money from a U.S. Department of Labor grant, we started a new alternative school, High School Redirection, in Denver. This school was operated under the auspices of the Denver Public School District for four years and was based on a set of assumptions that differed radically from those stated in the previous paragraph.[1] First, we believed that the one-size-fits-all apparatus for external control actually exacerbated the situation that was preventing most urban students from being successful in school: that is, their feelings of powerlessness, alienation, and anonymity. We designed our advisory system, which I shall describe in detail later in this chapter, to provide each student with an advocate, someone with whom the student could develop a relationship of mutual trust. These relationships took time to develop, but the fact that there was no staff turnover during our first three years enabled us to establish a climate of caring and consistency within which the students could learn to take control over their own education and, perhaps, their lives.

Our advisory system also allowed us to deal with our second point of difference with the conventional school system, the issue of discipline. We believed that all human beings, including students, were worthy of respect, even when their behavior might be unacceptable. Any misbehavior short of causing immediate danger was, therefore, treated as an opportunity for education rather than as a cause for punishment. The advisor, as the staff member with whom the student had the closest relationship, was expected to help the student to learn from the situation, to work with others who had been affected by his or her actions, and to develop alternative strategies for responding to similar situations in the future. The only discipline we were concerned with was self-discipline. Our goal was for all students to learn how to monitor and control their own behavior and, eventually, to have a positive effect on the behavior of others. An externally mandated set of rules and consequences would have impeded the attainment of this goal.

The notion that the curriculum for "those" students should consist of drill on the basics was our third area of fundamental difference with the conventional system. We discovered that our students were much better educated than was indicated by their previous school records, but the basics of school seemed to have had little relationship to the basics of their lives. Schooling and education were not synonymous; perhaps they had even become antithetical. We chose, therefore, not to teach reading, writing, and mathematics as subjects in themselves but rather to integrate them into interdisciplinary units based on themes that built upon the interests and strengths of the students. Students have always been involved in the shaping of their own education; our goal was to create an environment that actively engaged them in the shaping of their school.

In what follows, I will describe the three phases through which the school and its students developed during its first four years.

Phase I

Monique was one of the first students to enroll at High School Redirection. Her story, which she shared with her advisor in bits and pieces over four years, can represent the similar stories of Brenda, Cecilia, Layla, Letetia, and Tulonda, all of whom graduated from high school because they felt that they owed it to their children. The presence of a Child Development Center for their children right in our high school enabled them to accomplish their goal.

Monique had dropped out of school for three years before she discovered HSR. During those years she had run away from home, committed herself to a psychiatric ward, gotten married, had a baby daughter, worked full-time at the age of sixteen, been divorced, and moved back home. As far as the school system was concerned, however, she was just another ninth grader, or maybe not even that.

Monique's description of her development at HSR parallels the development of the culture of the school itself. She was shy at first, feeling that she would be behind the other students and worrying that she would be disliked because she had dropped out and been married. At first she took advantage of the freedom allowed her to just hang out and make friends. She says that she was waiting for someone to suspend her or drop her from the school altogether. Instead she was given trust and support. She found that it was her choice to become a leader and a role model by taking responsibility for her own learning and by holding up her part of the relationship with her advisor. She had moved through freedom *from* being told what to do into freedom *to* create the path that was right for her. This is what we came to call phase I.

Phase I for the school community meant taking the time to develop an environment that would be supportive of our beliefs within a school building controlled by believers in the old paradigm and within a school system that wanted immediate evidence of improved student "achievement." The High School Redirection staff had decided to limit our first year's enrollment to 150 ninth graders so that we could build our own school culture over four years; this also relieved us for a time of the need to concern ourselves with graduation expectations. The staff had a two-week workshop for team building and curriculum writing before the students arrived, and one outcome of that workshop was a schedule for the first semester that attempted to include enough planned activities that the students could be productively engaged but not so many that they would feel powerless to influence the future direction of the school.

Nurturing the staff, especially during the early stages, was essential. They had all been students in conventional schools and then they had taught in them, so they had a great deal of unlearning to do. My experience in a similar situation had convinced me that they would have an easier time adjusting to their new advisory role than they would have in becoming members of interdisciplinary teaching teams.

Survival as a creative teacher in a conventional school had meant shutting your door and doing your own thing, but new strategies would be necessary if we were to model the behavior that we wished to see in our students. Due to the outside money and also to the fact that our target population was primarily students who had dropped out or were at risk of doing so, we were able to staff our school at a ratio of fifteen per staff member. From among the thirty-three applicants we chose two teachers from each of the following disciplines: language arts, mathematics, reading, science, and social studies. In addition to these ten, we hired a full-time social worker to serve as our liaison with the many agencies that impacted the lives of our students and their families, a secretary, an assistant principal whom I would help to become my successor. I was the principal.

For our own mental health, we decided to limit the number of activities expected of each staff member. We also decided that we should work in pairs or larger groups as often as possible. This was especially difficult for the compulsive types who had been outstanding soloists in their previous jobs, but it remained part of the culture throughout our four years. We chose to pair by subject area for advising but across subject areas for teaching.

The school day began with an extended advisory group session to allow students to share their stories and to develop connections with each other and with the staff. The day closed with a brief advisory group session for students to write in their journals and to discuss their evaluations of the day. The only two classes that we offered were a science-social studies combination and a language arts-mathematics combination, with each student expected to participate in one in the morning and the other in the afternoon. The reading teachers joined each combination periodically and worked with individual students *by student request* at other times. All of the classes were encouraged to get out of the building as often as possible to avail themselves of such community resources as museums and recreation centers. The only other aspect of our schedule that was unique was that students had to attend only in the morning on Wednesday so that the staff could meet in the afternoon for mutual support and for continuing the planning process. Students were welcome at these meetings except when a particular student was being discussed, but only a few took advantage of the offer.

Midway during our first semester we held a meeting in the evening so that parents and other interested citizens could join students and staff members to determine the outcomes we wanted for our graduates. The question that I posed was, "If we could create an ideal school, and your child were an ideal graduate of that school, what would be the characteristics of that person?" We divided into small groups to generate as many ideas as we could and then we combined the results into a comprehensive list with much overlap and with obvious clusters. The most dramatic result was that in each of the small groups words such as caring, curious, and confident appeared before any academic outcomes, and in the total list such words outnumbered the others by better than three to one.

During the next two weeks, students and staff members helped me to condense the list to a manageable number that was still responsive to the overall intentions of the evening meeting. We decided to have an equal number of expectations from the character domain as we had from the intellectual. Figure 1 lists the seven C's and the seven I's.

The agreement on graduation expectations was the culmination of our phase I as a school community. The completion of phase I for each individual student would be accomplished when she or he had written a self-assessment on each of the fourteen expectations and created an individual learning plan for meeting these expectations at a personally appropriate level. This step made sense in our school because of the advisory relationship. The levels had to be mutually agreeable to the advisor and the advisee. By the end of our second year we were able to create written guidelines for phase I (see figure 2) and we began to hold a ceremony to recognize those students who were about to make the transition into phase II.

Zane was one of these students. He claims that he was attracted to High School Redirection by my positive approach to learning and by

Figure 1
Graduation Expectations

Character	Intellect
1. Knowledge of inner resources	1. Information/language/communication
2. Caring for self and others	2. Science/technology/environment
3. Sense of justice, fairness, ethics, and integrity	3. Mathematics/problem solving
4. Risk taking/self-challenge/ adaptability to change	4. Sense of history/political power/ global awareness
5. Appreciation for richness of cultural diversity	5. Expressive arts
6. Persistence/commitment	6. Practical arts
7. Long-term employability/en- trepreneurship	7. Critical thinking/decision making

Figure 2
Phase I: Introspection

Phase I for most students lasts one semester. It is the first step on your way to the goal of becoming self-directed, possessing the skills and desire to continue learning for the rest of your life. In this phase you will be working more on the character expectations than on the intellectual, but you will be helped to become aware of both aspects of your being.

The following set of expectations make up your first passage, *introspection.* Once you have successfully met each of the expectations, a celebration will be held that will include you, your advisor, your parents, and anyone else you wish to invite to confirm your readiness to advance to phase II.

1. Establish a relationship of mutual trust with at least one staff member.

2. Maintain a portfolio that includes daily journal entries, a detailed autobiography, dated examples of your work, self-evaluations of completed activities, and your first end-of-semester self-evaluation.

3. Set goals for attendance with support from your advisor and demonstrate your ability to attain these goals.

4. Obtain a Denver Public Library card.

5. Obtain a social security card.

6. Obtain a first aid card.

7. Read a daily newspaper on a regular basis.

8. Improve your reading skills and enjoyment by reading at least two books: at least one at your most comfortable level and at least one other that is a challenge for you.

9. Explore the job bank, take the CASAS Survey, and document completion of a career "shadowing."

10. Document the process of obtaining a pen pal in another country and show at least one copy of a letter from you and one to you.

11. Document at least one project completed by you as a member of a cooperative learning group.

12. Document at least one project completed independently.

13. Complete at least 10 hours of community service, in or out of school, individually or as part of a group.

14. Complete a self-assessment on all 14 graduation expectations.

15. Identify, with the help of your advisor, one of the 14 graduation expectations which you feel is an area of creative talent for you. Document completion of an activity or project that demonstrates growth in this area.

16. Document understanding of personal responsibility as it relates to sexuality.

17. Demonstrate the ability to explain effectively the differences between High School Redirection and conventional schools.

18. Create, with your advisor, a mutually acceptable program for a nine-week learning block and document fulfillment of your short-term goals, at least one character and one intellect.

19. Develop an individual learning plan with long-term goals for both character and intellect and estimate your probable date of graduation.

my statement that every student is gifted and talented and that the job of the school was to help each individual to discover his or her gifts and then to nurture the development of them. He had found his previous school boring, a sort of assembly line of knowledge, with no chance for creativity. He saw HSR as a place where he could learn a lot about one subject instead of vaguely learning parts of many subjects.

Zane's memories of his phase I included a visit to my former school, Jefferson County Open School, where he saw small classes, students making choices, and student involvement in all aspects of the school. Having seen a working model, he knew that he could help to make it happen at HSR. When students expressed a desire for an art class, and he discovered that none of the original staff had ever taught the subject, he worked with one of the language arts teachers to create a silk-screening class which he taught to her and to the other students.

Phase II

Phase II for the school began when we became the prime occupants of our building at the beginning of our second year. We added seven staff members: music, art, physical education, home economics, computer science, psychology, and industrial arts/vocational education. To maintain our student-to-teacher ratio we added 105 more students, mostly ninth graders, with a few tenth graders joining our returning veterans. From the original 150, 145 of whom had been labeled as probable dropouts, 113 returned to us, another 18 transferred to different schools, and 19 apparently dropped out. As the year progressed we added 37 more students to replace those who did not return.

The additional staff enabled us to offer a much more diverse educational program, the new batch of students had a larger percentage of students without labels, and being the landlord rather than the tenant meant that I would no longer have to expect a visit from the police whenever a bunch of students were hanging out in the halls. The new problems that we encountered were: communication became more indirect because of our size, there were more new students than old ones so the new ones unduly affected the culture, and the integration of new and old staff did not proceed as smoothly as we would have liked.

Pauline, the assistant principal, pointed out that when I consulted for larger schools that were dealing with similar situations I usually recommended a "house" structure as a solution, so why shouldn't we try it at HSR? We discussed whether we administrators should form the staff teams or whether the staff members should organize themselves, and we chose the latter strategy. Although there was some initial resistance, they did form four houses: two houses each of five teachers and their advisees, one of four, and one of three. They also decided that for a trial period virtually all of a student's school activity should take place within his or her house.

There were problems caused by this new structure but it did actually solve the ones it was created to solve. Each house had both new and old staff who had to learn to work together on behalf of their advisees, communication of important messages took place within the smaller unit provided by the house, and new students joined the house rather that the larger school, which eased their entry and their impact considerably.

"Impact" may seem to some readers an unusual word to use regarding students, but we were located in the center of gang territory and the students told us that we probably had a higher percentage of the student body belonging to gangs than any other school in the city. Also, as a city-wide school, we probably had members of more different gangs than any other school. Before we changed to the house system we would have a tense couple of days whenever we brought in new students. We still had occasional flare-ups afterward, but they were no longer connected to student intake.

One measure of the maturing of our school culture from phase I to phase II was the relative frequency of fights and the response to them by noncombatants. During the first year, when we were unwelcome guests in someone else's building and before we had developed trust within our own community, we not only had quite a few incidents, but they were inflamed by students not directly involved. During our second year, although we had almost doubled in size, the number of fights decreased and noncombatants tended to avoid any involvement. By phase III, in the latter half of our third year and into the fourth, fights were very infrequent and other students often broke them up and acted as mediators. It takes time!

There was another dramatic measure of how much we had grown as a community in our second year. At my monthly principal's meetings I had often heard one of my colleagues describe a student who seemed to be the scourge of his school, but because he was a special education student the principal had felt powerless to deal with him. Toward the end of the first semester I was asked by this student's parents if their son, Colin, could visit HSR for a week to see if he might want to transfer. I asked one of our teachers who had a special education background if she would include him in her advisory group, and at the end of Colin's visit she asked her fifteen advisees whether they thought that HSR was the right place for him. They all said yes, but Pat pushed them by asking if that also meant that he would be part of their advisory "family," and again they were unanimous in committing themselves to work with him. He wasn't easy, anymore than they had been when they first enrolled, but with their support Colin became a well-liked, productive member of our school community.

Their Curriculum, Our Curriculum

Educators reading this chapter may be wondering when I am going to write about the curriculum at HSR, but that is precisely what I have been doing. The inclusion of outsiders and responses to violence are important parts of what I call "the students' curriculum." What happens to the student outside of school, as well as what happens to the student inside of school but outside our intentions, has always been part of their experience but seldom considered part of their formal education. If we ignore *their* curriculum, is it any wonder that they choose to ignore much of *ours*?

At HSR we developed a definition of curriculum that provided us with a theoretical basis for our program. Curriculum is that process whereby the school facilitates the integration of a student's experiences, in school and out, planned and unplanned, into a coherent framework which has personal meaning for that student. The two-by-two matrix embedded in this definition and illustrated in Figure 3 expands the conventional idea of curriculum beyond the upper-left cell (see Figure 3) of in-school, planned activities; what "we" do to students. This is still *part* of our job, but the other three cells of the matrix, the students' curriculum, respect the importance of other influences on the student's life, especially that of their parents. What is needed is a balance, a sort of negotiation between the two "curricula" that is possible only if we really know the students with whom we work.

Figure 3

	In School	Out of School
Planned		
Unplanned		

Arnold Langberg

Monique remembers phase II as a time when the advisory relationship expanded into more than just a personal support system. She continued to have her one-to-one time with Amie, her advisor, right up until she graduated, but the other fifteen advisees had developed into her family, and every morning they would read the newspaper together and then discuss world issues. She claims that this did more to improve her reading ability and motivation than other more conventional attempts, and she still reads the paper on her own every day. With our change to a house structure, Monique also became part of an extended family, which brought new friendships and new learning resources but also brought new conflicts. Sounding boards, panels of at least three students and two teachers, had been used occasionally during our first year as a means of resolving conflicts, but they became an essential part of the functioning of each house. Monique had been able to resolve her own conflicts either through direct communication or with help from her advisor, but she did serve on a number of sounding boards to help others deal with their problems. She remembers listening to all sides of a disagreement and learning to ask probing questions before trying to arrive at a recommended course of action. The purpose was not to place blame or to hand out punishment but rather to educate, so the disputants themselves often helped to create the solution.

In those few cases where the recommendations of the sounding board were ignored or when a student refused to go through the process, I would become involved. I would invite the parents to join the student and me in creating a solution that usually included time out of school, either through home study if the student and advisor were willing, or a furlough, during which time the student was expected to get a job or engage in some otherwise productive activity. In either case, the student would have to petition for reentry, and evidence of productive activity would be the major portion of the petition. Even here, in a situation where the school had apparently not been successful, the student was expected to take an active role in shaping his or her education.

Monique lists desktop publishing, geometry, parenting, political action, and peer counseling as the most important classes that she took during phase II. By working in groups in geometry, she came to the point where she wasn't afraid to ask for help, which is why she believes that she did so well in that course. Although Monique was comfortable learning desktop publishing in a class, she observed that most students were more comfortable working with computers in their advisory group, so she became a computer teacher for many of her family members. Parenting and peer counseling laid the groundwork for her focus in phase III and beyond, and political action helped her to become an articulate spokeswoman for her school.

The experience that Monique remembers most vividly from this time was a five-day trip to the Canyonlands of Utah. Her advisory group grew closer as a result of this common experience in a challenging environment that was so far removed from their "comfort zone." She had to help set up tents in the dark, hike a long distance in intense heat, and overcome her fear of heights. "I stopped the group and let them know that I was afraid and that I wasn't going to go across. The group then started reassuring me and one of the boys carried my backpack across. When I was done crossing I felt relieved and not so scared anymore." After her first shower in four days she was able to reflect on the beauty and peace of the site and to say that even though it was a "life-surviving trip" and it was kind of awful, she wouldn't change it.

Evaluation

The details about Monique and Zane come from copies of their final transcripts, documents which were the culmination of our unusual evaluation system. This system evolved from two more of our fundamental beliefs: realistic self-evaluation is an essential component of taking responsibility for one's own learning, and character development is at least as important as intellectual development.

The latter belief, which is reflected in our graduation expectations, created a dilemma for us when we looked at conventional methods of evaluation. How could we give credits and grades for "Knowledge of Inner Resources" or any of the C's? But if we gave them only for the I's, for mathematics and social studies, then the students would know that those were obviously more important. Our decision was to replace the entire grade/credit system with a system of portfolios and graduation by demonstration. We also developed a series of fifty "be-able-to" statements that gave students more specific objectives within the fourteen general graduation expectations (see figure 4).

The former belief is an outgrowth of our mission statement: HSR will help each student to develop both the skills and desire to become a self-directed lifelong learner. This necessitates overcoming the "good boy" syndrome with which many of us were raised. Our parents told us when we'd been good or not, and our teachers continued this through the shorthand of letter grades. We performed for their approval. The final period in this game was graduate school where we

Figure 4
High School Redirection
Graduation Expectations

(Every statement under each of the fourteen headings is introduced by the phrase
"Be able to.")

Character	Intellect
C1. Knowledge of Inner Resources	**I1. Information/Language/ Communication**
• write a self-evaluation that details specific experiences, the learning that has taken place from these experiences, and a realistic appraisal of your own performance.	• communicate effectively in both oral and written language.
• identify your strengths and build upon them.	• locate needed information and adapt it for personal use.
• challenge yourself by expanding your "comfort zone."	
• identify your limitations and develop ways of overcoming them and/or compensating for them.	
• demonstrate flexibility and resourcefulness in dealing with unexpected obstacles, changes in plans, and bureaucratic red tape.	
C2. Caring for Self and Others	**I2. Science/Technology/ Environment**
• assess and enhance emotional, mental, and physical well-being.	• apply the scientific method as one form of logical inquiry.
• demonstrate understanding of individuality within relationships by developing a meaningful relationship with at least one other person.	• demonstrate understanding of the vocabulary of the various branches of science and the nature of each area of investigation.
• document the experience of giving to others without expecting something in return.	• demonstrate understanding of the concept of technology and the social, economic, and moral implications of technological development.
• demonstrate a repertoire of positive responses to stressful situations.	• demonstrate environmental awareness through a documented pattern of reduced negative personal impact.
C3. Sense of Justice, Fairness, Ethics, and Integrity	**I3. Mathematics/Problem Solving**
• describe values and principles necessary for making moral decisions, and demonstrate personal application of these principles.	• organize the data and perform the calculations necessary to maintain control of personal finances and economics.

Continued

Figure 4
Continued

Character	Intellect
C3. Sense of Justice, Fairness, Ethics, and Integrity, *Continued*	**I3. Mathematics/Problem Solving,** *Continued*

C3. Sense of Justice, Fairness, Ethics, and Integrity, *Continued*
- demonstrate the ability to put yourself in the place of someone with whom you find yourself in conflict.
- demonstrate awareness of the effects of your behavior on others.
- document having effectively functioned as a mediator in a dispute in which you were not personally involved.

C4. Risk Taking/Self-Challenge/ Ability to Change
- do something for yourself that you formerly depended on others to do for you.
- document successful completion of an adventure satisfying the following components:
  1. It was created by you with support from your advisor.
  2. It was designed as a personal quest.
  3. It was planned as an appropriate challenge to enable you to transcend your normal limitations.

C5. Appreciation for Richness of Cultural Diversity
- demonstrate knowledge of your own cultural background and understanding of the contributions your culture has made to the larger society.
- document specific experiences that have made you aware of the unique contributions that have been made to the larger society by at least three cultures other than your own.
- demonstrate awareness of stereotypes and document at least one experience that caused you to change your former beliefs about another person.

I3. Mathematics/Problem Solving, *Continued*
- demonstrate understanding of arithmetic, albegra, and geometry, their properties and relationships.
- demonstrate proficiency with measurement through reasonable estimation as well as by correct use of appropriate devices and instruments.
- solve problems by generating hypotheses and drawing upon a repertoire of creative approaches to test these hypotheses.

I4. Sense of History/Political Power/Global Awareness
- place an issue of current interest into its historical and geopolitical context and develop at least two alternative futures for that issue.
- document participation in a political campaign for either a candidate or an issue of personal concern.
- demonstrate awareness of other political, social, and economic systems, their relationships to each other and to the system in your own state and country.

I5. Expressive Arts
- document experiences with at least three different forms of creative expression.
- demonstrate an appreciation of art forms derived from diverse cultures.
- demonstrate openness to new ideas and differing points of view.
- make aesthetic judgments based on critical analysis of one's own work and that of others.
- demonstrate a willingness to take risk and to learn from mistakes as necessary aspects of creative process.

Continued

Figure 4
Continued

Character	Intellect
C5. Appreciation for Richness of Cultural Diversity, *Continued*	

C5. Appreciation for Richness of Cultural Diversity, *Continued*
- describe relationships that you have developed that crossed racial, national, and generational boundaries.

C6. Persistence/Commitment
- demonstrate the willingness to make commitments to yourself and others, and the ability to fulfill these commitments.
- document successful experience in setting goals, determining priorities, and managing time so as to complete tasks on schedule.
- document specific examples of your persistence and perseverance in dealing with bureaucratic red tape and overcoming obstacles in order to complete your task successfully.

I6. Practical Arts
- prepare a nutritious meal for yourself and at least one other person.
- demonstrate the ability to function as a prudent consumer.
- document successful completion of an approved course in first aid and one in C.P.R.
- document completion of CASAS survey of employability skills.

C7. Long-Term Employability/ Entrepreneurship
- fill out a job application without errors and, using the word processor, prepare a personal résumé and write a business letter, both of which will also be free of error.
- document participation in an interview during which you were able to present the skills and personal traits that you possess.
- document at least one set of skills that could lead to immediate employment, habits of punctuality and dependability necessary to maintain employment, and the motivation to grow and advance within an area of employment.
- demonstrate knowledge of the concept of entrepreneurship through the development of a detailed plan for starting and managing your own business.

I7. Critical Thinking/Decision Making
- document the setting of both short- and long-term goals, the attainment of the former, and progress toward attaining the latter.
- demonstrate the ability to define a problem, to identify possible underlying irrational beliefs, to outline an array of options for solving the problem as well as the possible consequences of choosing each option, and to evaluate the results of any choice for the purpose of modifying future behavior.

142

would spend the first few sessions trying to figure out what the professor wanted so that we could be reasonably sure that we would receive the award of credit when the final buzzer sounded.

Changing the focus from the teacher's wants to the student's needs was why we called phase I "Introspection." Every student in our school was expected to write in his or her journal every day, indicating what had taken place, how it felt, and what had been learned. The advisor was expected to respond, in writing, at least once a week, though most of the advisors found it important to read the journals every day and to try to write a brief response daily as well. Time was provided at the end of the school day for the students to make their journal entries, but many students preferred to take them home to write in them at night. The prime purpose of the journals was to develop the habit of self-evaluation, but it often served as a way of enabling the students to communicate concerns that they might have had difficulty conveying in a conference. The journal was not limited in any way other than to maintain confidentiality between the student and the advisor. It could deal with issues directly related to school as well as situations that had no apparent school connection at all.

The second level of portfolio development was the self-evaluation at the conclusion of any learning activity. I use this phrase rather than "course" because teacher-centered activities comprised only about one third of the learning experiences. Trips, jobs, independent research, and service projects tended to be even more profound learning activities for most of the students. Whether it was a course, a service project, or a trip, the students were expected to write a detailed self-evaluation of the activity, including what they had done, what they had learned, how they might have behaved differently, how the leader of the activity functioned, and how the activity might be improved if it were to be repeated. Then the leader of the activity was asked to provide a written response to the student's evaluation. If there were a major discrepancy between the two viewpoints, the advisor would arrange a meeting to discuss the differences so that this also became a learning experience, rather than assuming that the student's response was less valuable than that of the teacher. The more formal aspects of the curriculum generally ran in six- to nine-week blocks of time, so we would take a day at the end of each block to give students time to write their self-evaluations because we considered these to be an important part of the learning process.

Twice a year, in January and in May, we would take the time for students to write an extended self-evaluation that would attempt to summarize the previous semester. The focus would be on patterns of behavior more than on the specific learning experiences. Had the student started many things and completed few? Had the student discovered that an antipathy toward mathematics was based on unpleasant previous experiences rather than any inherent dislike for the subject? Did he or she find out that he or she was more effective doing one thing at a time, in depth, rather then trying to do many things simultaneously and with less attention to excellence? The advisor would write a response to this document and this would become the basis for a plan for the ensuing semester.

Zane emphasizes field trips as one of the most powerful influences of his time at HSR. From a walking tour of the surrounding neighborhood during phase I when he studied the architecture and history of the area as well as the natural environment, to trips to Pueblo, Colorado, and Santa Fe, New Mexico, to help others learn about our school and where he learned to appreciate the Indian and Hispanic cultures, he realized that learning experientially helped him to make connections that he had not been able to make in the classroom. When he visited Leadville, Colorado, he understood the conflict between its mining history and its need to develop a new economic base, probably around recreation. When he visited the Rocky Mountain Arsenal he saw an enormous wildlife refuge that included a breeding ground for bald eagles in close proximity to the most polluted square mile on earth, where the residues from the production of nerve gas had been stored. These trips, and what he gleaned from them, led him to one of his phase III research projects.

An equally important influence on Zane was his interest in drafting and technology, which led him to enroll at the school district's Career Education Center (CEC). His instructor was as enthusiastic as Zane about learning and creativity and he encouraged Zane to follow the paths of his own inspiration. During his two years at CEC Zane won many awards for his drafting and one for his design in a Statewide bridge-building contest. The project that dominated his life for three years, however, was the result of seeing the movie *Back to the Future, Part 2*. He was fascinated by the hovering skateboards that were powered by two tiny jet engines, and he decided to design and build his own jet engine. It was this project that convinced his advisor of his readiness to enter phase III.

Phase III

Phase II for the school community had been the time necessary to define ourselves and our goals as well as to establish the structures that we would need to help the students to do the same thing for themselves. The fifty "be-able-to's," the sounding boards, annual trips such as the service project where students planted fruit trees on the Navajo Reservation, and most of all the acceptance of the advisory system as both an individual and group support structure, were evidence of our completion of this phase. Phase III for students would be the time to demonstrate that they had not only acquired the skills and developed the desire for self-directed lifelong learning, but that they could use their skills, actually apply them in real-life situations.

The structure that we developed for phase III evolved from work that we had done at my previous school. Each student would create three challenging projects which we called "passages," in the sense of a rite of passage to adulthood. Proposals for these three passages, global awareness, career exploration, and creative expression, would be presented to each student's personal graduation committee, which would include the advisor, at least two other teachers, the parents or some other appropriate family member, at least one phase II student, one person from outside the school community, and me. (See figures 5, 6, and 7 for the guidelines for the three passages.) The committee would grant approval if they felt that the student's proposals were challenging but attainable. It was left to the advisor to help the student incorporate any modifications that members of the committee would want for them to give their approval. The committee as a whole would be reconvened only when the student and advisor agreed that the passages had been successfully completed, the final transcript written, and the student was prepared for an oral examination on the graduation expectations.

Monique's global awareness passage was a study of child abuse in the United States and Canada. In addition to a great deal of reading on the topic, she visited a local crisis center and interviewed the director and attended a seminar on sexual abuse. She contacted a Canadian educator who had visited our school, and he helped her to find information about how his country was dealing with the problem. After all of this research she volunteered her time to work with abused children before she felt ready to compile her research paper. She explored a career as a social worker by shadowing some and conducting interviews with others in a variety of settings, and then she arranged a three-month internship. She also checked into the education necessary to pursue this career, and in the process she was awarded a scholarship to a local community college. Monique demonstrated her creativity by printing and binding a book of pictures that had been drawn for her by the abused children with whom she had worked. Each picture

Figure 5
Career Exploration

1. A few students enter high school with clear career goals, but many students do not. Whether you are one of the few or among the many, your preparation for this passage will include spending time in Room 2, learning about the resources available through Job Link, and taking the CASAS Survey.

2. The next step is to choose a particular job that you wish to learn more about. Your advisor can help you reflect upon your experiences in Job Link, in other school activities, and in your life outside school as a way of reaching a decision.

3. Once you have chosen the job, use your advisor, the Job Link personnel, or any other appropriate contact to help you make arrangements to shadow a particular person who is working in that job. Keep a journal during the shadowing and, when it is complete, write an evaluation of the experience and share it with the person whom you were shadowing.

4. At the next level of preparation you should begin to distinguish between a job and a career, and your advisor can help you set up a community learning apprenticeship. This will last longer than the shadowing, it should be broader than a single job, and it will have you actively involved in contributing to the work situation, but not initially for pay. Your "pay" will be the learning that takes place, which you will document in your daily journal. Upon completion of the apprenticeship you should write an evaluation and ask the community teacher to write a response to it.

5. If you have not yet held a paying job, this would be the time to do so. If you can get one in the career field of your main interest, that would be best, but this may not be possible. If not, any paying job would be acceptable as long as you keep documenting your learning in your daily journal. Of particular importance are your relationships with supervisors and fellow employees as well as your understanding of wages, benefits, taxes, etc.

6. By now you should be ready to write a proposal for your career exploration passage. Indicate what career area you will be exploring, why you are choosing this career, how you expect the exploration to proceed, what questions you will need to have answered, what resources you may need: individuals, organizations, books, magazines, and professional journals, and an estimated date of completion.

7. Upon approval of your proposal by your Graduation Committee you can begin the process of answering the questions through interviews, research, and other such activities. Be sure to keep detailed documentation, including dates, to facilitate the writing of your final wrap-up.

Continued

Figure 5

Continued

8. Specific information that you should include in your final wrap-up:

a. *Education and/or Training:* How long will it take? How much will it cost? Where can you get it?

b. *Salary:* What is the expected starting salary? What is the highest possible salary and how long will it probably take to get there?

c. *Constraints:* Is this career open to everyone or are there restrictions? Are there locations where you would have more or less opportunities to pursue this career?

d. *Employee Organizations:* Are there unions or associations connected with this career? How much does it cost to join? Do you have a choice? What are the pros and cons of joining?

e. *Future Trends:* What is the likelihood that the number of openings in this career area will be increasing as your prepare to enter it? How do you know?

f. *Related Careers:* Describe at least five other careers that you could enter with minimal retraining if, for some reason, you could not pursue the one you have explored.

9. The final wrap-up should be a narrative describing the details of your total career exploration. If there were changes from the proposal, be sure to describe them and give reasons for making the changes. In most passages a number of surprises occur, experiences that you have not planned for. Include these in your paper and indicate what you learned from them. Finally, what effect did this passage have on your career plans? What are your next steps? Will you pursue this career? Why or Why not?

---

was accompanied by a poem that she composed in response to the picture.

The final transcript is primarily a personal narrative that attempts to draw together material from the student's journals, learning activity evaluations, semester self-evaluations, and passages, into a single document that describes this student and the educational journey that has led to his or her graduation. Writing it is a difficult, time-consuming process, but we have found that it serves to unify a program that may have previously appeared fragmented. It is also a reality check on the importance of written communication because it will be the core of the student's permanent record of his or her high school education.

A process for developing this narrative that has been used by many students begins with them writing down all over the paper, as nonlinearly as possible, words or phrases that will remind them of key

Figure 6
Creative Expression

1. Each passage has two major purposes: To demonstrate your ability to apply, in the real world, those skills that you have acquired in school, and to challenge yourself to the fullest to continue to stretch and grow. Your creative expression passage might be either a significant development and expansion of a talent that you have previously demonstrated, or an intensive exploration of an area that is a new interest for you.

2. Your initial preparation for this passage occurs during the process of introspection when you do your self-assessment on the graduation expectations. As you discuss your responses with your advisor, the two of you should be able to identify at least one area of strength where you have confidence in your creative ability. Although the expressive arts category is a likely possibility, you should not limit yourself to conventional notions of creativity.

3. At a more advanced stage of preparation, you should choose to explore an area of creativity in which you might feel you lack talent. There is evidence to suggest that many of us possess talents that go undiscovered because we have not been in environments that nourished their development. Risk taking is an essential part of a true creative process.

4. You should now be ready, with the help of your advisor or other staff members, to choose the specific project you will do for your creative expression passage. You should then draft a written proposal indicating your choice of project, the materials and equipment you might need, a budget for the project, possible sources of funds and materials, an estimated date for completion, and a procedure for providing an appropriate critique of your work.

5. It is particularly important that you document all phases of this passage. Journals, photographs, audio- and/or videotapes, slides, any combination of these that can help your committee to understand your creative process, will be as important as the final product.

learning experiences. When they do this first from memory and then they fill in from rereading their previous documentation, they are usually surprised at how many activities they have not initially recalled. I believe that this is because the word "transcript" evokes thoughts of classes and conventional school experiences, and the advisors often have to remind their advisees of out-of-school learning as well as their involvement in hiring their own teachers, helping to recruit students, making presentations at conferences, university classes, school board and legislative hearings, and helping other alternative schools get started or get back on track. Work, travel, and relationships have all contributed to their becoming who they are, and these also need to be included.

Figure 7
Global Awareness

1. Choose for your topic a problem that has global impact but one that also has personal interest for you. Ask yourself, "If I could solve just one world problem, what would it be?"

2. Write a draft of a proposal stating why you chose this particular topic, at what level you will research it in America (local, state, or national), what resources (human or other) you have already identified, what other country you think might be dealing more effectively with this problem, and what you might do for a service project to help solve this problem at a local level.

3. Give a copy of the proposal to your advisor and at least one other staff member, and arrange to meet with them to agree on what revisions would be necessary to make it into a formal proposal. You might include another student on this support team.

4. Type the formal proposal on a word processor, if possible. If you do not know how to use a word processor, a neatly written proposal will be acceptable, but the research papers will have to be done on the computer. Be sure to include in the formal proposal when you expect to complete each part, including learning to use the computer, if that applies to you.

5. If you haven't yet done a library search, this would be the time. The main public library on Broadway and the Auraria campus library have the most complete collections, although some specialized libraries might be helpful later on. Be sure to identify books, magazines, newspapers, and journals that you might use, as well as appropriate films, videotapes, and audio-tapes.
When you use any of these resources, be sure to write down the title, author, publication date, volume number if it is a magazine or journal, and even the page number if you decide to quote directly. It's a pain to have to go back and find these out later.

6. If you haven't yet contacted human resources, this would be the time. There are government agencies at all levels, private organizations, public nongovernmental groups, and just plain individuals that are working on whatever issue you have chosen, and they can provide information and, perhaps, ideas for your service project. If you are going to do interviews, you should plan out your questions and practice on a teacher before taking up someone's valuable time. If you would like to tape-record the interview, be sure to ask permission, and be sure to practice using the recorder.

7. By now you should have gathered sufficient materials to be able to begin putting your project together into a paper that describes what is being done, how well it is working, what changes might be needed, and what major forces exist for and against solving the problem. Share a rough draft of this paper with the same people who helped you in step 3, and you should then be ready to type the finished paper, including suggestions from your support team.

Figure 7
Continued

8. The paper on another country could be put off until now, but it would be smart to begin the research back around step 3 or 4. Once you have chosen your country, you should try to learn a little about its geography, history, population, its vital statistics, so that you will have some background for understanding the current situation. The library might be of some help, but if it's not, find a local person from that country to help make contacts. Perhaps there is a consulate in Denver or you might have to write or call the embassy in Washington. This all takes time, so don't wait too long to start preparing for this second paper.

9. The writing of the second paper will follow the same procedures as the first. Complete your notes, write a rough draft, share it with your support team, and then type the final version, including suggestions from the team.

10. Your service project may be started at any time during these steps, and it may be finished before you have completed your papers, but usually it will be the culminating activity of the whole Global Project. It, too, should have the prior approval of your support team, and you should keep a journal of your experiences during your service, including photographs, if that is appropriate. Written responses from those you serve, or something equivalent, would provide the final touch.

The next step in this process is the search for clusters. In almost all cases, students can find a focus to their school lives that they might not have noticed before. As many as one third to one half of their experiences may fit into that major cluster. Often there is a second cluster, sometimes a third, and usually there are a few activities that stand alone. The rough draft begins with the student writing about the major cluster which is an easier and more exciting place to begin than "In my freshman year . . ." From this draft the advisor and others can help the student refine the narrative, and it usually can be completed in from three to five rewrites. The final transcript actually includes the student's personal narrative, which may run from twenty to forty pages, a short description and history of the school that I have written, and support letters from the student's advisor and at least two other people who know the student well.

Zane had difficulty limiting himself to exploring just one career. He had worked part-time during high school as a heating and air-conditioning repairman, and he plans to continue in that line as a way of earning money for his university education. He thinks that he will major in mechanical engineering with an emphasis on mechanical drafting or engineering design. I think that he ought to write a book, to be entitled "How I Designed and Built a Jet Engine When I Was Sixteen Years Old." His global awareness passage was a comparison of the legacy of waste being left to our children in the United States and in Germany and how we might learn from German attempts to find innovative solutions to the problem. For his creative expression passage he designed and built, over three months, a mahogany entertainment center for his mother's house. I guess she didn't need a jet engine.

High School Redirection and the Denver Public Schools

During the four years of High School Redirection's existence as a Denver Public School, we underwent three external evaluations for our school alone and we also took part in two others that the U.S. Department of Labor sponsored for all seven of the Redirection replicas across the country. The first was done before we had completed our first year, and it reflected the lack of coherence that we experienced that year. It recommended an increase in staff development, more attention to academics, that the data should be considered as a baseline upon which to measure growth in the future, and that a longitudinal study should be implemented to help us build on our strengths and reduce or eliminate our weaknesses.

The second evaluation was done one year later as we neared completion of our phase II as a school. This team's recommendations included postponing the next evaluation for three years to allow at least one class to complete its full cycle in the program, that the criteria for that evaluation be mutually developed by the school and the system, that greater specificity be added to the fourteen graduation expectations, that assessment measures be developed to demonstrate student achievement and progress toward those expectations, that the relationship between HSR and all the other secondary programs in the system be clarified, and finally, that HSR be recognized as an experimental school within the system working toward a goal of becoming the laboratory school for the system within three years.

The third evaluation was going to be the official visit of the accreditation team from the North Central Association. It had been arranged for February of our fourth year, but the district withdrew its support for that visit in December without involving our school in the decision. The chairman of the team chose to continue with the evaluation on an unofficial basis and at the team's own expense, and fifteen people visited us for two days in early May of 1992. The following statements are taken verbatim from their unsolicited report to the Denver School Board and central administration:

"High School Redirection is a unique institution. While many aspects of its program are replicated in one or another Denver or suburban school, no other institution, to our knowledge, attempts to combine such a broad range of alternative approaches to secondary education.

"The evaluation team believes that High School Redirection is a unique asset for the Denver Public Schools and unanimously recommends that it remain open as one of several alternatives available to young people.

"We believe that the faculty and student body of HSR should remain together. It takes many years to develop a faculty and student body with a shared vision, and HSR is one of the few that we have evaluated where such a vision exists.

"It has taken four years to create this educational experiment, a unique school culture based on self-discipline and mutual respect, to develop a staff that shares a common set of goals and philosophy, and to build a learning community of students, parents, and staff. The school has suffered grievous wounds with the cutting of 7 staff and all the negative publicity connected to its possible closure, but we still found a deeply dedicated staff and student body. We recommend that the institution be brought up to full staffing again. We recommend that High School Redirection become a teacher training laboratory school, working in close conjunction with UNC, UCD, CCD, UCB, and Metro State, and serve as a center for the Denver Schools to identify, recruit and begin training its own future teachers."

The reports from the Department of Labor could not be obtained because they are part of a continuing study of all seven sites. However, informal discussion with the evaluators indicated that their views were similar to those expressed by the other teams.

The reader may wonder if Monique and Zane were exceptional cases rather than representative ones. My response is that they are both. If any school would take the time to create the structures to truly educate each of its students, I believe that school would find what we have found: all of its students are exceptional.

I chose Monique as a representative of teen parents, a group that has a very high dropout rate. I named some of our other mothers but I purposely omitted Takita and Nakia until now. The presence of our Child Development Center contributed to their success, the success of both mother and child brought the fathers to our school as well, and both of those young men also graduated. They are both African Americans, and the dropout rate for that group might be even higher than for teen mothers.

I chose Zane as a representative of students whose obvious talents fall outside the narrowing range of acceptability within the conventional school system. I believe that that system must take responsibility for the development of some of society's gifted criminals because of its inability and unwillingness to create positive avenues to help them express their gifts.

According to a survey done by a Denver newspaper during our fourth year, we had a more diverse student population than any other high school in the city: 41% Hispanic, 27% black, and 32% other. Perhaps the best measure of our school's success is the breakdown of our forty-three graduates: 37% Hispanic, 28% black, and 35% other!

Why did the Denver School Board and central administration close our school? The three issues that they raised publicly, space, money, and evaluation, were each shown to be untrue. The district had just completed a study that named many underutilized buildings where our program could have been transferred as a whole; we kept a large number of students in school who would not have otherwise been counted for state reimbursement; and the "evaluation" that was referred to had been done without our knowledge or participation, the evaluator had never visited the school, and the report contained many inaccuracies and faulty comparisons. Furthermore, at no time did I, as principal of the school, ever receive any written communication stating what specific changes we would have to make in order to keep our school open.

I believe that the issue was one of political power and an unyielding school culture. I had originally been hired by a superintendent who was being deposed at the same moment that the board approved acceptance of the $800,000 grant from the U.S. Department of Labor by a four-to-three margin. The administrator to whom I reported had recommended against acceptance, yet he remained my supervisor. The idea that students and parents would be able to choose whether or not to attend HSR violated the role that alternative schools had historically played for the system: a dumping ground for those who were not "making it." No previous alternative school had ever been allowed to grant diplomas. They had been just "repair and return" operations; the students were broken, not the system. By accepting the grant, they accepted the fact that HSR would grant its own diplomas.

We were hampered in informing prospective students about our existence because the official channels of communication were controlled by a system that "referred" students rather than informed them of their options. As a result, most of our first year students were sent to us having been told that they had to enroll with us until they were functioning in a way that would be acceptable to the system. At that point they would be allowed to return to a conventional school. We told them, however, that they did not have to attend our school unless they wanted to, and if they chose to enroll with us they would not have to return to their former school unless they really wanted to. It was at this moment that their education began. I am sure that most of them signed up because of their dissatisfaction with their previous schools rather than because of our special attraction for them. In time, however, they became the ambassadors that helped recruit future students with our own positive message.

For our first year we were assigned to a building that was underutilized, but we shared it with the program for which it had been built. The principal of that program would send a weekly memo to my supervisor indicating in great detail what *my* students had done to *his* building. During our second year, the new superintendent had dropped by for a visit just as I was standing in the street in front of the school with blood all over my coat from a fight I had just broken up. She turned and left and never returned.

There are probably hundreds of other incidents, but the reasons for closing the school must have been very deep-seated for the board and administration to have been able to ignore the results of the external evaluations, the impassioned testimony of students, parents, and staff members, and the letters of support for us that they received from around the world.

But all is not lost! We reopened as an independent school the following October with one teacher, an assistant, and twenty students, and we recently established a partnership with an agency that receives public funds to educate students outside the bureaucracy of the regular school system. We are beginning to plan for the future, not just to return to what we were, but to move forward to a new ideal!

Notes

1. In part because of these differences, High School Redirection was denied funding by the Denver Public Schools in the fall of 1992. In October of 1992, however, the school reopened in partnership with an agency that receives public funds to educate students outside the public school system. More details about the school's recent history are presented in the conclusion of this chapter.

7

Linking Classrooms and Communities: The Health and Media Academies in Oakland

Larry F. Guthrie and Grace Pung Guthrie

School dropouts, low academic achievement, drug abuse, and teenage pregnancy continue to plague American education. In many American high schools, a demoralized staff, poor teaching, compromised standards, and a haphazard curriculum are the norm (Cusick, 1983; Powell et al., 1985; Sedlak et al., 1986). These problems are often most acute in the inner city, and Oakland, California, is no exception.

Oakland Unified School District has been besieged with problems for the past several years. In addition to high dropout rates and test scores that are among the lowest in the state, the district has contended with "cronyism, incompetence, fraud, abuse, and mismanagement" (Maynard, 1989: B4). The district teetered on the edge of bankruptcy, and employees were charged with crimes ranging from forgery to grand theft and embezzlement. At one point, the state Department of Education imposed a trustee on the district.

In the midst of the turmoil, two of the high schools continued to search for solutions. Unwilling to give up on their students, they experimented with ways to reorganize the high school experience for inner-city youth so that the number of students who graduate, get good jobs, or enroll in college will increase. One approach has been to set up school-based "academies," the Health Academy at Oakland Technical High School and the Media Academy at John C. Fremont High School.

Building upon a concept originated in Philadelphia and successfully replicated elsewhere, the schools link up with resources in the community to provide students with an academic curriculum focused on a career area in a school-within-a-school setting (Academy for Educational Development, 1989; American Institutes for Research, 1984; Snyder and McMullan, 1987; Stern et al., 1988). The Health Academy, which graduated its first cohort of students in 1988, prepares students for postsecondary study in the health professions in conjunction with health facilities in the city. The Media Academy, begun a year later, works with local newspapers and television stations to give students experience and training in both print and electronic media.

Earlier versions of the academy models had a clear vocational focus. The Philadelphia academies, for example, provided potential dropouts with experience and training in the electrical, business and commerce, and health areas. Using a school-within-a-school format, the program enrolled cohorts of about fifty at-risk students per year in a specialized, work-related curriculum. Work experience and field trips were integral to the program, and business and the community were involved in its management (Snyder and McMullan, 1987). In replicating the program, the Oakland schools maintained most of these features, but shifted the focus of the intervention away from entry-level jobs and toward preparation for postsecondary education.

In 1988–89, staff from Far West Laboratory studied the Health and Media Academies through observations of classes and interviews with teachers, students, and community professionals involved with the programs.[1] In this chapter, we extend earlier work (Guthrie and Guthrie, 1989) in which we described the design and implementation of the programs and drew comparisons on several dimensions. Reporting on the results of additional analyses, we argue here that a key to the success of the Oakland academies has been the close collaboration between the schools and their community partners.

Our research was guided by a theory of dropout prevention based on the concepts of "educational engagement" and "school membership" (Wehlage et al., 1989). Educational engagement refers to students' involvement in academic tasks and the process of learning. Schools need to find ways to relate the work of schooling to the real world. Instruction needs to go beyond the superficial coverage to include projects and other reality-based activities.

School membership refers to the sense of belonging that students develop as they participate in school activities and form social bonds with peers and adults. As students become "members" of the school, they come to see a purpose for schooling.

In our study, we found that the two Oakland academies successfully incorporate these two key concepts in their design and implementation. However, we found the concept of school membership too limited to capture the complex of influences on participating students. As we suggest later, a comprehensive idea of "community membership" more adequately describes how students develop relationships with adults not only in the school but in the professional communities outside the school. Within the school, the academies provide a community of support that builds a sense of school membership; at the same time, the work experiences, field trips, and other connections with the broader community foster a sense of belonging there as well.

The Oakland Academies

The Health Academy

The choice of health as a focus for the district's first academy was a logical one since the health industry is the largest employer in Oakland, and Oakland Technical High School is within walking distance of "Pill Hill," the site of several hospitals and health care facilities. In addition, the area surrounding Oakland enjoys a steady growth in the health-related biotechnology industry. Yet only a fraction of public school graduates in Oakland typically qualify for work in the local health industry. The birth of the Health Academy, therefore, represents a deliberate effort to link school and community.

It is also a direct result of school-community partnership. Once the district had secured a planning grant from the state and a project director was chosen, the new director met with the head of a nearby hospital and the director of the Samuel Merritt College of Nursing, only blocks away. Soon a steering committee representing seven hospitals was formed; in jointly developing a plan for the academy, they helped solidify the agency ties with the school. They went a long way toward outlining the curriculum as well. Personnel directors, for example, provided valuable insights into what hospitals and other medical facilities typically seek in employees.

Situated only a few blocks from downtown, Oakland Technical High School faces a busy thoroughfare. The school enrolls approximately 1,800 students, 94% of whom are minorities (73% blacks, 17% Asian and Pacific Islanders, 3% Hispanics, and 1% Filipinos). Over one third of the students qualify for Aid to Families with Dependent Children assistance.

157

The Health Academy involves nine teachers under the leadership of Patricia Clark and serves approximately 120 students in grades ten, eleven, and twelve. Each year, students are block-programmed into academy courses in science, English, and math that cover the same curricular objectives as others in the school but emphasize medical or health issues whenever possible. The core of the curriculum is the science sequence of biology, physiology, and chemistry. Each course has an accompanying lab, usually scheduled the next period. More advanced students may take chemistry in their junior year and then enroll in physics as seniors. Others can take an advanced health occupations course as seniors that covers the basic skills and medical terminology required for hospital technicians, clerical workers, and nurses' aides. In the second semester, these students are provided work experience at a local hospital, rotating through twelve different departments a week at a time.

In academy English, students read novels and stories that have a health or biological orientation. A library adjacent to the academy's main classroom contains multiple copies of health- and medicine-related novels, as well as a collection of popular nonfiction books on relevant topics.

Local businesses and the community are involved in several ways. Students take frequent field trips to the nearby hospitals, work at part-time or summer jobs, and participate in seminars at the Merritt College of Nursing. In one set of field experiences, for instance, students signed up in groups of two to four to attend clinical laboratory classes at the Merritt College of Nursing. The laboratories ranged from one to four hours in length and included hands-on training in medical techniques and the nursing of adults as well as lectures on leadership and medical research. Guest speakers at the academy have included administrators, faculty, and students from several hospitals and universities. In addition, students often attend the taping of *Vital Signs*, an educational television program produced by the nursing college (for more detail on the Health Academy, see Guthrie and Long, 1989).

The Media Academy

The Media Academy was begun a year later as part of the effort of the Oakland Unified School District to extend the academy model to three other high schools. The district's three academies offer concentrations in media, business and finance, and computer technology. The

Media Academy, built on the existing journalism program at Fremont High School, is directed by Steve O'Donoghue. Media is a logical choice also for Oakland Unified School District, for Oakland has its own well-known daily, the *Oakland Tribune*, at least four local TV stations, and a number of radio stations in the area. Since most journalism or broadcasting jobs today require a college degree, the Media Academy is designed as essentially an academic preparation program.

The Media Academy represents a new direction for the academy model, a direction that holds considerable promise. It offers students the opportunity to practice journalism as part of their school experience. O'Donoghue's students not only publish the school paper, but put out a bilingual community paper, *El Tigre*, as well. In 1988–89, the electronic media portion of the curriculum was added to the academy, and students produced an AIDS education video with the support of the local YMCA. Such school-community collaboration goes beyond the usual one-way support of community to program—the students actually provide services in return for community support.

John C. Fremont High School is located in a low-income area of southeast Oakland. The school enrolls about 1,700 students, of whom 98% are minorities (54% blacks, 32% Hispanics, 8% Asian and Pacific Islanders, 3% Filipinos, and 1% Native Americans). The Media Academy occupies two portable classrooms near the back entrance of the school; one of these serves as the academy office and O'Donoghue's classroom. The school newspaper, the *Green and Gold*, is produced in the academy office, which is also home for several computers, a typesetting machine, a new digital scanner, and a darkroom. Much of the Media Academy's "wealth" comes from the generous donations and fund-raising activities of media professionals (and their organizations) who serve on its advisory panel.

The second portable classroom serves as the classroom of English teacher Michael Jackson, who works closely with O'Donoghue. The proximity of these buildings makes block-scheduling of students and coordination between the two teachers easy to manage. The new instructor for video production is another key staff member. Two social studies teachers and a librarian are also involved in the program, but because of their commitments to other school activities, they participate less actively.

The Media Academy serves approximately 120 students in three grade levels. Students are block-scheduled in English and journalism classes in the morning and move through the rest of the school day as a cohort. The Media Academy curriculum is designed to help students develop and apply reading, writing, critical thinking, and technical skills through the hands-on production of school newspapers, magazines, and radio and television projects.

Currently, the Media Academy Advisory Panel includes the editor and president of the *Oakland Tribune*, local radio and television personalities, and communications faculty from the University of California-Berkeley and San Francisco State University. This group provides guidance and publicity for the academy and offers occasional lectures. Several corporations also contribute time and equipment to the academy, as noted earlier. (For a more detailed description of the program, see Guthrie and Guthrie, 1989, and Wehlage et al., 1989). This community of learned, successful media professionals (role models) has contributed much to the sustained academic engagement of many of the students in the Media Academy.

Academy Students

During the years we studied the academies, their ethnic composition generally reflected that of the respective schools. The Health Academy enrollment was nearly all African American with a small percentage of Asian and white students. At the Media Academy, over half the students were African American, and roughly one-third were Hispanic; the rest were Asian. Nearly half the Media Academy seniors said they spoke a language other than English at home.

Most of the students came from disadvantaged homes and lived in the lower-income neighborhoods around the schools. Their backgrounds and experiences reflected inner-city life. They came from single-parent homes and encountered crime, drugs, and prostitution daily. Only about a third of the Health Academy students and slightly more than half of those at the Media Academy lived with both parents. The school principal said that the Health Academy students were some of the "hardest core" in the school.

School staff selected students for the academies who were at risk of dropping out of school. Many had a record of poor attendance, disruptive behavior, or involvement with drugs. While their prior grades were usually average to low, they were judged to have the potential to be successful. And, although school staff described some of them as "average" in achievement, at these two schools, "average" could mean students who were three or more years behind grade level.

Findings

Given the family lives and history of school failure of the students, the two academies face a tremendous challenge. They are attempting to undo several years of unproductive schooling and bad experiences. In other schools, many of the students would be allowed to leave so teachers could focus on students with greater potential. However, by making school relevant and linking it to not only the students' community, but the larger community of work and career, teachers in the academies have kept them in school and prepared them for later life. In this section, we present findings about how students changed as a result of their academy experiences. The discussion covers four areas: attitudes toward school, academic performance, social bonding, and future orientation.

Attitudes Toward School

Many of the students recruited for the academies had a history of poor attendance and disruptive behavior, were disaffected with school, and were at risk of dropping out. The academy experience, however, appeared to have had a dramatic effect on how they thought about school and academic work. Although bored and uninterested in school before, after three years in the academy, more than three quarters of those interviewed reported having developed a more positive attitude toward school. Several even described themselves as "driven," "motivated," and "ambitious." In retrospect, they seemed to agree that the academy experience had helped them focus themselves and their goals.

Academy students' improved attitudes were revealed in their study habits and classroom behavior. They were less disruptive in class and able to work in cooperative groups. One of the English teachers noticed a definite change from their sophomore to senior years. At first, "they kept bouncing off the walls, and I kept wondering how [the director] had gotten them together at all. By the time they were seniors, they were a sharp class." Another teacher observed that "you could pick them out all over the campus—they're a little better mannered."

While some of their improved behavior might be attributed to their having grown older, comparisons with nonacademy students provided further evidence of the program's effect. One teacher, for example, described the Health Academy students as "more serious" and "more productive" than their nonacademy peers. "They don't complain about the difficulty of assignments," she said. The physiology teacher in the

Health Academy noticed a "different attitude toward school—more like that of the top academic kids in other classes." They "really want to know things" and "show genuine interest," he added.

Another aspect of their improved attitudes was revealed in the feeling of ownership students had for the academy. "We represent the academy," said one student, "so we have to do well. It's tough sometimes." In a variety of ways, students were willing to pitch in to make the academy a success. At the Media Academy, for instance, students answered phones or straightened up the academy office. When deadlines were near, students came in early and stayed late to make sure the paper went out on time. With regular exposure to and ongoing relationships with the community of media professionals, these students seemed to have learned what it meant to be a professional—taking responsibility and doing what's necessary to get the job done.

Academic Performance

Indications of improved academic performance for academy students were found in their completion of assignments, improved grades, increased self-esteem, and improved attendance.

At the Media Academy, only seven students from the initial cohort of fifty failed to graduate. Of these, two got married and left school to work; the others left because of a variety of personal and family-related problems. As ninth graders, all but one Health Academy student scored below the fiftieth percentile in both English and math on the Comprehensive Test of Basic Skills (CTBS). By the time they were graduating seniors, twenty-four of thirty-two (75%) of them were accepted at four-year colleges; thirteen of these met the entrance requirements for universities in the California system. Table 1 compares CTBS scores for the three cohorts to the schools' and district's scores for the school year 1986–87. In all three areas (reading, language arts, and mathematics), academy students scored better than others in their respective schools and the district.

Over half the Health and Media Academy students reported their grades had improved after joining the program. Between the sophomore and senior years, 63% of students graduating in 1989 had an improved grade point average (GPA). Of these, ten improved a full grade or more. Many who entered the academy with a D or low-C average graduated with A's, B's, and C's on their transcripts. While the aggregate GPA for each of the three cohorts didn't show much change between sophomore and senior years (from a low C to a high

Table 1

Average CTBS Scores for Academy, School, and District Students
1986–87 School Year

Subtest	Media Academy	Fremont H.S.	Health Academy[*]	Health Academy[**]	Oakland Tech. H.S.	District
Reading	42	25	53	51	30	33
Language Arts	49	26	49	55	37	37
Mathematics	54	41	54	62	53	51

[*] 1985 cohort
[**] 1986 cohort

C average), the ten students entering with the lowest GPAs for each cohort made remarkable progress. As sophomores, they had low *D* or *F* averages, but by the time they were seniors, they had raised their GPAs to a high *D* or low *C*. Based on what we know about at-risk students, it is likely that these ten students would have dropped out had they not received the personal and focused attention of the academies. In fact, one student who raised his average from *D*-minus to *C* admitted that he would have left school had it not been for the Health Academy.

It should be noted that the academy curriculum was more demanding than what students would have taken had they not enrolled in the program. Students took more advanced courses and reported that academy courses in general were more challenging than their nonacademy classes. Transcripts showed, for example, that in the Health Academy the chemistry and geometry classes brought down the GPAs of many students. In both academies, however, more than half attended summer school in order to bring their grades back up.

Students attributed their improved grades to the additional support they received from teachers or pointed to the teamwork and cooperative arrangements in classes. Some students, however, reflecting on their personal development, drew a connection between their growing self-confidence and better schoolwork. This notion was echoed by an English teacher at Oakland Tech: "They're much more willing to tackle things and give it a try. They're less afraid to make mistakes. ... I think they're a lot more mentally healthy than the average group of seniors that I would see." Here too, however, the sense of belonging that goes with being part of a team seemed to be a factor; students trusted their peers and felt comfortable taking risks they might not have in another class.

Academy students completed their homework and submitted it on time. According to the physiology teacher, Health Academy students might not have been "academic whizzes," but they could always be relied upon to turn in their assignments. "The proof is in the gradebook," he said, pointing to pages filled with grades and checks for completed work.

Attendance was a serious problem at both high schools, but not within the academies. In fact, as the director of the Health Academy pointed out, the number of students who came to school on a given day was often greater in the academy courses, despite a smaller initial enrollment. In nonacademy classes, it was not unusual for only twelve of thirty-five students to show up, while all twenty academy students would attend their class.

A key element in students' better academic performance was the improved self-esteem that accompanied participation in the program. In fact, membership in the academy itself was a source of pride. There was clearly something special about being part of the program. In addition, more challenging classes and teachers' higher expectations had a tendency to make students feel better about their accomplishments. Also, the support students received from teachers and peers helped to reduce fear of failure. As their teachers pointed out, academy students were not afraid to speak up in class or take a chance. Finally, the care and support demonstrated by the academy advisors and the students' role models in the media field must have had an strong impact on students' self-esteem.

Social Bonding

The academies gave students and teachers a chance to get to know each other well and to develop a sense of group membership. Several students spoke of the familylike atmosphere which brought them closer to teachers and fellow academy students. In describing the Media Academy, for example, one student remarked that "you feel as comfortable here as you do at home when there are several people cooking in a small kitchen." Another said he liked the teachers because they "don't have an image of being God." "It's nice being here," said another. "I sometimes wonder what I'd be doing if I were not here."

The Media Academy director summed up the success of the program with these words: "We're not doing anything radical educationally. What makes it work is that there are a few teachers that know all the kids real well, and the kids know each other real well." Many students, in fact, credited the academy for their continued enrollment in school. As one student put it, "The bond between students, parents, teachers, and the principal kept me from being a dropout. I am so different from the way I was before."

Friendships among the academy students were common, and many reported that most of their friends were academy members. While the cohort scheduling contributed to their choice of friends, they said, working in groups and similarity of interests also influenced their choice of friends. The seniors described their academy friends as more serious than nonacademy students: caring, active, smart, ambitious, motivated, and intellectual.

Most of all, the Media Academy provided these at-risk students a handy and proud label for self-reference. The annual rituals of breakfast, lunch, or coffee with mentors, awards dinner, and summer internship gave these students a visible group identity and a clear sense of belonging and being cared for.

Future Orientation

Whereas earlier versions of academies were designed to equip students for entry-level jobs, Oakland's Health and Media Academies emphasize preparation for postsecondary education. In these programs, students have been encouraged to look beyond a particular course, the current semester, or their high school diploma to the possibility of college and a career. Thus, students who otherwise might have finished high school with limited skills or who were contemplating leaving school altogether developed a more positive outlook on the future. With a growing confidence in their own abilities, more clearly defined goals, and a better idea of what it takes to succeed, students began to plan seriously for college.

The particular vocational focus of the academies attracted some students to the program in the first place. Several joined for the very reason that they were interested in becoming doctors, journalists, or veterinarians. The confidence, resources, and support they gained from the academy helped ensure their achievement of those goals. A Health Academy teacher noted, "I think a lot of them are getting into college that might not have. . . . Some of them would have anyway, but I think we've got a few more that would not have automatically, or would not have even thought about college."

165

Virtually every student interviewed had college plans. Of the sixteen Health Academy seniors, fifteen had applied to college and planned to attend. The one exception had decided to join the military first to gain additional experience. Of the twenty-eight seniors at the Media Academy, twenty-five had applied to college. The other three wanted to work for a year or so before making up their minds. Academy students were accepted at many of the University of California and California State University campuses, as well as several other local and out-of-state universities. Fifty-eight percent of the 1989 graduating Health Academy seniors took either the Scholastic Aptitude Test (SAT) or the Academic College Test (ACT) compared to only thirty-two percent of the school and forty percent of the district seniors. About fourteen percent of all academy students (both health and media) took the SAT more than once. In some cases, students took it three times; one student took it five times.

About half of the students indicated that they were going to attend a junior college before transferring to a four-year institution, even though several already had been accepted. They felt their current skills weren't quite strong enough for survival in the university and that a junior college would ease the transition. These students seemed able to assess their skills and limitations objectively and realistically; others were confident enough not to let any supposed weaknesses discourage them. When asked about her career plans, one girl replied, "If I'm going to be a nurse, why not a doctor?"

Academy students also learned the importance of planning. They learned that if they planned early and made the right preparations, they could successfully attain their goals. A Health Academy senior, for example, was interested in pursuing a career in physical therapy. A self-described potential dropout before joining the academy, he researched schools that would best serve his interest. Once he found a university he felt would provide him with the best opportunities, he contacted the dean of the School of Physical Therapy to ensure that he could meet all the requirements.

All the seniors who were interviewed said they would recommend the academy to another student, and an important reason for this appeared to have been the emphasis the academies placed on preparation for the future. As one student put it, the academy "will help you find a direction in life." More specifically, students said that the academies taught them about career options (30%), improved their skills (23%), and provided them with alternatives in life (14%).

Discussion

What was it about the academies that might have contributed to these changes in behavior and attitudes toward school? When we asked the academy students to explain, more than half pointed to the caring and supportive teachers; others felt the companionship and teamwork with classmates was a factor. In fact, our observations and interviews with adults provided evidence for both these explanations, as we will attempt to demonstrate in this section. We will expand on these hypotheses and attempt to identify those features of the academies that had an impact on the students and their school performance. A recurring theme in this discussion is the concept of "community membership" discussed earlier. In important ways, the academies expose students to a wider community of work; belonging to that real-world community appears to be an ongoing incentive for students both to work hard and to persist.

We have identified five key elements of the academies that seemed to contribute most to developing community membership: (1) a relevant and challenging curriculum; (2) work exposure and experience; (3) field trips and special events; (4) support services and resources; and (5) restructured schooling.

A Relevant and Challenging Curriculum

A fundamental principle of the academy model is to provide students with a relevant and challenging curriculum. Whatever the particular focus, courses are designed to emphasize a common vocational or career theme. In their interviews, students in both the Health and Media Academies said they were able to see a purpose to the courses and were seldom bored. They confirmed that their academy courses had connections to one another and to the real world.

One way the academies accomplish this is through the hands-on application of what students learn in academy lessons. For example, because the Health Academy science classes were followed by a laboratory period, students had a chance to practice the skills taught in the previous hour. Students practiced hospital procedures in a mock "recovery room" adjacent to the Health Occupations classroom. Similarly, at the Media Academy, students were often able to apply their journalism skills in other courses. In an assignment for their English class, for instance, students wrote a news story about the death of Julius Caesar. Furthermore, skills and lessons learned in the academies were useful and directly applicable at the students' after-school jobs or summer internships.

The director of the Media Academy stressed the importance of a relevant and interesting curriculum in improving attendance. If the students are excited about what they are learning and see the relationship between it and their everyday and future lives, they will come to class. "If there's one subject that will draw students into the school and keep them there every day, then you have a chance the other five periods of the day." A few students, in fact, admitted that on days when they felt "tired of school," they would attend only the academy classes.

Most students felt the academy classes were more difficult than those in the regular program and required more work. Because teachers demanded more, the students said, they were more challenged and thus worked harder. Some academy students even believed that the more challenging classes were easier to pass. Their explanation for this apparent paradox was that because the classes were more interesting, the academy teachers more supportive, and the relevance to the world of work more readily apparent, the students were motivated to work harder.

The potential benefit of the increased effort was not lost on the students. As one girl put it, in the Media Academy, "you feel better about yourself . . . you feel you've earned the grade." In other classes, she continued, work was "thrown at you" and the classes "just aren't a challenge, with just book, paper, and pencil. It can get boring; there's no learning." In other classes, she continued, grades were given simply for attendance.

In the academies, peer pressure against school success, as is often found among inner-city students, was rare. The physiology teacher at the Health Academy, for example, commented on how the academy students "really want to know and are quite a bit more motivated and less alienated." In the academy, "it's really okay to want to do well in school." In nonacademy classes, on the other hand, "it's okay to give smart answers to the teachers, but it's not okay to have *A*'s." Many students made similar observations. One student said she and her Health Academy classmates were considered "bookworms" by their friends, but that she didn't mind. Another said she preferred the academy classes because students in the others were "half asleep" and "don't worry about school."

Work Exposure and Experience

Through experiential learning, the academies strengthen the connections of the curriculum with the real world. Field trips, internships, mentoring, and the like give students the opportunity to see what working in the field of medicine or journalism is really like. In a variety of ways, the academies make it possible for students to interact with professionals in their fields of interest. Health Academy students, for example, participated in a wide range of seminars, tours, and other activities. Several nearby hospitals, medical facilities, and the Samuel Merritt College of Nursing provided opportunities for students to visit classes, attend lectures, and shadow professionals. In 1987–88, for example, the local Red Cross chapter provided students with sixteen hours of instruction about AIDS and then trained them to instruct their peers at Oakland Tech and other schools on the same material. Another interesting example was the twelve-week class in health occupations. In the first semester, students learned the basic skills used by hospital clerical workers, nurses' aides, and X-ray technicians. In the second semester, the teacher arranged for the students to work twelve weeks at Kaiser Hospital, about three blocks from the school. The students rotated through twelve different departments or areas (e.g., pediatrics, admitting, and medical lab) and, based on their work performance, some were offered summer jobs at $9 an hour. The maturity and workplace behavior of the Health Academy students prompted the hospital administrator to request more student workers. He even commented on how they had set a good example for the other employees.

In addition to seminars and simulated work experiences, Health Academy students sometimes shadowed medical professionals, observing and asking questions about what their subject actually did during the course of a day. Such experiences fleshed out the image students had of particular careers, a process that led some to change their minds altogether. For example, one student thought he wanted to be an anesthesiologist. After having spent some time with one at Kaiser Hospital, however, the student switched to sports medicine.

At the Media Academy, periodic visitors from local newspapers or television gave seminars and other presentations. Media Academy students also toured and met with the staff of organizations like the *Oakland Tribune*. Guest speakers not only provided students with additional information about career options, but also provided students with role models. A reporter from the *Oakland Tribune*, for example, led a discussion on tracking down leads and developing a story. Many of the professionals had experiences to which students could relate. They told the students, "I made it, and you can too."

Field Trips and Special Events

Field trips and special events play an important part in developing school membership and educational engagement. An important event each year in the Media Academy, for instance, is the three-day field trip to Yosemite National Park. In 1989, forty-five students and five adults made the journey. This excursion represented the first experience in the mountains for many of the inner-city students; some had never left Oakland before. To O'Donoghue, however, the field trip was more than just a chance to expose students to the natural world; he structured the three days around a variety of journalism activities. After a hike, for example, students wrote up descriptions and then critiqued each other's work. This past year, in addition to the four school faculty members who went along, a practicing freelance journalist accompanied the students. He not only provided them with guidance and feedback on their stories, but gave them insights into the life of a professional reporter.

In June, the Media Academy held its annual "Academy Awards Dinner" at a local hotel. The principal, school board members, academy teachers, students, and their parents attended the event, where the program included an invited speaker, a local TV anchor, and media and community dignitaries. The three key teachers gave students various awards for achievement and as incentives to work harder in the coming year. The testimonials from the graduating seniors were genuinely touching and confirmed the importance of knowing that "someone cares." This experience and others helped to rekindle the researchers' faith in the power of education to transform lives and communities or, rather, the importance of schooling being closely connected with the larger community of professionals.

Support Services and Resources

The academies also provide students with extensive support in the area of college counseling and planning. A nonacademy English teacher commented that he was pleasantly surprised by the way the Health Academy students were "very aggressive about seeking me out and asking me about scholarships, turning in applications." In his judgment, while the academy students might not have the best GPAs in the school, as a group they were better prepared for college.

College applications are made available, and counselors and teachers help students fill out forms and answer questions. At times, students are brought to nearby colleges to attend a class and talk to college students. For example, when Health Academy students went to a biology class at the University of California at Berkeley, they talked to biology majors and learned about what it takes to be accepted by the university and how to stay in. In addition, job listings, workplace contacts, and career options are discussed, and students are taught how to write resumes and behave during job interviews.

Through such firsthand experiences, students learned how education applies to the world of work. They learned the requirements for college entrance and the demands of a career in medicine or the media. At the same time, they are shown the significance of school through a variety of "nonbook" experiences. As a result, they feel more confident, assured that they can confront and handle difficulties that might arise in the future.

Restructured Schooling

The two academies represent bold efforts to restructure the schooling experiences for truly disadvantaged youth. In both their design and their implementation, the programs incorporate the latest thinking and knowledge on preventing students from dropping out. Research and practical experience, for example, have led to a set of strategies that schools can use to develop school membership and educational engagement (Guthrie et al., 1989).

For one thing, the academies involve businesses and the surrounding larger communities in sponsorship, mentoring, tutoring, seminars, field trips, work experience, and other activities. The natural connection between the particular vocational focus of each academy and the community and business agencies has made establishing partnerships easier. The academies acknowledge that schools alone cannot meet the needs of at-risk youth.

Perhaps more important, business and the community are involved in substantive ways. All too often, business contributions are limited to short-term, superficial kinds of activities. In the academies, however, the involvement is ongoing and real. Advisory panels play an active role in planning, developing, and guiding the programs. They also represent the academies to the district, often arguing for added support. The relationship between the Health Academy and the Merritt College of Nursing has grown increasingly close. Building upon a joint project funded by the California Postsecondary Education Commission, these two institutions have collaborated on several other shared ventures.

The academies are structured to provide students with a more personalized experience, an alternative to the anonymity and regimentation of most schools. Classes are kept small, and as school-within-a-school programs, the academies enroll fewer than 150 students at a time and are block-scheduled through academy classes. This creates a familylike atmosphere and enables students and teachers to get to know each other better, thus minimizing the impersonal atmosphere of the typical urban high school. On at least one occasion, the Health Academy director took several students to her home and helped them type up their college applications. Such personal attention made an indelible impression on the students.

Because of the block scheduling, students take most of their classes together and really get to know their instructors and their classmates well. The instructional day isn't always cut cleanly into fifty-minute segments either. Laboratories are linked with content classes, journalism merged with English, and field trips provide opportunities for experiential learning outside the school. Block scheduling also seems to facilitate academic performance in that lessons are connected thematically. As one student put it, "you can use all the information learned from all four classes to do your homework, which really helps." It also fosters continuity in the curriculum. As the Media Academy director explained, "Learning is not necessarily divided up in people's minds and in life."

Conclusion

The majority of students served by the two academies came from communities populated by the "truly disadvantaged," where poverty and crime were common. In this context, getting a good education is often impossible. In fact, educating inner-city youth stands as perhaps the greatest challenge facing today's educators:

> The development of cognitive, linguistic, and other educational
> and job-related skills necessary for the world of work in the
> mainstream economy is . . . adversely affected. . . . Teachers be-

come frustrated and do not teach, and children do not learn. A vicious cycle is perpetuated through the family, the community, and through the schools. (Wilson, 1987: 57)

High school academies like those in Oakland may be the key to breaking the vicious cycle. Even though the two academies in the Oakland Unified School District are not without problems in actual implementation, and even though the academies did not succeed fully in graduating all their students, both the Media and the Health Academies have nevertheless accomplished the nearly impossible with a significant number of urban at-risk youth. The interviews conducted with the graduating class in both academies revealed a group of confident, interested, and ambitious young adults.

In the academies, students are neither patronized nor treated as buddies. Instead, the faculty, and especially the directors of the programs, treat their students as mature, responsible adults. They show genuine concern over students' development as a whole; they never lower standards or strike bargains (Sedlak et al., 1986). Despite the time commitments of being educational entrepreneurs, whose creativity and hard work garnered crucial financial and technical assistance from local businesses and the community, the directors are, in the words of at least one student, "always there" for them.

Many of the academy students came from broken homes and an inner-city environment in which few people and few things gave them positive messages about themselves. Moreover, in more typical inner-city high schools, less successful students lead lives of anonymity, where no teacher knows them really well (Sedlak et al., 1986). The academies, however, help these students develop an identity and expose them to the larger world beyond the "mean streets" of East Oakland. Frequent contacts with researchers, observers, and other visitors complement the familylike relationships with their teachers, mentors, and fellow academy students. These potential role models, unlike some adults in the students' home neighborhood, respected the students, and thus affirmed their own self-worth.

In many urban high schools, peer pressure against academic success has a strong influence on minority students (Fordham, 1988; Fordham and Ogbu, 1986; Ogbu, 1974). In fact, the peer pressure for academic noninvolvement and nonconformity is often given as a reason for unusually high dropout rates and academic failure. In the academies, on the other hand, success in school is respected; and an orientation toward college is almost universal. As one teacher pointed out, the Health Academy students didn't have the "don't be a nerd" pressure, while for other, nonacademy students, including those who were "much more academically trained," giving smart answers was okay, but getting good grades was not.

While other students may have drifted toward academic nonengagement for fear of being perceived as "acting white" (Fordham and Ogbu, 1986), the academy students had pride and a sense of ownership in their program. To uphold the reputation of the academy in the presence of the researchers, they even admonished each other to pay attention or to do better in class.

The experiences and changed attitudes of the Health and Media Academy students show that it is never too late to provide effective interventions for at-risk youth. The physiology teacher at the Health Academy summed up the program best:

> The academy has two purposes. The first is about taking some specific students and really trying to give them the ability to get along with the school and the skills and courses that it will take to get them to do something they wouldn't otherwise have gotten to do, whether to go to college or go to a training program. On another level, the goal is to show . . . what it takes to get students, like minority students in Oakland, to really respond to school, [and] to really think about what it takes. It takes some connection to careers. It takes some enrichment so that school isn't so dull. It takes some extra tutoring. It takes really pushing on these kids in the sense that they are special, and they can do it. It takes smaller classes so teachers can really get to know them. This is the kind of thing we ought to be doing if we're serious about wanting students like Tech students to feel themselves to be productive in society and not be on the margins.

Schools can make a difference in the lives of disadvantaged urban youth and break the cycle of failure if only educators dare to be creative in designing and adapting programs to meet their needs. Schools can no longer rely on a strictly academic program of remediation, nor will a focus on building self-esteem suffice. Today's disadvantaged youth know the streets and are looking for a way to survive. By offering them membership in a larger community of professionals and a world of careers, the academies have uncovered a powerful strategy for bringing their students into the larger society.

Notes

Work on this chapter was supported by the Office of Educational Research and Improvement, Department of Education, under Contract No. 406–28–25 to the Far West Laboratory for Educational Research and Development, San Francisco, California, and under subcontract to the National Center on Effective Secondary Schools, University of Wisconsin, Grant no. G008690007.

1. Ethnographic methods (Guthrie, 1985) were used to document and understand the operation of the academies fully. During the 1987–88 school year, our research team observed a variety of classes and other academy activities, such as field trips and advisory board meetings for the academies. A few academy and nonacademy classes, taught by the same teachers, were also observed and compared. During all these visits, we were able to speak informally with teachers and students in a variety of settings. The site visits enabled us to note student behavior, attitudes, and levels of interest. Over the 1988–89 school year, semistructured interviews were conducted with students, teachers, school administrators, and advisors in both school and nonschool settings. We also attended special functions, went along on field trips, and served on the district's "Super Advisory Committee" on academies.

   Furthermore, in order to fully assess the impact of the academies and gather more in-depth data on student changes in attitudes, achievement, and future orientation, all academy seniors were interviewed a few weeks before graduation. These interviews provided a three-year perspective on students' academy experiences. The interviews included twenty sets of questions divided into five categories: student background, experience in the academy program, friendship patterns, prior school experiences, and future plans. Sixteen Health Academy students and twenty-eight Media Academy students were interviewed in May and June of 1989.

   Finally, student transcripts were reviewed in order to gather data on grades, Comprehensive Test of Basic Skills scores, and Scholastic Aptitude Test scores. The transcripts also showed where students went if they left school before graduating (e.g., dropped out, transferred, or left temporarily).

References

Academy for Educational Development (1989). *Partnerships for learning: School completion and employment preparation in the high school academies.* New York: Author.

Larry F. Guthrie and Grace Pung Guthrie

American Institutes for Research (1984). *Replication guide for the Peninsula Academies*. Palo Alto, Calif.: American Institutes for Research in the Behavioral Sciences.

Cusick, P. (1983). *The egalitarian ideal and the American high school*. New York: Longman.

Fordham, S. (1988). Racelessness as a factor in black students' school success: Pragmatic strategy or pyrrhic victory? *Harvard Educational Review* 58 (1): 54–84.

Fordham, S., and Ogbu, J. (1986). Black students' success: Coping with the "burden of acting white." *Urban Review* 18 (3): 176–206.

Guthrie, G. P. (1985). *A school divided: An ethnography of bilingual education in a Chinese community*. Hillsdale, N.J.: Lawrence Erlbaum Associates.

Guthrie, L. F., and Guthrie, G. P. (1989). *Providing options for at-risk youth: The Health and Media Academies in Oakland* [final report]. San Francisco: Far West Laboratory for Educational Research and Development.

Guthrie, L. F., and Long, C. (1989). *The Health Academy of Oakland: Expanded opportunities for at-risk youth*. San Francisco: Far West Laboratory for Educational Research and Development.

Guthrie, L. F., Long, C., and Guthrie, G. P. (1989). *Strategies for dropout prevention*. San Francisco: Far West Laboratory for Educational Research and Development.

Maynard, R. C. (1989). A school system gone awry [letter from the editor]. *Oakland Tribune*, September 3, B4.

McCollum, H. (1990). A review of research on effective instructional strategies and classroom management approaches. In M. S. Knapp and P. M. Shields (eds.), *Better schooling for children of poverty: Alternatives to conventional wisdom; vol. II: Commissioned papers and literature review*. Washington, D.C.: U.S. Department of Education. XII.1–XII.32.

Ogbu, J. (1974). *The new generation: An ethnography of an urban neighborhood*. New York: Academic Press.

Powell, A. G., Farrar, E., and Cohen, D. K. (1985). *The shopping mall high school: Winners and losers in the educational marketplace*. Boston: Houghton Mifflin.

Sedlak, M. W., Wheeler, C. W., Pullin, D. C., and Cusick, P. A. (1986). *Selling students short: Classroom bargains and academic reform in the American high school*. New York: Teachers College Press.

Snyder, P., and McMullan, B. J. (1987). Philadelphia high school academies. In B. J. McMullan, P. Snyder, S. Rosenblum, D. Gruber, and J. Tyler (eds.), *Allies in education: Schools and business working together for at-risk youth, volume II*. Philadelphia: Public/Private Ventures. D.1–D.61.

Stern, D., Dayton, C., Paik, I. W., Weisberg, A., and Evans, J. (1988). Combining academic and vocational courses in an integrated program to reduce high school dropout rates: Second-year results from replication of the California Peninsula academies. *Educational Evaluation and Policy Analysis* 10 (2): 161–70.

Wehlage, G. G., Rutter, R. A., Smith, G. A., Lesko, N., and Fernandez, R. R. (1989). *Reducing the risk: Schools as communities of support.* Philadelphia: Falmer.

Wilson, W. J. (1987). *The truly disadvantaged: The inner city, the underclass, and public policy.* Chicago: University of Chicago Press.

8

International High School: How Work Works

Terrill Bush

> . . . you can watch the process, how people cooperate with each other. It's the only school where you can cooperate and work with other students. Maybe it is because we are immigrants, the teachers don't want us to be closed inside ourselves.
> —sixteen-year-old Russian girl, six months in the United States

If you visit the International High School in New York City, located among the offices, service areas, and classrooms of LaGuardia Community College, you will be impressed with a certain élan about the people, adult and younger, who live there: it is clear that they feel safe, valued, and fortunate. Young people who are admitted to International have been in this country less than four years, and score below the twenty-first percentile on the English version of the Language Assessment Battery. They have come from the trauma of immigration to a sheltering time and place, where they can remake their lives and prepare for college.

International High School, founded in 1985, is the second high school on the campus of LaGuardia Community College. The first one, Middle College High School, founded in 1974, has had remarkable success in graduating and sending on to college 85% of its students, all of whom are judged to be at risk of dropping out of school when they enter. Middle College found that it was unable to serve the hundreds of immigrant children with limited English proficiency (LEP) who asked for admission each year. So the college, in collaboration with the New York City Board of Education, responded to the needs of this equally vulnerable group of students.

Like Middle College High School, International has also found that careful structure, hard work, and a collaborative support system make for success. In 1992, the school enrolled about 450 students in four years of high school. More than two-thirds of the students come from families whose income is below the poverty level. The daily attendance rate is above 90%. The graduation rate is 96%, and 97% of graduates go on to college, 85% of them to four-year colleges.

How It Works

A visit to the school will soon reveal both the workings of a community of young immigrants with their teachers and other helpers, and the physical and human resources active in support of their work. It is work that draws on the riches of the many languages and cultures the students bring. The school is led by faculty who are given every support for building a curriculum that engages both teachers and students in a continuously developing process. There is an ambiance here in which literacy is motivated, for adults and students, by the need of the community for public exchange of information and experience. A good example of the marriage of the ideal and the pragmatic that is characteristic of International's curriculum is to be found in the Personal and Career Development program, which will be described in detail in the second half of this chapter.

High school on the college campus has several advantages: collaborative agreements with the college allow International's students to share college facilities such as the library, gymnasium, cafeteria, and laboratories. Students are free to come and go as they would be in college, and they may stay in the warmth and safety of the campus until ten o'clock at night if they need to.

Students are able to take courses in the college when they qualify for them: this year, 150 International students are taking college courses. The arrangement is like advanced placement: high school credit is awarded for the college courses, and college credit is given when students enter City University or other postsecondary institutions.

Because International follows the daily schedule and calendar of

LaGuardia College, class periods are seventy minutes each. Longer class sessions have made it necessary to rethink teaching approaches in order to introduce variety and maintain interest. In that context, cooperative learning has become not only desirable, but necessary, and the longer time periods make group work approaches very comfortable.

Teaching That Draws on the Riches of Many Languages

A visitor to the school would naturally ask students, some of whom have been in this country only a few months (including a few who have never been to school), how this school is different from those they attended in the past. All will answer that the important difference is that here, *the teachers help you.*

The instructional program is the result of a seven-year struggle to help a widely diverse group of students to master English through content courses and to be comfortable in American culture. Teachers, in addition to being duly licensed, must speak at least one other language; among the present staff of thirty-eight (twenty-four teachers), thirteen languages are spoken, including Spanish, Chinese, Korean, Farsi, Finnish, French, Haitian Creole, Hebrew, Portuguese, Russian, Greek, Dutch, Italian, Pashto, and Yiddish. Many teachers have had experience in teaching English as a second language, even though that may not be their subject matter specialty.

The Faculty Runs the Show

> . . . In this school, rather than accepting what is, we have always tried to imagine what might be—what students need, and then respond to that . . .
>
> —A senior teacher at IHS

Just as students have found the space, time, and adult guidance they need to reorient themselves in a new world, so do teachers at International find themselves in a world they may have only imagined in their previous professional lives. The New York City public schools are infamous for their dysfunctions (which result in a very high dropout rate from the comprehensive high schools). Members of International's

180

faculty, having experienced these problems in other, dysfunctional schools, are happy to find themselves in a professional situation where teaching and learning can thrive.

Committed to an experiential view of learning, the faculty seeks to order its affairs so that they themselves experience the cooperation and collaboration they wish to foster in students. The teachers, looking to their own adult need for community, have structured their faculty affairs in governance and teaching so that mutual respect and demo-cratic collaboration are the coin of exchange. The school's work is informed by a vision of a cooperative, interdependent, supportive community in which the challenges of schooling in a new language can be negotiated with confidence, and eventually, with ease.

Founding principal Eric Nadelstern, himself a former ESL teacher and kibbutzim, has a rare talent for low-key leadership which over seven years has produced a faculty that dares to dream what might be. He has assigned all policymaking for the school to its faculty: committees of the faculty direct the ongoing development of the curric-ulum; the appointment, continuance, and tenure of faculty and staff; the disbursement of discretionary funds; and relations with parents, the college, and the board of education. The principal and other admin-istrative staff have defined their roles as supporting the faculty's work. These governance arrangements have nurtured a highly committed faculty and engendered high morale.

Work That Engages Student and Teacher

Teachers of a second language become intensely aware of the power of their example for students in every respect, from pronunciation to how to ask a stranger for the time. Over the years, teachers at Interna-tional have taken the role-model challenge a step further. They dream of presenting an example of a good life to students: a life in community and cooperation.

What is missing in many of the New York City schools from which the teachers came is work that engages student and teacher, work that is related to the lives young people wish to build during their adolescent years. This faculty, seizing the opportunity that came with inventing a new school, has structured a program of academic work whose value in real life is apparent. Teachers also strive to demystify both language learning and other academic tasks by posing them as problems to be solved collaboratively, and by making the processes through which they are undertaken public.

Many classes at IHS are taught collaboratively by two teachers in the same classroom, where live examples of the processes of collaborative, multidisciplinary instruction provide a model for young people of how adults work together, how they negotiate their differences. Students find such examples immediately useful in the many cooperative learning activities they undertake in their courses. In every endeavor, these processes are made explicit. Great care is taken to hear and respect minority or divergent points of view, both in faculty affairs and in classroom work. The focus on process rises to the level of philosophy, for it is believed that understanding group process creates an ambiance of acceptance which fosters effective participation in the work of the community.

Principal Nadelstern has made it clear that instruction is the primary task of the teacher, and has insisted that the work of curriculum building and teaching be recorded and made available to peers. It follows that curriculum development and staff development are one and the same, an idea with which faculty have come to agree.

The school has found it possible to structure its affairs to serve this priority: time for curriculum development is built into the schedule, and support for it is forthcoming. Personnel decisions about reappointment and tenure are based in part on the teacher's curriculum development work. At the heart of this process are faculty peer groups. Modeled on higher education collegial relations, these groups are made up of four or five teachers who have chosen to work together and support each other. Faculty peer groups seek to foster teacher growth so that individual satisfaction will serve the interests of the school.

Continuous Evolution of the Curriculum

Curriculum work at International has been subject to continuing assessment and modification as faculty have sought to structure tasks and projects for more effective learning. Unusual formats are often employed to great advantage. The Integrated Learning Center offers a series of core courses that orient students and reinforce basic language skills, leading them to complex tasks of the kind they will meet in college; the Motion curriculum was the first powerful example of a block program that integrated disparate fields successfully; and the Personal and Career Development program sends students out of school to the wider community, where they broaden their view of themselves in society and become aware of options available to them.

The Integrated Learning Center

The Integrated Learning Center (ILC), at the core of the instructional program, is a resource center that offers concrete help and skills in the transitions to school, society, and academic language use. Its courses, which fulfill the school's English requirements, engage students in small-group interdisciplinary learning activities designed to supplement content area studies and promote personal growth. They begin with two trimesters of Orientation to School and Society, and continue through Communicating across Cultures, Cross-Cultural Studies, Structural English, and two trimesters of College Prep in which the focus is writing. The second trimester course in the series, called Immigration, provides opportunities for students to share and reflect on their immigration experience, a rich source of cross-cultural insights and material for writing. Reading materials for Learning Center language courses are available at two levels: regular texts, and those that have been modified for ESL students. All Integrated Learning Center courses require daily writing.

A course called Research prepares students for the tasks of selecting and applying to colleges. Students learn to take notes, skim, paraphrase, outline, and summarize while using resource books to find needed information about higher education. A course in Advanced Language Skills gives students practice in reading and writing English in preparation for the New York State Regents Competency Tests.

The Motion Program: A Generative Model

The Motion course, presently in its fourth year, is an interdisciplinary curriculum made up of a set of connected courses exploring the concept of motion from the several points of view offered by physics, mathematics, literature, and physical education. A cohort of students travels together from class to class for an entire trimester. Students receive credit in the four subject areas through a combination of individual and group work, displayed in a final portfolio that demonstrates their mastery of the concept of motion. The physical education component consists of Project Adventure, a community-building program in which games and activities teach trust and cooperation. The team of teachers (including a college instructor) works closely together to ensure the coherence of the program and to monitor student progress.

This past year, the culmination of developments of both supportive, collaborative governance and exemplary curricula and instruction has fostered an exponential change to the curriculum. Faculty instituted several new interdisciplinary, team-taught, theme-centered block programs modeled on the Motion prototype. Faculty and student response has on the whole been positive, although tempered with the recognition that change on such a scale clearly necessitates further complex adjustments to program and governance. Early in the 1992–93 school year, the faculty decided to begin moving the entire curriculum to a block program format in which cohorts of students would travel through the same program together daily.

The Internship Program

LaGuardia Community College, founded about twenty years ago in working-class, warehouse-rich Long Island City, was conceived as an internship college. All college students, not only those who are enrolled in technical and vocational programs, spend one trimester of each year engaged in internships, which pay them the minimum wage. Over the years, the college program has been refined and expanded so that the transition from school to work is seamless in some specialties and is eased for all students. The college works closely with local business and industry to mutual benefit.

The goals of the two high school internship programs differ in that they are meant to broaden the students' views of themselves in society and to make them aware of the options available to them, rather than to prepare them for specific trades or careers. Internships require a significant commitment. Students report to work daily, four days a week, and evaluation and credit for the trimester is based on their performance on the job. Middle College High School students spend the entire day on the job, attending seminars at school one day each week with the teacher-counselor who directs the program. Though internships are unpaid, they sometimes lead to summer or weekend jobs.

International's faculty planned the internship component of the Personal and Career Development program (PCD) on the Middle College model, making use of the same parameters and many of the same sites.

But as the program developed, it became apparent that immigrant students just getting their bearings in a new school found a trimester away from teachers and peers too disruptive. The schedule was modified to allow mornings on the job and afternoons in school. For students, the program provides a bridge between the work of the school and the broader social and economic environment. Yorlene, a senior this year, summed it up when she said, "It's a good thing for us, because we don't really know what work is like until we do this." Teachers have reported that the PCD is good for students' course work as well. Following the internship, students often demonstrate better attendance, more punctuality, more assignments completed, and higher grade point averages.

As the program has been refined, faculty have found sites that will reinforce and utilize students' native language skills and cultural background or stimulate and reinforce English language skills. Most of the 300 sites also provide opportunities to practice technical skills and to develop social skills. While the program is not presented to students as a community service activity, about two-thirds of the sites are in nonprofit agencies such as schools, hospitals, and community centers. About half of the service sites are at the college or the school, but students are allowed only one such placement, usually the first internship, because faculty want them to try their wings outside the school. The remaining third of the placements are at commercial sites, where special care is taken to assure that supervisors take their teaching responsibilities seriously and do not consider the students simply free labor.

Teachers who work in the PCD program develop the internship sites, coordinate the program with site supervisors, direct the preparatory seminars, make regular visits to each site, and coordinate student participation in placements and seminars. They meet weekly to monitor overall progress and developments and are currently at work on modifications to the program which will make the contemplated school-wide move to block-programming smooth, while preserving the special functions of the career program.

Internships are only part of the comprehensive Personal and Career Development program. Prior to each ten-week internship, ninth-, tenth-, and eleventh-grade students are required to take a PCD course. These three courses help identify interests, aptitudes, and values, and demonstrate how students can work together to identify personal strengths and interests. The goal is to help students understand that there are differing right choices for each person. The tone of the class work ranges from serious to earnest, but visits to the classes reveal students experiencing the satisfaction and camaraderie that come from doing important work with others.

The ninth-grade PCD course includes a formal introduction to psychology, presented in a project-oriented, small-group format using the theme "myself." If you dropped in on the class, you would find students gathered in a windowless basement room, picking up the work they left the day before, prior to the teacher's arrival. Carefully constructed posters displayed on the walls show family trees, personal time lines, lists of goals, and cartoons. Abundant on the tables are copies of books produced in semesters past, with colorful illustrated covers bearing such titles as *Almost Normal Life, Hammer-Head's Life, Beginnings of International H.S., The life of MARTA* by Neneng, *A Long Way to the Wonderland: Poland —> USA "dirty N.Y. didn't fill in her dreams."*

Materials are available in the classroom for making all these things: magazines, crayons, markers, glitter, pencils, colored paper. A filing system is at work: folders color-coded for work completed, guidelines for projects, student work from past terms, and so forth. During one visit first-year students are at work on their first major assignment, a biography of a classmate. An outline has been given to them, providing major categories and questions to be asked. At the end of the book each student produces, there is a section entitled "about the author" in which the writer, following another model, gives a brief biographical statement. This later becomes the basis for an expanded autobiography each student will undertake. The biographies are used as the basis for oral presentations in small groups. A poster is built from the biography, using clever cartoons and collages from magazines, and is used as a prop for a presentation to the class about the classmate-subject.

On this day, Charlie, the teacher, is at work with Rafael on his statement of goals. He observes, "OK, that's your first goal: 'I want to get good grades in all my courses.' OK—how you gonna do that?"

"Work."

"OK. 'By working hard on my projects.'" Charlie writes on the boy's paper then looks to a neighboring student. "Do you know how to do goals? OK, I want you to help him. Make sure he has a 'by' to finish each goal. Remember to think about short-term and long-term— for life—goals."

A few minutes later, Charlie gets the attention of the class. He has a twinkle in his eye. "You want to see a nice time line? Who wants to see a nice time line?" All move to see the work of a shy Vietnamese girl who has made her time line on music staffs. When asked if she is a musician, she says, "Yes, but I need a piano."

The tenth-grade course, whose theme is "work," focuses on sociology and offers more detail about careers in preparation for the second internship. Students are directed to investigate available options; they then write a letter to the teacher explaining why they chose the internship. They must go to an interview at the prospective site before they are assigned to the job.

A visit to this classroom reveals that International students, like many New York City kids, take up their work in the computer room wearing baseball caps and jackets even though it is warm and they have lockers. Migdalia, the teacher, is directing a girl in Spanish to go downstairs and get a folder from a locked cabinet in a classroom. Students are at work, using a catalog, *Learning and Working*, which lists the internships available. Two of the 300 items:

3064 Reporter/Journalist
Youth Communications
29 W. 21st St.
New York, NY

Qualifications: Good writing skills; a willingness to travel around the city alone; good verbal skills.
Duties: Working as a reporter for New Youth Connections. Attend a weekly writing workshop; receive training in interviewing and research skills; some clerical.

3133 Furniture Refinisher's Apprentice
Louis Agusa and Company
32–05 Greenpoint Ave.
Queens, NY

Qualifications: Interest in working with wood; good manual dexterity.
Duties: Stripping, sanding, staining, spraying, compounding, buffing, repairing broken furniture. Clean up.

Someone asks why they have to write an essay on their first choice. Migdalia explains that if there are several requests for the same internship, teachers will have to decide who gets the assignment based on what they say about their interests, skills, and understanding of what the job involves.

"If you don't finish today, leave it in my box tomorrow," Migdalia reminds them as the work session ends. Some students stay to continue working, while others go on to the next class.

The eleventh-grade PCD course, called Decision Making, focuses on values and seeks to develop the skills needed to explore career possibilities and to begin considering a choice of college. This course is given in conjunction with the Integrated Learning Center course called Research, mentioned earlier, which deals with skills that support both personal and academic research. The goal of these courses is to show students how to make informed decisions in a new culture, and to help them to bridge the gap between the cultures of school and home as they plan their future schooling.

All the work for these courses takes the form of projects that have some personal relevance, such as investigating a career field or an undergraduate major, and are undertaken in small cooperative groups. Students are required to do daily writing assignments that are carefully structured to help them explore the questions they have chosen. They share their work and get feedback as they revise research projects continuously on the computers.

What the Internship Experience Brings

During the internship term, students participate in a seminar in which they share their experiences and learn and practice certain job skills. Nancy Dunetz, director of the Personal and Career Development program, describes the initial responses:

> Students do not automatically perceive the career education program as valuable. Initially, many are resistant to confronting the personal issues raised in PCD1. . . . Personal issues are similarly examined in . . . courses dealing with orientation and immigration, literature courses, human development, leadership group, and in biology. Students are regularly asked to relate their learnings to their own experiences.
>
> Some students are reluctant to embark on their first internships. Some do not perceive a relationship between internship and their (traditional) concept of school. . . . Others experience serious anxiety over the prospect of losing the support system they have grown so comfortable with at school. They are afraid to

go out on their own, and to be separated from the school. They are afraid of being in a totally English-speaking environment of a different culture from their own. They are afraid of using the telephone, not only in the context of their jobs, but even to call their supervisors to report that they will be absent or late. And they are not certain that they will be able to deliver what is expected of them.

Many students return to school after their first day on internship requesting a change. The reasons they give range from boredom to weather. Students are encouraged to give themselves and the situation a chance. They are guided by their internship teachers to articulate their problems clearly. . . . If the situation proves to be unreasonable, a change will be made. The most important part of this process is for students to learn how to negotiate with their superiors and coworkers rather than turn their backs on problems and difficult situations (Dunetz, 1992).

Offering a Hand Up

If you stop into Internship Seminar III, you may see third-year students reporting on their experiences to younger students preparing to select their first internships. During one visit, three groups present an overview of a field of interest, supported by posters and charts.

Mariuz, the first spokesperson for the business group, explains that at NSA Software, a programming and head-hunting company, he has done office work and "C" programming. He presents a chart showing the structure of a business and observes that the role of business in our society is to produce goods to earn money. He then introduces the other members of his group.

Gino describes his work in the college computer center and is followed by Annie, who reads a report she has written about computers in business. Annie occasionally turns to Mariuz to ask how to say a word. She goes on to discuss her earlier work at the courthouse. When she doesn't understand questions asked of her, another Chinese student interprets for her. Annie concludes by presenting a chart, "How to Start Your Own Business."

The teacher asks Mariuz to tell the class how he chose his internship. "I wanted to learn programming. . . . It's good, because the boss knows a lot, and he doesn't have that much to do, so he teaches me all the time."

"Is programming hard?"

"Yes. It can take one month to write 100 lines and then one comma can crash the program."

Speaking for the education group, Rita, poised and obviously very well prepared, introduces Janie, Ronny, and Lorena. She then offers a definition of education and presents a chart showing income compared with education. "It's hard to compete with people on the market for people who don't have education. Also, some people don't think about a good philosophy of life, but only about making money."

Ronny, who works as assistant to the gym teacher, describes gym classes and his duties. He says he thinks about becoming a teacher and offers advice to those considering an internship in education. "It's going to be a serious job—you'll have to be responsible. . . ."

Lorena has been a teacher's assistant at PS 11, a bilingual school. She explains that ". . . it's not just to talk Spanish, but write and explain to others how to write it—it's different. . . . I never went to school in the Dominican Republic. . . . The teacher helped me—she gave me a book to read and then showed me how to write in Spanish, so that I could help the kids."

Jenny works for Kids Meeting Kids, an international peace organization run by kids. "It's to make the world better. . . . Pen pals get to exchange ideas. . . . I recommend it to people who like to have peace, to organize and work hard."

Rita reports that she assists the physics teacher, doing experiments, helping kids with language, showing them how to use computers. "It is not just formal—I contribute something, I am needed. It's for a person who likes science and hard work. If you don't like kids, don't choose an education internship."

A tenth grader who has not yet taken an internship asks, "What do you think about having an internship instead of a class?"

Jenny answers, "The internship gives you experience of the outside world, a chance to speak English and work with people, to see adults, how they work, to get an idea about the future."

Edyta introduces herself and the health group, then proceeds to a description of her work as assistant in the physical therapy department of a hospital. She likes the work because it means using her hands and seeing adults, patients, and professionals. She transfers patients from one department to another, does exercises, and talks with people. Carol works as admissions office assistant in a different hospital, where she does paperwork, uses the computer, and files records. She helps by interpreting for patients and doctors, and she once saved a man's life because she could speak his language. Iffath describes his work at the Biglow Pharmacy, noting that he enjoys the clerical and sales work.

Writing It Down for the Future

Writing is necessary in the PCD program. In the careful crafting of curricula, literacy is motivated. Just as teachers at International recognize the need to write about their curriculum work so that it will be available as a resource to others, so students come to see the need to write about their experience so that it can be shared publicly. The central project of the seminar requires students to produce a booklet that reports on the internship. The booklet is directed to other students who may be considering taking the internship they are completing, and it includes advice about what can be gained from the site and who should choose it. The student writers have themselves enjoyed the help of such booklets, so as they begin the group work for feedback and proofreading, they have a clear idea of what is needed. Selections from the internship booklets follow.[1]

Monika worked in a photography studio and prepared a booklet entitled, "YOUR FUTURE—in your hands!!" The attractive, colorful cover shows a drawing of a girl thinking and a balloon which says, "Now I know what I like to do . . ."

People in my internship are very quiet, they do everything with their thoughts, they always listen to slow music like a Bach. They are always relaxed, understanding, patient with one other. They are happy with their work, because that's what they like to do, even if it's boring. My supervisor is a very understanding person, he joke around with everybody and everybody respect him, he is taking advices from his assistant when ever he is trying to decide something.

What I have learned about myself!

I know about myself that I'm a responsible person. . . . I like that kind of work on my internship, but in different way I hated it, because it was so boring, it's taking a lot of attention. On the beginning I thought that I would love this internship but as soon as I started I just like it. I don't want to be a photographer in my future, I want to be a doctor.

What I have learned about the world of work:

I think that people at work are more serious than people at school, they are responsible, they know that they have to do a work that somebody gave them. People trust each other. People in my organization worked for money but they love this kind of jobs they do. Everybody do some work that they don't enjoy, that's the way it is a world.

Letter of Advice:

Dear Students!
I'm writing this letter to let you know that I'm really happy with that internship, even if it's boaring. If you really interesting in the photography, this is a excellent place for you to start, you'll learn a lot of new stuffs so it will help you to get a real job in your future. Chose this internship, because it's really interesting. If you don't like to work in the office, this internship is not gonna be good for you, so think about this. I hope you all will enjoy your internships in the next cycle. Good luck.
The author, Monika K.

Robinson reported on his work in a pharmacy:

These people are nice and really smart people they all like to work and they care for the Pharmacy they are patient, friendly and caring for example my Supervisor John he is a funny man he likes to make jokes. In my work place the people are relaxed, calm, understanding also they are happy. All the workers show a lot of respect for each other.

What I have learn about myself:

I think I learned a lot of things about myself like I didn't know before that I was a dependable person and that I always don't need somebody to tell me things I do than by my own. Now that I finish this internship I feel more mature than before. The kind of work I like to do most is active work and varied work.

Teresa wrote the following regarding her work in a law office:

What I Have Learned About Myself:

What I learned about myself is that I can do anything if I put my mind to it. This internship was a very challenging experience for me. . . . Before I took this internship I thought that it would be boring because it is in an office. I was wrong! I do so many miscellaneous things. I go around in the neighborhood. Sometimes I take the train or go to court. Then in the office I do different work every day. I learned that I am interested in becoming a lawyer.

Personal and Career Objectives:

I think that I have achieved my . . . objectives as best as I can. My typing has improved. I know almost all the files in the office. The fax machine is no problem. I learned the neighborhood and went to the Surrogate's court once.

Letter of Advice:

My advise to you is that if you are interested in law, then you should definitely take this internship. It shows you a lot about what lawyers do and how you need to be when you are around them. There are a lot of things you can learn on this internship. They can help you tremendously in the future.

Ruampon was placed in a local post office and made the following observations about his placement:

Vocabulary I'm Learning: Certification/Deliver/Priority

Dear Students,
I think this work will be very good for you whoever are interested in mailing and who like clean and easy work. The supervisor and other co-works are very good and kind. So do not worry to get in any problem. . . . Do not choose this job because it is going to be very borring work when you have nothing to do. For students who has interested in this job, the most things that you has to know are you should be skillful and able to learn quicly and how to get along with adults. It will be good to know how to get along with adults.

Sincerley, Ruampon

Danny reported on his work in an engineering firm:

Terrill Bush

My Internship Goals

—One of my goals during this internship is learn how to read the plans of a building and be able to make typical details by only looking at the plans.
—I also intent to see if I'm going to be able to handle the Engineering career, which I like, by sticking around my supervisor and seeing what an engineer life is like.

What I Have Been Learning About Myself:

Firstable you won't believe all the responsibility I have over my shoulders. I have to work with the intern, getting him to help me on my tasks, I have to order supplies, I have to deal with the company that prints drawings for us, I have to deal with the company that runs messages for us, I have to keep record of petty cash, and many other things. . . . this teaches me that I'm true hard worker and that I can do what I want as long as I have my mind to it.

I've also learned about myself that I'm not like other kids. I'm more mature than most of my peers. The opportunity of being hire at my internship has made me realize that I should not full with my time or play games while I could be doing something helpful because I have special talents and I'm not going to waste them.

Dear Students:

I find this internship a very good, but challenging internship. I felt very comfortable working at this office and my skills and knowledge grew more and more each day that past by. The part I like the most was that I was doing something different almost everyday.

I think that the kind of personality you shall have for this internship is an assertive personality. If you are quit and limited, you will find out that after a while you will be doing only easy tasks. But if you try to do better than what you were ask, you will find out that you will be given more and more challenging tasks. Depending on how well you are doing, you will be promoted.

These writings speak for themselves about how students grow through the experiences that come to them in the PCD/Internship

194

program, how their understanding of the world grows, and how they learn to share what they are experiencing through what they can write.

They report as only peers can about the features of the experiences: "You speak English a lot." "It's going to be a serious job." "If you don't like kids, don't choose this one."

The growth that comes from trying out the world of work is clearly described as well: "I know I'm responsible." "I thought I would love it, but I just like it." "I can do anything if I put my mind to it." "Everyone does some work they don't like." "If you do better than you were asked, you will find out you will get more."

And their observations on the adults they meet are patently valuable: "You learn how to get along with adults . . . how [they] work, how they relate to the boss." "They are patient." "They are good and kind people."

The PCD program is central to the experiential, collaborative curriculum the faculty have imagined for these young immigrants. It provides a program of activities in which they step into the outside world to participate in what is there, returning daily to the peer support and teacher guidance that helps them to interpret the experience. They gain in maturity, as evidenced by more responsible behavior and higher grades the semester following the first internship. For students and teachers, it offers good work that engages them in the real world uses of literacy, responsibility, and mutual support.

Conclusion

It often happens that urban youths settle into a limiting provincialism focused on their peer group and neighborhood. Immigrant adults and families are also inclined to limit their scope because they naturally seek the comfort of establishing themselves in a new place, and look for some relief from the recent trauma of drastic change. In the PCD program at International High School, faculty guide students out of their self-limited spheres and direct them to reach out and explore a wider world. All adolescents grapple with questions of vocation and self-definition. This experiential program provides a stucture by which students explore career options and gain a realistic view of both the adult world of work and of how their own interests, skills, and personal resources might fit into that world.

Terrill Bush

Notes

1. These quotes are from the booklets the students produced, given here with their original grammar and orthography, both in the interest of accuracy and to demonstrate the remarkable clarity in written English that some students achieve in only two or three years.

References

Curriculum Committee, International High School (1987). *The International approach: Learning English through content area study.* Long Island City, N.Y.: International High School.

Curriculum Committee, International High School (1988a). *Beyond high school graduation requirements: What do students need to learn at the International High School?* Long Island City, N.Y.: International High School.

Curriculum Committee, International High School (1988b). *The International approach: Learning English through content area study, volume 2.* Long Island City, N.Y.: International High School.

Curriculum Committee, International High School (1990). *Insights: Thoughts on the process of being international.* Long Island City, N.Y.: International High School.

Dunetz, N. (1992). The Personal and Career Development program. Unpublished report to the CUNY Chancellor.

Gregory, L., and Strong, M. (1991). *An evaluation of the City University of New York/New York City Board of Education collaborative programs.* Philadelphia: Center for Urban Ethnography.

Nadelstern, E., and Hirschy, D. (1991). Response to Circular #41, Educational Plan. Unpublished report, Fall 1991. Long Island City, N.Y.: International High School.

Personnel Committee, International High School (1991). *Personnel procedures for peer selection, support, and evaluation.* Long Island City, N.Y.: International High School.

9

Turning In: Community Schools as Enclaves

Robert B. Everhart

After a twenty-year lacuna, the emphasis upon an increased sense of community in education seems ascendant again. A reading of much of the current educational "reform" literature evidences this ascendancy in many ways—parental involvement, schools as parts of communities, site-based management, parental choice in education, teacher empowerment. All of these dimensions and more point to language that reflects a search for elements of community for the schools of the twenty-first century.

Yet even in this resurgent process, one is struck by the evasive nature of what constitutes community education, as well as the characteristics of an educational community. We witness now a flood of "reform" that passes as an attempt to reconstruct community, while what comprises community remains ill-defined. In Oregon a recent piece of omnibus educational legislation well typifies this trend. This legislation provides the outline for a variety of educational changes from preschool through postsecondary education and details a rather unusual balance between mandatory state standards on the one hand and an impetus toward local school-based councils to develop and monitor those standards on the other hand. This translates into a major initiative for school site councils to be the primary policy agencies for schools, the assumption here being that policy decisions moved to the school and classroom levels will naturally result in more responsive and participatory decisions from the larger community which the school serves. Following this line of argument still further, schools where decisions about school-ing are made collectively and widely by diverse constituents will begin the process of reconstructing salient dimensions of community.

In this legislation, however, the relationship between community-based decision making and community schools is scarcely addressed. Does the presence of participatory decision making constitute a com-munity school? If not, what are the consequences of treating matters such as shared decision making and school empowerment as if they were the same as community education? Do schools that undergo reform as an attempt, in part, to create an educational community actually inhibit attainment of their objective due to the very reforms that are adopted? Do the means eventually supersede the ends? This chapter begins a discussion of these questions.

Community Education: What and Why?

Why does there exist the almost fanatical allegiance to principles of educational community? What is so appealing about the concept that drives educational sloganeering to the stage of unrelenting acceptance? Answers to these questions rest, I believe, in the underlying belief that a broad-based, integrated, and active community of support is crucial to the educational progress of youngsters. Such a community of support must occur not only at the school level, but must also be representative of corresponding principles of support within the family and the micro-community within which the student lives. Educators use the concept of schools as communities in part as a metaphor to link schooling to a broader social context. In this sense then, the term "community" represents a bridge between what has been and what can be. The concept of educational community, then, serves as a keystone between the past and the future.

It is useful here to articulate more clearly the meaning of the term "community" in this chapter. It focuses on both structural and norma-tive dimensions. Structurally, a community has defined boundaries and processes for maintaining those boundaries. Yet community involves more than, for example, administrative mechanisms designed to en-hance certain organizational ends (e.g., "shared decision making"). It refers both to a unit of society and to the aspects of the unit that are valued if they exist and desired if absent. Community then exists because of an articulated and shared value and normative structure. As Joseph Gusfield notes,

Human beings, in their activities, select out from the manifold potentials of events those which fit their ordered patterns of perception and relate to their interests and purposes. . . . This perspective emphasizes the situations in which experience for the actor is conceived as communal or societal rather than the existence of the communal as a *ding on sich* (thing in itself). (Gusfield, 1975: 30)

Community in this sense is indivisible from human actions, purposes, and values.

Ironically, embracing the building of community comes at a time when the actual community that is preferred and valued appears but infrequently. As most Americans struggle to accumulate enough resources to live or to meet their dreams, they have less to do with the traditionally conceived "community." Working, commuting, and consuming become the surrogate communities within which Americans spend most of their time, leaving little room to construct the connections to what was or consciously work toward what might be. Instead, the majority of Americans do what they can in order to maintain their present lives, all the while struggling to preserve some semblance of human connectedness based upon vaguely defined but deeply felt human values. In the absence of explicitly articulated and shared values, lurches and overtures toward creating community are made, thereby symbolizing a cherished collective extending beyond the individual and the family.

What then does "creating community" mean in actual practice? While the concept may conjure romantic, almost Rockwellian images, in our present context community takes on a considerably different meaning. Community, for the most part, does not exist. Most individuals are not embedded within and do not have ready access to a support network linking them through past and future core value structures. As Robert Bellah and his associates note (Bellah et al., 1985), most Americans struggle with the concept of community within a larger social structure that fragments rather than integrates experiences and ways of knowing. In this struggle, they reach for an image that does not exist in practice and, at the same time, attempt to move that image into practice within a somewhat unreceptive environment. Building community in American society is too often akin to the biblical passage about the man who built a house on sand. When the rains came and the winds blew, that house collapsed because it was not built on a firm foundation. Likewise, we strive for a firm and reinforcing relationship between education and community, one that has "rocklike" interrelationships. All around us, however, are the sands of discontinuity—economic, political, structural—that shape the type of community we are able to build. Still, the quest for community education is important, primary, and laudatory because this search and the process of working toward shared communal values define, as Gusfield (1975) noted earlier, the very social construction of community.

Yet, in the construction of community, directions are taken that often block and inhibit communitarian practices. Unaware as we sometimes are that a different path has been taken, we are also unaware that essential energies are devoted to the means by which we attempt to achieve community rather than community ends themselves. This transformation of means into ends is particularly troubling for those of us with progressive visions. We want to believe that, because our intentions are so noble, our strategies so based upon what we view as clear objectives, that we know better than to convert means into ends. Yet there are too many examples of such basic processes occurring as frequently in progressive organizations as they do in any other organization. An example of this is the classic case examined by the French political scientist, Robert Michels (1959), wherein he described how the French Socialist party changed from a progressive political movement to one that deflected the interests of the rank and file and concentrated its energies on organizational maintenance activities protective of the managerial elite of the party. Similar patterns are found throughout the literature, in a variety of organizational contexts (Gusfield, 1975; Swidler, 1979; Zald, 1967).

Yet relegating the shortcomings of the community-building process to technical capacity—means/ends confusion—is overly simplistic. More fundamentally, as I will subsequently argue, educators are often unaware that what is being sought in community schools is not being achieved. Still, they forge ahead in directions that are counterproductive to the very intentions of community. This is not due so much to inattention, but to an ideology about community that masks or disguises more basic factors that interfere with the building of community. In this sense then, our consciousness about community affects the way in which we build community and ultimately shapes the form of community we come to accept.

In the next section, I will outline how an ideology about community rests at the base of many of the impediments to greater integration of school and community. I will then discuss how the presence of ideology about community is related to the culture of individualism, a culture that has always been a pervasive force within our society. Next I will turn to a discussion of the process of the formation of ideologies in community schools. In this section, I will chronicle the process observed in one progressive school wherein the ideology about community contributed to the eventual, flawed attainment of progressive objectives. In the final section, I will discuss community schools as "enclaves," drawn into themselves, thwarting the very community fabric sought. I will conclude with some suggestions about minimizing ideology-based outcomes.

Ideology about Community

Americans have always had a singular notion about the relations between education and community, one that has changed remarkably little since the early days of the republic, and one that continues to have a decided impact upon the evolution of its social institutions. Horace Eaton, Vermont's first superintendent of schools, noted in 1846:

> Let every child in the land enjoy the advantages of a competent education at his outset in life—and it will do more to secure a general equality of condition than any guarantee of equal rights and privileges which constitution or laws can give. (quoted in Welter, 1975: 285)

As Eaton proposes, it is through the individual education of children that society is constructed and enhanced. Through this individualized process, each child attains the benefits thought to be available to all of the larger society. Education came to be viewed as the institutional embodiment of American freedom—an act of public authority that guaranteed freedom to all. Fundamental to this perspective is the acquisition of education solely through *individual* activity, education gained primarily through self-determination. Education then was viewed as a commodity available within a marketplace environment, and because markets are inherently individualistic, then, ironically, schooling in America had embedded within it the very antithesis of community.

Individualism has within its root assumptions a steady process wherein private life steadily subsumes public life. In this process, Richard Sennett argues that a developing secularism as well as emerging capitalism contributed to the view of man as author of his own character (Sennett, 1974), separated and removed from the social forces defining that character. This trend line has been developed by such varied social commentators as Alexis de Tocqueville (1969), Frederick Turner (1947), David Riesman (1954), and most recently, Robert Bellah and colleagues (1985). All of these observers, in one way or another, describe the individualistic spirit that has characterized the American landscape through the nineteenth century and into the twentieth and the manner in which that spirit has defined and reinforced emerging American institutional frameworks, including, of course, education. Institutions that encourage and reinforce individual ingenuity, initiative, adaptability, and determination are viewed as productive of beliefs and behaviors associated with the American character.

How does the context of individualism affect the manner in which we build community within our schools? As discussed earlier, Horace Eaton (cited in Welter, 1975) believed that access to education served as the primary guarantor of equality and one's station in life. The principle underlying this belief is that individuals are the fundamental unit within society, that they are able to negotiate their way through life, in control of the material and nonmaterial assets gained through the educative process. Fundamentally, then, individuals move through the life course by using, but minimally committing to the social institutions through which they pass. Tocqueville noted that individualism "disposes each citizen to isolate himself from the mass of his fellows and withdraw into the circle of family and friends; with the little society formed to his taste, he gladly leaves the greater society to look after itself" (Tocqueville, 1969: 37).

Excessive individualism, then, influences the formation of the American community as a fragmented community, one that may contain dimensions of community but is not productive of a culture of community. It is a community that exists through particular relationships, constructed to serve specific functions. American society generates and supports individual atoms which coalesce in microgroups, but are only loosely connected to the greater constellation of matter.

Much of the basis for the fragmented nature of American contemporary communities rests in the equally fragmented society in which those communities exist. But as historian Robert Wiebe noted some twenty years ago, what has always called forth the greatest sense of the term "community" has been the economic system's capacity to "guarantee each constituent group a regular flow of rewards, a predictable payoff. Weak and strong alike combined to defend it against any radicals who might jeopardize these crucial procedures of distribution" (Wiebe, 1975: 26). Maintenance of the economic apparatus to continue this flow of goods and services is the primary source of unity within a largely segmented society. Schools play their role in this process, preaching the gospel of individual achievement and organizing schools in a manner that reinforces the individualistic ethic.

So, if Americans are anything, they are "free"—free to choose, free to join, free to be separate. The nation was founded upon the very principles of freedom and liberty, principles that clearly outline the rights of individuals and collectives of individuals to pursue their economic, religious, and personal interests. The assumptions found in such cornerstone documents as the Declaration of Independence and the Constitution are that the common good is served best when individuals are free to pursue their individual self-interests. If self-interests are better served through some collective, it is assumed then that free individuals will form such collectives for the "common good." Conversely, free individuals should not feel compelled to maintain collective efforts that no longer serve the purposes for which they were formed.

This concept of freedom corresponds closely to the economic principles of entrepreneurial capitalism, as Max Weber (1948) indicated over a century ago. The juxtaposition of a philosophical system that translates natural rights into individual rights and further links them to an economic system emphasizing the allocation of resources based upon market (i.e., "natural") conditions is an ontological system unto itself. Herein we see freedom from a different perspective, especially as it helps us to understand the construction of community. As Tocqueville noted, free individuals "form the habit of thinking of themselves in isolation and imagine that their whole destiny is in their hands" (Tocqueville, 1969: 37). In the pursuit of the "natural" freedoms said to be "inalienable" to every human being then, the common and collective good often becomes ill-defined, fragmented, and difficult to sustain. In the American culture, with the distribution of economic rewards as the primary glue of our society, collective enterprise is especially difficult to sustain. Thus we struggle with enterprises such as community schools, attempting to craft an educational community in the face of a culture wherein "freedom," interconnected with the fervor of a market economy, inserts itself as the first-order principle upon which community becomes defined.

There is, however, ample reason to challenge the view that freedom is the sine qua non of liberty and personal fulfillment. Orlando Patterson notes that freedom in Western thought has a dark side to it— a side that has justified lords, kings, sovereigns, indeed nations in their perceived right to dominate and subjugate others to their own ends. He traces the concept of freedom to early Greece, and argues that throughout much of Western history, freedom has come to mean the freedom to rule over others (Patterson, 1991). The most visible illustration of this point in our own history is the institution of slavery. Herein the individual liberties accorded to the planter class, connected with the "natural" processes of an emerging international capitalistic system, were used to justify the enslavement of untold thousands from another continent.

Schools usually reinforce these historical traditions through a social-constructive process in which individualism and the concept of personal freedom serve as a backdrop. Any attempt to define, initiate, and build schools as communities, for example, will be affected by the manner in which community is viewed. While elements that constitute community are, in fact, part of the efforts of many schools to form a more integrative, participatory culture, what passes for community often is but a surface-level attribute, the acceptance of which halts a search for the more deep-seated attributes. When a concept that is to some degree an accurate description of reality serves to disguise or cover up a more basic or fundamental representation, then that concept is said to serve an ideological function.

Ideology as a Concept

Few terms in the social science lexicon generate more confusion than does ideology. Such confusion exists in part because the concept has grown to become all-inclusive of virtually anything to do with thought or ideas. Sociologists often talk about ideology as a belief or system of beliefs about a social category (e.g., class, family, etc.) (Parsons, 1964), while anthropologists discuss ideology in the context of culture (Barnett and Silverman, 1979). Sooner or later, however, one runs into Marx (Marx and Engels, 1975).

To discuss ideology is to confront Marx, who justly put the term into prominence in political and social thought. Marx's use of the term was not always consistent, a fact that has pained Marxists and non-Marxist scholars over the years. Yet Marx was one of the earliest thinkers to move ideology and its ontological roots toward a deep analysis of the very nature of thought and the context within which the origins of thought can be empirically (rather than ideally) documented.

In Marx's writings ideology is seen as consciousness, but more specifically false consciousness. Consciousness is false to the extent that it is based on ideas that are believed to exist independent of material practice. Consciousness is also false to the extent that it rests with the individual *qua* individual, rather than the individual as part of a larger class structure. Thus ideology consists of the failure to invert appearances and recognize that the superstructure of ideas is used by the ruling classes to rationalize and thereby reinforce the material base from which it draws its power and from which surplus value is extracted.

But if ideas are merely the reflection of man's relation to the productive forces, then what constitutes the truly authentic nature of man as a species being? What criteria do we use in order to identify this authentic relationship? Marx would reply that history indeed reflects a rational process, and "its apperception by man . . . must necessarily be the apperception of absolute truth—the truth contained in history as the vehicle of man's emancipation" (quoted in Carlsnaes, 1981: 43).

Yet it is an error, I believe, to accept too literally Marx's concept of ideology as "false" consciousness, as if to contrast it to "true" consciousness. There cannot be an ideological continuum consisting of verified and verifiable statements on the one pole and unverified or unverifiable statements on the other. Ideology can, however, prove a powerful concept as it focuses upon the appearances of apparent "truths" that may be held by all individuals in all social contexts. Ideologies, then, are not false appearances in the sense of *illusory* appearances, but rather they constitute a surface level of meaning that covers over a more fundamental meaning. To the extent that such "representations signify a set of relations that are real, but which hide another set of relations no less real" (Sharp, 1980: 92), then an ideological relation exists.

What form do ideological relations take in the community-building process? Can community building as a process serve to turn against itself so as to reinforce the very patterns it is designed to overcome? We will address these questions in the next section, through an illustrative examination of the dynamics of Metropolitan High School.

Ideological Relations in Community Schools

Metropolitan High School is a public alternative school with an enrollment of 450. It serves as a magnet high school in a district with a student enrollment of some 40,000 students. Metropolitan is designed to draw from the district's seven high school areas, and serves students who find the traditional curriculum of the high school to be too structured, too inflexible, and not sufficiently engaging. Because the school is located near the downtown core, the school places much emphasis upon the city as a laboratory for the education of students. Local libraries, art and historical museums, public social service agencies, and offices of the city and county governments serve as locations where students spend considerable time linking classroom work to applications in the real world.

Metropolitan's vision focuses upon building educational community within urban communities. This agenda is set forth in the school's mission, which delineates formation of an "educational and social community of shared purpose." This community is intended to transcend academic learning and create and sustain new collectives of "students of all ages willing to assist, support, teach, and learn from each other in an environment of commitment and mutual support." In this context then, the Metropolitan school envisions the young and old working together to create a less hierarchical, more communitarian learning and social environment.

The heart of the Metropolitan experience is the learning community, whose major purpose is the integration of academic knowledge and everyday life through organized subcommunities of students, teachers, and citizens in the larger community. Learning community agendas are carried out through major projects or activities that all students share. In the fall of 1990, for example, fifteen different learning subcommunities centered one month of their work on the study of the economics of the community. While each of the groups defined this topic somewhat differently, each subunit established a project centering upon economics not as an abstract discipline, but as part of the daily life of the larger community. The fundamental objective of each subcommunity was to use the theme "economics in the community" as a mechanism to assist in the formation of a communitarian microsociety. In this sense, learning about economics was to serve as a mechanism to help foster commitment to mutually defined goals of economic equality, justice, and responsibility.

As an illustration, one of the fifteen subgroups adopted a focus on the economics of food and agriculture in the local region. Thirty students designed a project around the theme of "Food: Who Sells, Who Buys, and Who Gets?" Students spent the first week conducting background work, after which they dispersed for the next five to seven days to study and visit farms, food processing plants, distribution centers, supermarkets, and food banks and charity kitchens, all in an attempt to provide multiple perspectives on basic economic questions.

Being involved in the activities at Metropolitan for two years, I was not surprised to discover that what emerged was similar to efforts I have reported elsewhere (Everhart, 1988). Teachers and students emphasized designing learning activities embedded within surrounding communities. An explicit link between elements of school and the community, through such projects as that on economics, stood behind this effort. Metropolitan teachers justifiably took pride in the initiative of students, their active participation in the community as they discovered the manner in which the food production and distribution system worked, and the collaboration necessary as the projects were woven together. School members actively supported a forum held at the end of the unit, wherein all fifteen learning communities presented their findings. This forum was attended by over fifty parents and citizens, many of whom also participated in the learning community activities.

Alternative ways of learning are prominent at Metropolitan and are viewed as a necessary element of community building, yet their attainment provides only a partial sketch of the community-building process. Constructing a learning community within a school does not necessarily contribute to the social and intellectual skills necessary to build community. That requires exploration of and conscious commitment to interdependent links between the normative and value structures developed as part of the school community–building process. At Metropolitan, such links were only infrequently present. While the learning communities were, to a considerable degree, participatory in nature and student work roles more diffuse than in most schools, the fundamental value structures reinforced within the learning communities reflected mainstream societal values.

The project on the economics of food and agriculture illustrates this conclusion. The impetus toward learning communities proved to be successful as an initial step, yet their further development slowed at a point short of the necessary explorations necessary to produce a communitarian value system. For example, students in one of the learning subcommunities discovered that in many of the food distribution companies, financial remuneration was concentrated within a small number of positions, and that individuals in high-profile positions received extensive "perks" (high-ticket company cars, well-furnished offices, a large number of support staff). At the same time, students also observed that most of the production line employees were women or minorities, individuals with low wages, modest benefits, and who worked in jobs that were repetitive, stressful, and which provided little opportunity for advancement. These disparities, as they reflected the basic underlying principles of a market-driven, hierarchical economic system, rarely become part of the dialogue at Metropolitan. The instructor in the one subcommunity I observed addressed the matter only once, and while he acknowledged the student comments about these matters, he passed them off as being "just the way it is." Commenting to one student having difficulty finishing his project, he noted: "Work hard, Tom, and maybe you'll end up in Consolidated's corporate office someday." Thus one of the most critical economic issues, that of the political economy of the labor process, remained unaddressed and absent from the constitutive process of community building at Metropolitan.

Why did Metropolitan's development slow down at this critical point? Primarily because the school's espoused value structure, wherein organized learning communities were meant to challenge the individualistic normative structure so common in most school settings, was only partially established and minimally reinforced. The mere existence of an alternative learning community came to be accepted as the creation of community, when in actuality it was only an initial step. As much as Metropolitan attempted to establish itself as a community school, it served more as an enclave focusing on a local version of community formation which too infrequently addressed the question "community for what?" Emphasis upon the curricular and instructional dimensions inherent in community building (e.g., participatory decision making, diminished authority structure, broadened definition of school learning) resulted in avoidance of the value conflicts that inevitably will arise from school activities such as the unit on food distribution.

These normative/value dimensions receive too little attention because community schools often experience identity problems. They strive to be different, struggle to be accepted, and hope ultimately to be models for other schools. Community schools, usually under close scrutiny by outsiders, emphasize the process of becoming distinct as a way of making a quick mark. In the process, such schools can lose sight of their original purposes and be overcome by organizational maintenance activities which deflect the schools from attention to the normative structure that is so fundamental.

Metropolitan, from the beginning, articulated the importance of a normative community with a commitment to economic and political justice, equality, and opportunity. This commitment was to be carried out in part by merging the boundaries between school and the larger society. Metropolitan emphasized that the school should serve as the locus for students to play an active role in the construction of a small community, unbounded by the limitations of conventional learning. A new, distinctive education community was the selling point, and a school set apart served as the rallying point. If one's son or daughter was disenchanted with school, if parents were concerned about their child's lack of commitment to school, if they had a vision of a small community in which a more distinct value structure was present, then Metropolitan was perceived as a school with a difference. The fundamental question, however, is whether Metropolitan's difference was enough of a difference.

When seemingly progressive directions are subsumed by valid but more superficial initiatives, the ideology of community schools takes over. In almost an infectious fashion, the language used to describe one form of reality in the school colors and shapes the dialogue about other perspectives on schooling. At Metropolitan this infection spread through a too uncritical acceptance of egalitarian-centered pedagogical processes that stressed openness, flexibility, and negotiative elements. At the same time, the language used to describe how these processes were necessary steps toward building community attracted parents and students and reinforced the myth that the normative vision being sought was an actuality. However, the pedagogical routine—the means to the desired end—too easily took over the minds of families and educators, thereby subsuming the more critical normative elements so critical to the community-building process.

In discussing how ideologies become mental constructs rooted in lived social conditions, it is important—indeed critical—to note that there is nothing inherently "wrong" with the schooling process as it evolved at Metropolitan. Indeed, focus on such pedagogical processes is a fundamental objective of virtually all community schools. Gary Wehlage and his colleagues note that to be successful, "school programs must help students overcome isolation and alienation, help them succeed in school and, optimally, develop an interest in continued learning" (Wehlage et al., 1989: 112).

The omnipresence of ideology, however, causes us to look deeper into schooling practices. It forces us to examine the degree to which acceptance of the "truth" of student commitment and investment deflects examination of more fundamental issues of schooling.

The case of Metropolitan illustrates that the fundamental roots of an educational community—the normative and value-oriented dimensions—are critical, and school participants cannot be sidetracked by accepting too wholeheartedly other "truths" that obscure fundamental issues. At Metropolitan, student processes of involvement in and understanding of the food distribution network were important to the evolution of community building, as was a participative environment. But student involvement and an egalitarian decision-making structure do not, of themselves, constitute a community. An ideological relationship led to Metropolitan deflecting the more fundamental issues about food distribution: who profits, to what extent, and why? Or, who loses, to what extent, and why? Indeed, such are critical issues if students are to learn from participatory initiatives and to develop skills in constructing new normative dimensions in the larger society. The premises underlying an educational topic being addressed must be considered, as must the pedagogical processes that are part of this examination. Failure to examine both halves of the sphere tells only half the tale, and half the tale is what ideological thinking is all about.

Toward "Turning Out" in Community Schools

In this brief snapshot of Metropolitan school we see the manner in which the language of community building can absorb the intended actions, and in which the best intentions can go unrealized. The fact that the same patterns exist in other progressively oriented schools alerts us that good intentions and progressive goals are necessary but not sufficient ingredients in the community-building process.

I am disappointed by the shortcomings at Metropolitan and in other similar settings. I wish that a school such as Metropolitan could be perceived as an aberration, a situation where something had simply "gone awry," a situation demanding to be fixed and which could be fixed through some simple organizational manipulation. I am disappointed because most progressive schools are schools with whose philosophy I am in basic agreement, schools whose staff I personally admire, and schools that I hope will succeed. I am an unabashed booster of these schools, not because they always do the right thing, but because they usually raise the right questions and struggle in a search for answers.

Yet there are no such easy fixes, and my conclusions as to how progressive schools sometimes operate have not altered my personal affinity for them. Unfortunately, however, ideological thinking does grow out of historical and cultural contexts. The distortions that ideologies create exist because they center on a partial reality—partial because those distortions come from and are shaped by a given history and culture. We are all, then, subject to ideological relationships. Progressive schools are no exception, no matter how well intended they are, no matter how much we may agree with their educational philosophy, no matter how hard they try to overcome the errors of the past.

It is not too difficult to understand how structural and historical factors influence the ideological development we sometimes see in community schools. Progressive-minded individuals in community schools, for the most part, tend to be well-educated, middle-income, and politically liberal individuals, who are staunchly independent about their personal life. They reject much of what they consider to be the more distasteful parts of American life (e.g., consumerism, an economy based on waste, normal party politics, and other elements). In order to adapt to a society that many find alienating, progressives often follow a route of personal and economic freedom, emphasizing relative independence from other individuals or social agencies. To this end, many such individuals are self-employed, most believe in but are not necessarily activists in collective causes, and most believe strongly in principles of individualism.

Yet the heavy coating of independence and individualism that pervades our national character has its limitations. Its adherents ostensibly seek out community, yet a culture of semirugged individualism emphasizes a community of individuals united in their dedication to the maintenance of personal autonomy but who do not always advocate for a collective/normative framework to guide actions. This somewhat incomplete sense of community convinced Metropolitan participants that they had achieved genuine community and had overcome, to a considerable extent, the dysfunctional patterns that existed in other schools. An aura of distinctiveness as it existed at Metropolitan can appeal to school and community members because they believe that by being distinctive their school is indeed communitarian in practice. At the same time, however, acceptance of a partial truth of what community schools are can obscure attention to the more fundamental normative dimensions that underlie community. This leads too often to such organizations following individualistic principles and a turning inward.

For schools to turn out and confront the reality of community they must be able to unmask the ideological nature of constructing community. Community, as the essayist Wendell Berry has noted, "is a concept like humanity or peace, that virtually no one has taken the trouble to quarrel with; even its worst enemies praise it" (Berry, 1987: 179). By this seemingly offhanded statement, Berry points to the manner in which community is symbolic and metaphorical. As in all semiotic relations involving symbolic language, the use of the term "community" often leaves to chance how the term is used and what attributes are accepted as valid elements of community. For community schools to be more than a collection of individuals who reject other modes of education, a deeper, more complex articulation of community needs to be embedded in everyday school life.

What might characterize such a complex, deep-structured articulation? Fundamentally, there would need to be clarity that community is more than just sharing some general beliefs or opinions about one segment of everyday life, such as schooling. True community must involve nothing less than a normative structuring of life's multiple dimensions, including education. This is a difficult objective to achieve in a highly individualistic society, one within which virtually everything is predicated upon specialization, segmentation, and the misplaced assumption that each individual is exclusively responsible for his or her own destiny. In most of the contemporary Western world, lives are parceled out into a home life, unrelated to a work life, vaguely tied to recreational life, and usually removed from one's educational life. Ours is not an economic or social system that encourage community, nor does it provide many structural alternatives to reverse this pattern.

It is romantic and naive to believe that we can create a Rockwellian community in modern America, one in which individuals actively build an interlocking culture of shared values. Such a belief reflects a condition that has rarely existed in America, the land of moving on. On the other hand, we can create a greater sense of community in community schools and concurrently develop the necessary worldviews that become the glue of a prospective community. We know, as did Metropolitan, that we cannot divorce student life inside the school from many parallel dimensions outside the school. Education, work, health, and family (to name some examples) are inextricably intertwined, and such interdependencies should be celebrated, acknowledged, and incorporated into the routine of community schools. Such a fusion can occur in diverse ways: through the presence of child care facilities on-site, the integration of school and workplace internships, and a genuine commitment to incorporate parents in the daily life and governance of the school. Through this process, and with an eye toward the specter of ideological relationships arising, building community can become truly a more integrative process.

To change how we conduct the business of school will, however, require a worldview that looks outward as well as inward. We must press for a social ecology of everyday life, one that recognizes and celebrates the core threads that constitute our human existence. Recognition of the public nature of everyday life, the fact that we must develop a communitarian ethic that undergirds all that we do, is one dimension of such a social ecology. Such an emerging collectivity must also reassert the importance of civic responsibilities. Community schools must provide the model of this social ecology and in so doing move beyond presenting only slices of life that are only tangentially attached to other elements. Community schools can become a catalyst in building an incorporative life, a catalyst that, in the words of Alan Trachtenberg, is truly "an association of individuals bound together in a corpus—a body sharing a common purpose and one which, historically, serves the public good" (Trachtenberg, 1982: 38). To take such an approach begins the process of turning out in community schools and moving beyond ideology.

References

Barnett, S., and Silverman, M. G. (1979). *Ideology and everyday life.* Ann Arbor: University of Michigan Press.

Bellah, R., Madsen, R., Sullivan, W. M., Swidler, A., and Tipton, S. M. (1985). *Habits of the heart.* New York: Harper and Row.

Berry, W. (1987). *Home economics.* San Francisco: North Point Press.

Carlsnaes, W. (1981). *The concept of ideology and political analysis.* Westpoint, Conn.: Greenwood.

Everhart, R. B. (1988). *Practical ideology and symbolic community.* London: Falmer.

Gusfield, J. (1975). *Community: A critical response.* New York: Harper and Row.

Marx, K., and Engels, F. (1975). *Collected works.* London: Lawrence and Wishart.

Michels, R. (1959). *Political parties.* New York: Dover Publications.

Parsons, T. (1964). *Essays in sociological theory.* New York: Free Press.

Patterson, O. (1991). *Freedom.* New York: Basic Books.

Riesman, D. (1954). *Individualism reconsidered, and other essays.* Glencoe, Ill.: Free Press.

Sennett, R. (1974). *The fall of public man.* New York: Random House.

Sharp, R. (1980). *Knowledge, ideology, and the politics of schooling.* London: Routledge and Kegan Paul.

Swidler, A. (1979). *Organization without authority*. Cambridge, Mass.: Harvard University Press.

Tocqueville, A. de (1969). *Democracy in America*. New York: Doubleday.

Trachtenberg, A. (1982). *The incorporation of America: Culture and society in the gilded age*. New York: Hill and Wang.

Turner, F. J. (1947). *The frontier in American history*. New York: Henry Holt.

Weber, M. (1948). *The Protestant ethic and the spirit of capitalism*. New York: Scribner.

Wehlage, G., Rutter, R. A., Smith, G. A., Lesko, N., and Fernandez, R. R. (1989). *Reducing the risk: Schools as communities of support*. New York: Falmer.

Welter, R. (1975). *The mind of America: 1820–1860*. New York: Columbia University Press.

Wiebe, R. (1975). *The segmented society*. New York: Oxford University Press.

Zald, M. (1967). *Organizing for community welfare*. Chicago: Quadrangle.

10

Schools in Communities: New Ways to Work Together

Toni Haas

A Place Where Everybody Knows Your Name

Why do we search for community? The search for the good community is a quest for direction and purpose in the collective anchoring of the individual life. A community is a place where you know and are known. It is through healthy communities that we will build the good society, exemplifying the values of peace, prosperity, freedom, and justice. America's young people will be the architects and inhabitants of this good society, and we need to provide them with the tools, skills, and desire to build it. Across America there are schools and communities that are recapturing this vision of social transformation, a vision too often ignored in our current preoccupation with economic competitiveness.

In schools where this vision has taken root, walls between the classroom and the community are no longer barriers, and the teachers feel an obligation to return the public's investment in their work by becoming partners in the development of the community. In these places, schools construct themselves as resources to families, seedbeds of economic and community plans, and as stimuli for the physical and cultural regeneration of the neighborhoods that surround them. In this process, their teachers invent new ways of thinking about curriculum, instruction, and the purposes of education. Their students become infused with the determination to create new jobs and futures for themselves.

This chapter recounts stories that are part of a national ground swell of private and collective action leading to fundamental redefinitions of education's purpose, process, and participants at the end of this century. They recapitulate an ancient idea, placing learning in the community and using the community as a focus of study. Learning was indistinguishable from living throughout most of human history. It is only relatively recently, within the last century and a half, that we separated learning and "real" life, segregating young people inside specialized buildings. In the schools described here, educators have taken steps to overcome this segregation and reconnect children to the life of the adults they will become. In doing so, they have set aside the "factory" model of schooling that has dominated educational thought throughout much of the twentieth century and are creating examples of real school reform.

What Does Real School Reform Look Like?

While the politically driven educational reform agenda of the last ten years has been focused on making the factory turn out a better product at a lower cost, it has been to little avail. The Center on Organization and Restructuring of Schools collected data from three large sources thought to represent cutting-edge practice and thinking[1] and concluded:

> These three studies, taken together, indicate that the elements
> of school restructuring (student experiences, the professional
> lives of teachers, school governance, and collaboration between
> schools and communities) are not being widely adopted. Both
> the number of participating schools and numbers of restruc-
> tured areas are still small. . . . Negligibly few schools are em-
> barking on changes in governance and relationships with the
> larger community. (Center on Organization and Restructuring
> of Schools, 1992: 4)

What follows are three models for restructured schools that are embarking on fundamental changes in governance and relationships with the larger community. In fact, for these schools it is the relationship with the community that is driving changes in governance, in curriculum, in instruction, in school organization, and in the roles of parents, teachers, and students.

Schools as Family Resource Centers: Coordinating Services for the Whole Child

Life in the last decade of the twentieth century requires a different model than a factory for a number of reasons. The first is that young human beings are not analogous to raw materials. Factory production requires standardization and a level of predictability that is impossible to guarantee in human students. Social changes in the fabric of domestic life for American children mean that the youngest students are coming to school with wide variations in what they know, what they have experienced, and how they have learned to learn. Additionally, there is less agreement on common values between parents and teachers and fewer safe assumptions about shared concerns and priorities. The gap between the out-of-school circumstances and experiences of education professionals and many students has increased during the last decade, as educators have become richer and children poorer. While much of the education establishment has bemoaned the fact that "kids just aren't ready for school," in fact the institution of school has failed to adapt itself to students who don't mirror the race, gender, and class of the faculty and administration.

Replacing the notion of school as factory is a new metaphor of school as an extension of a child's family. Schools that embody this vision of themselves provide the scaffolding for children's growth and development that relatives and neighborhoods used to provide. Called variously "Schools for the Twenty-first Century" or "Family Resource Schools," the schools acknowledge dramatic changes in the nature of families, the disappearance of social infrastructure, and the out-of-school factors that interfere with young people's ability to learn (Kreck, 1992). They are concerned with the physical and psychological needs of the whole child and provide many of the same services as settlement houses at the turn of the century.

These institutions offer a single point of contact for families to access a variety of services and skill building opportunities, from food stamps to child care, from employment training to exposure to the arts and dance, from parenting training to gang-prevention workshops, from health care to food and clothing banks. They exist in several states; Kentucky, Texas, Connecticut, New Jersey, and Colorado are among

217

the leaders. The teacher plays the roles of skill builder, coordinator and case manager, diagnostician, and partner with parents on meeting young people's needs, among others. Colorado's first lady, Bea Romer, has been deeply involved in the movement in her state and succinctly expresses the difference between these efforts and more traditional social services: "Care must be taken not to tell families what to do or how to be—that's not what works" (Kreck, p. 15).

Acknowledging research which indicates that primary students acquire most of their literacy, problem-solving, and human relations skills before entering school, educators view parents in this model as partners with the school in educating the child and as the primary experts on that child (an idea that owes much to the activist parents of children with disabilities). The student plays the role of learner; he or she is a person with a complex set of needs that must be addressed for intellectual growth to take place. The community is welcomed into the school to provide help, encouragement, expertise, services, and support to students and families.

Curriculum and instruction are not explicitly addressed in this model, but the organization of the school changes as hierarchies are replaced by more collaborative decision making grounded in expert, rather than position-based, authority. Financing comes from the local school district sources and is supplemented by pooling funds from sources like Head Start, tuition and fees, in-kind support from training institutions that use the schools and centers as on-the-job training sites for students, handicapped and preschool funds, state and federal reimbursements for food service, and grants.

As an example of the range of services provided, in Denver's Family Resource Schools there are before- and after-school programs including community study halls with volunteer tutors, family math, family read-alongs, swimming, guitar, community gardening, and cultural activities. There are adult education and skill building classes, including adult basic education, GEDs, English and Spanish as second languages, conflict management, employment workshops, and parent education. Seminars are held on topics such as positive discipline, sex education, and gang prevention. Family support services are provided, including on-site case management, alcohol and drug prevention, child care, baby-sitting co-ops, food and clothing banks, mental health services, and women's support groups. The school also sponsors community and business partnerships. Local utility company employees participate in school governance and act as volunteer tutors; student and parent scholarships are funded by a local supermarket chain; before- and after-school child care is provided at the YMCA; and adult education classes are offered by the Community College of Denver.

Metropolitan areas are not the only places where families are in crisis. High in the Rocky Mountains in the small mining town of Leadville, a child-care crisis was created in 1988 when the mines shut down and 5,000 people were laid off. Many moved away, but those who stayed found work in Vail and Copper Mountain working at low-paying service jobs in the ski industry. Kathy Brendza began The Center, six blocks from Leadville's West Park Elementary School, to provide preschool and day care with a creatively negotiated waiver from Head Start. That project has blossomed into a multifaceted general store of services, including a child-care component that opens at 5:00 A.M. and stays open until the last parent comes to collect his or her child (sometimes at 7:30 P.M. when there is a snowstorm), English as a second language classes for Hispanic families coming to Leadville to work in the ski resorts, a dollar-a-day pregnancy prevention program for at-risk teens, an outlet for the Colorado Food Share program that trades food for community service, a parenting skills opportunity for high school students who assist with the younger children, family life skills classes, and enrichment programs from scouting to archery to belly dancing.

The schools as family centers idea breaks down the walls between school and community by reaching out to families and demonstrating that their needs are important, and simultaneously working to make more fluid the boundaries between public and private youth-serving agencies and coordinating their efforts. Whether as part of the district structure (as in Denver) or as a freestanding center, the message is, "It takes a whole village to raise a child, and we are here for you. The children of this community are the responsibility of all of us." This is a profound restructuring. Bea Romer says, "If I could find a way to do it, I would make family resource centers a part of school reform. . . . There should be a family resource center in every neighborhood" (Kreck, 1992: 17).

Many, although not all, of the needs that family resource center schools meet are born of hard economic times. A second model of community involvement addresses this issue directly as it makes economic development an organizing framework for the school.

Schools as Incubators for Economic Development

The second reason that the factory model no longer works is that the economy no longer needs factory-type workers. "The emergence of the information society requires initiative and self-reliance rather than the setting of standardized tasks and centralized control" (Grunwald, 1992). Every American family has personal evidence that the old rules that governed economic advancement and social mobility no longer work. We need new ways to think about how young people become economically productive, self-supporting, taxpaying members of post-industrial America. If one purpose of school is to prepare people to support themselves and if the fastest growing economic sector is small business, then let's teach students to create and manage businesses. Furthermore, let's use this process as a carrier, an organizer for the rest of the curriculum for all of the students.

Based on economic development work in this and other countries, entrepreneurial schools have as their purpose teaching young people how to create jobs as well as how to work for someone else. The teacher's role is coach, information giver, advisor, and consultant. The student's role is entrepreneur, researcher, planner, designer, manager, and owner. Parents provide psychological support for this most practical approach to education. The community's role is multifaceted: market, source of venture capital, site of apprenticeships and other training programs, and fountain of expertise and advisors.

The curriculum is interdisciplinary, focused on providing knowledge learned "just in time," when it is needed, and growing organically out of tasks. For example, the class that Jean Helmer and Mike Pangborn team-taught on rural economic development in South Dakota was in chaos as the students argued about what kind of a business had the most potential. One of the sophomore students turned to them and said, "What do we do now? How do we get people to shut up and listen to one another?" which prompted a three day seminar on parliamentary procedure.

Obviously instruction changes in this kind of school. Large groups, small groups, and individuals work as necessary, meeting with teachers and a wide variety of community members whose expertise makes them appropriate advisors. Instruction takes place both in school and out in the community. Organization of the school day changes as well. The school day is divided into larger blocks of time, teachers as well as students work together and share decision making, and decisions are made closer to the people who will be affected by them.

Financing comes from the local district but may be supplemented by vocational education and training funds. Partnerships between schools and businesses may play a larger role as students serve internships, do work-study jobs, or are apprentices. Examples from successful programs follow.

REAL Enterprises: Real Kids Doing Real Work

Jonathan Sher, Paul DeLargy, and their colleagues at the University of North Carolina's Small Business and Technology Development Center and North Carolina REAL Enterprises are the pioneers in the REAL Enterprises approach. Launched in 1986 with a grant from the Mary Reynolds Babcock Foundation and from UNC's Small Business and Technology Development Center, REAL Enterprises has grown to a national program whose components include market development, membership and partnership in select states, course and materials development, organizational development, and training in intensive summer workshops for teachers and managers and local community members (REAL Enterprises, 1989: 1).

At the center of the REAL program is a specific, discrete course, offered as an elective. Students prepare and implement comprehensive business plans for student-operated ventures. They then seek the involvement of a cross section of business people, professionals, and local leaders who serve on community support teams and act as advisors to, and mentors for, the program participants. Course materials are generated jointly by the REAL Enterprises' staff and local participants, and REAL staff provides extensive training to participating teachers during the school year and the summer. Start-up capital is provided through REAL's own revolving loan fund; projects also receive substantial assistance in securing loans or investments from public and private sources (REAL Enterprises, 1990: 2–3).

More than fifteen working businesses have been started as a result of local communities and schools adopting the REAL Enterprises approach to student-created small businesses, including a child-care center, a feeder pig operation, a graphic design business, an ice cream shop, a fabric shop, a plastic production and manufacturing shop, and a deli. One recent addition is Footprints, in Beaufort, South Carolina.

KeAndra Johnson, Kalisha Young, and Tabatha Moore are co-owners and operators of the newest shoe repair business in Beaufort, an outgrowth of Jackie Parker's school-based enterprise class at Battery Creek High School. Originally the class thought about what businesses they might patronize: a record shop, a teen center, a children's clothing store, or a lingerie shop, but a market analysis turned up competitors for each of those ideas. Shoe repair was missing. When the owners of a dry cleaning shop offered joint venture space in the new shopping center, their research, consultation with local business leaders, and the business plan that they developed all paid off. They obtained a start-up loan with help from REAL Enterprises and purchased secondhand shoe repair equipment, which they learned to use. The young women hired their former teacher as bookkeeper, but carried out all their own negotiations and made their own decisions.

One of the decisions they made was to distinguish their store from the typical shoe repair shop, which they described as "dull and dingy." Dancing couples trip across the wall above the Footprints logo. A second difference is the respect and seriousness which the young owners have earned. When she was interviewed for *Rural Electrification* magazine's article on students who create jobs, KeAndra Johnson reported, "My daddy didn't even want to hear about it at first. He'd say, 'Oh yeah, right, please be quiet. How can you start a business? You don't have any money.' Now my daddy likes to hear everything I have to say about the business. When I come in, right away he asks, 'How'd your meeting go?' " (Gibson, 1991: 14).

Not every participating student will start a business, nor will any two students follow exactly the same course of study. However, common to all students and to every REAL classroom are the following goals and principles: All students experience the process of researching, planning, and operating economically viable small enterprises that meet a need in their community. The second, and equally important goal, is to give students the opportunity to develop critical thinking and life skills. The development of a business plan is the primary vehicle for achieving both goals. It is also a means for learning decision making, communication, and cooperation, as well as a vehicle for helping students assess their entrepreneurial capabilities.

REAL principles focus on the process by which the REAL course is taught. The work must reflect student needs, desires, and concerns and be infused from the beginning with student choice. Teachers assume the roles of facilitator, coach, guide, and team leader rather than boss. The instructor ensures the academic integrity of the program by creating opportunities for students to master certain basic competencies during the preparation and execution of the business plan. Learning activities are characterized by student action, and the process emphasizes peer teaching, cooperative learning, and teamwork. Connections between classroom work and the community are clear, and there is an audience for student work beyond the teacher. The content and competencies addressed in the course build progressively toward established goals. The value of entrepreneurial experience is acknowledged and modeled in interactions between teacher and students so that policies and practices that deprive students of opportunities to think and work creatively are resisted. Opportunities for conscious, thoughtful reflection (e.g., in journals) are provided throughout the program, and the program includes constructive, honest, ongoing evaluation of skills, content, and changes in student attitudes (REAL Enterprises, 1992).

REAL Enterprises has members in North and South Carolina and Georgia and provisional members or local sites in Vermont, Ohio, West Virginia, Alabama, Wisconsin, Minnesota, South Dakota, Oklahoma, Wyoming, Oregon, Washington, and Alaska.

*The Minnesota Model: Revitalizing Rural Communities and
Restructuring Rural Schools*

Minnesota is also growing student entrepreneurs, primarily in rural areas. Rural communities everywhere are plagued by a swarm of troubles. National policies have led to economic decline. The deregulation of the transportation system, for example, leaves many communities more isolated than they were fifty years ago. Agricultural policy that favors large-scale production companies at the expense of small-scale family farms has meant fewer farms and closed stores on Main Street. Communications systems that are incapable of carrying high-speed electronic data have prevented electronic entrepreneurs from accessing homes in entire counties, and from establishing their residences in rural communities. The result in Minnesota is the outmigration of rural people to urban areas in and outside the state. The Center for School Change of the Humphrey Institute at the University of Minnesota is working to reverse that trend and to improve schools at the same time. They have a substantial grant from the Blandon Foundation to help rural schools become partners in economic development by creating student entrepreneurs and in this way revitalize rural communities and restructure rural schools.

In Alden-Congers, the students have chosen to focus on food and sociability. They have just opened a restaurant that serves as a local spot for breakfast and lunch and as a social center for teenagers on weekend evenings. Involvement of industrial arts and home economics classes is providing hands-on learning in the remodeling process and in kitchen staffing. The enterprise emerged from a match between classroom discussions and a desire on the part of students and teachers to fill the need for a local meeting place for teens. In Delavan, students from the elementary school are entering their sixth year as owners and operators of their own "Mini Mall." An initial loan of $100 from a local bank president and facilitation by their sixth-grade teacher has helped the mall flourish. Students operate five businesses, including a consignment shop, a loan office, and stores selling candy, records, and school supplies. Their store is the only place within about ten miles where paper, pencils, and other school supplies can be purchased. In class, students study management, purchasing, inventory, and finances.

Hanska, Minnesota's elementary school is planning a Greenhouse Learning Center that will provide the local community with plants and offer elementary students lessons in science and community connection at the same time. The Learning Center will be staffed with both community members and students. At Staples High School, in western Minnesota, students operate a child-care program and build a house each year. The child-care program not only provides an on-site service for three- to five-year-olds, it also reaches into the community to work with the local Head Start program. The house building program is part of the construction trades curriculum: students pick the plan and materials, then they build and sell the house with support from the school board.

There are other efforts that fill less obvious needs. Plans are unfolding in Staples to reopen a local radio station, student staffed and programmed, in cooperation with a local couple. The most comprehensive effort is in northern Minnesota's Rothsay where student-operated enterprises are replacing closed local businesses. TIGER Inc. (Teenage Innovative Group Entrepreneurial Research) reopened Tiger Mart, on the site of a grocery store that had been closed. Operating capital came from a variety of student-generated sources including the local Rothsay Focus Fund, the Lions Club, the regional Initiative Fund, the city, the school district, the power company, and area churches. For the past three years the school has also owned and operated the Storefront— a hardware store and lumberyard—which provides students with additional opportunities for community business experience. The latest plan is to take over an empty motel and run it as a youth hostel/dormitory for foreign and local students (Hinz, 1991: 4–5).

The Minnesota projects are context-based with no common course or curricula (unlike REAL). As indicated earlier, the Center for School Change focuses on school reform and restructuring, using entrepreneurial projects as a means to that end. REAL's organizational technical assistance revolves around identifying likely participants and training them in REAL's approach, while the Center for School Change concentrates on nurturing local projects as one way to influence state education and development policy.

New Ways To Work Together

Alabama: Economic Development as "Learning to Dig Our Own Wells"

Another group providing the impetus for community outreach and economic development through public schools is the Program for Rural Services and Research (PRSR) at the University of Alabama. Through the PACERS Cooperative (a collective action organization that takes its name from an earlier PRSR effort, the Program for the Academic and Cultural Enhancement of Rural Schools), thirty rural schools stretching the length and width of the state and representing the poorest, most isolated, most racially diverse, and smallest public schools in Alabama have come together to learn to act collectively in their own best interests. The PACERS schools are engaged in a variety of projects. Of immediate interest is the program theme that focuses on identifying and meeting local community needs for food, housing, and good work.[2] It is this set of projects that represents the next logical evolution of entrepreneurial notions. Rather than exclusively benefiting the individual (REAL's focus) or the community (the approach of Minnesota's Center for School Change), the PACERS Cooperative strategy blends the two emphases.

PRSR staff asked teachers in a PACERS Cooperative planning meeting to consider the needs and circumstances of their students. "Many of our kids eat from their grandmother's garden, but they don't have gardening and preserving skills themselves. From whose garden will their children eat?" was the most haunting response. Dorsey Walker, consultant to the PACERS Cooperative and director of the Upper Sand Mountain Food Bank, echoed this tragedy. Even though his agency is located in a rural and traditionally agricultural area, he notes,

When people come in for food assistance we offer them seeds and plantings as well. Many young rural people don't know how to respond. They either don't have the land or the skills to grow their own food, or it just never occurred to them that it was possible.

Feeding oneself and one's family is obviously the first step. Student-conducted market studies have shown that people will gladly pay well for fresh, organically grown produce. The problem is finding an outlet for locally grown produce that is reliable, within reasonable transportation distance (to preserve the freshness of the produce), and has requirements that small operations can meet (unlike grocery chains that need

225

very large supplies from every source they deal with). The cooperative has received support from the Hunger Committee and the Church and Society Unit of the Presbyterian Church (USA) for a project that will establish food guilds in the churches through which the congregation will order and guarantee payment for selected produce from students, thereby providing a prepaid market. Additional marketing may be done in church parking lots to serve the churches' neighborhoods. The school in Wadley, Alabama, raised $10,000 from the Lyndhurst Foundation and local donations to buy eight acres adjacent to the school for the first stage of a school farm, and subsequently has received the donation of another three acres. Monroe Senior High School received land from the county board to expand a play and recreation area and for the proposed cooperative marketing/gardening projects.

Schools associated with the cooperative are planning to pair students with local residents in order to learn skills and provide services simultaneously. For example, students may help elderly residents put in gardens, tend farm animals, or preserve food in school-based canneries. And cooperative schools are reconsidering their role as food providers. In many Alabama communities, the school is the major provider of food assistance in rural areas, serving the large numbers of students who receive free or reduced-price lunches and breakfasts. Under discussion are topics such as how to provide better and more nutritious food, how to involve students and teachers in food planning and preparation, and how to extend school-based feeding programs to needy community members.

Housing is another crucial issue. Alabama has an enormous backlog of substandard housing stock, yet the Alabama outpost of the Farm Home Administration regularly sent funds back to the federal government because of a dearth of applicants who met their criteria for construction or rehabilitation funding. In 1991, PACERS met with FmHA representatives to determine how those funds might be made available to student builders, and agreements were reached for PACERS to demonstrate a project in which students are paid to build or rehabilitate homes for local residents eligible for FmHA financing. The first prototype house, constructed by students in Coffeeville, has 1,000 square feet. It includes a two-acre lot and garden plot, cost approximately $25,000 to build, and requires approximately $50 per month for utilities. Students have located a buyer for the house, his loan application has been approved by the FmHA, and he and his family will move in during the spring of 1993. Because the new homeowner has three children who will be attending Coffeeville schools, considerable money will come into the community, in addition to the home construction costs which were primarily incurred there.

Students also completed a rehabilitation project in Akron, Alabama insulating and adding a passive solar greenhouse to the home of an elderly low-income resident. So enthusiastic were the students and community residents that plans for the summer of 1993 include making the four students who acted as the principal workers on the home rehabilitation project team leaders of a team of students. Four teams will work together to build a greenhouse for the elementary school. The teams will then split up and each build another passive solar greenhouse to benefit a low-income resident.

The housing projects have attracted considerable interest in the community, with many residents expressing an interest in collaborating with students on housing construction or rehabilitation projects. The FmHA will finance student work to rehabilitate existing homes for eligible residents and sign an agreement to purchase (through which schools pay students and purchase materials) for all student-constructed homes that meet FmHA regulations. The FmHA state architect has agreed to work with schools and students to study and improve designs for low-cost houses. Because it so dramatically improves the agency's ability to serve a remote rural constituency, the FmHA has proposed making the effort a national demonstration project in 1993. Partners that have emerged from this pioneer effort include the FmHA state staff, all district directors, the state architect, the state housing directors, and many of the FmHA county directors. A draftsman and certified engineer are finishing a detailed manual for each school to follow in their house building and rehabilitation efforts. Focused not only on technical construction details, the manual links these skills to traditional math, science, and social studies curricula. It will be circulated to all faculty members for added comments about applicability to academic subjects (e.g., math teachers will add design pages of problems for students to solve, etc.).

One of the principles that guides the PACERS Cooperative is to make barriers between agencies or school districts more permeable by identifying common interests. The PACERS Cooperative itself is a living example that traditional divide-and-conquer rivalries can be put aside and outgrown as mutual interests become apparent. Within the set of PACERS schools, Cedar Bluff, Red Level, and Meek are creating a vertically integrated conglomerate for which Cedar Bluff students build computers, Meek students plan and implement marketing strategies, and Red Level students provide the print materials, manuals, and printing to support the other two efforts (Haas, 1992).

Other principles that undergird the PACERS Cooperative work include academic rigor and an attempt to contextualize student work. Academic work is linked to the immediate improvement of students' lives and their provision of basic services to the local community. Inclusive program activities pay close attention to at-risk young people and draw in a range of students and community residents, avoiding the marginalization of anyone. The school's activities improve the overall life of the community through appropriate development efforts that build capacity for understanding and contributing to community health in students, teachers, schools, and community members so the program efforts can be sustained over the long term. Finally, these activities are aimed at producing tangible public outcomes, attracting partners, and benefiting everyone involved (Lambert, 1992).

When teachers, students, and community members articulate and evaluate proposed work against these criteria, profound changes in public policy and activities take place. The PACERS approach looks at both education and economics as if people mattered.

Understanding Education and Economics as if People Mattered

Starting businesses is not the only goal of these economic development approaches. They are also deeply concerned with what young people are learning and how they can put this into practice. With David Orr (1990), proponents of this vision of schooling believe that education must be *for* something. Teaching economics without reference to the environmental or social consequences of economic systems, for instance, suggests that economic decisions are abstract, relatively simple, and belong in the hands of experts rather than ordinary people. What a different experience is had by students who research the flow of goods, services, and capital in their communities and market areas and learn to calculate gross community product. Not only do they have a more comprehensive understanding of the concept of gross national product, they have also gained insights into how their spending decisions have an impact on the entire community. Dave Versteig's Custer, South Dakota, economics class began by conducting an in-school survey of disposable income controlled by Custer High School students each year. The total, for a school of 250 young people, was roughly a quarter of a million dollars. Every school can collect similar data. Sharing this information with local merchants through the chamber of commerce should make an impact and change perceptions of young people from nuisances to clients, potential customers to be wooed. The next step for Dave's class was to research where that student-controlled money was being spent. Much of it left town in cars headed to the mall, an hour away in Rapid City. The students were savvy by this time about principles of local economic development. They created an audiovisual program about market leakage and the consequences of buying locally and presented it to the student body and to other community groups.

A partnership between the students and the Chamber of Commerce began. Chamber meetings were moved to the school so that the economics class could attend. Students were commissioned to conduct other market research studies for the chamber, including gathering data for a Farm Home Administration low-cost housing application. When the chamber was entertaining executives from a factory looking for a relocation site, students from the economics class squired their children around both the school and the town, enthusiastically promoting the area as a good place to live.

The economic development approach is not confined to high school students. In Wisconsin, Russell Gilbert teaches his fourth and fifth graders a unit on development that includes their designing and operating a company. As might be expected, the company often centers around food (one year it was tapping and making maple syrup, another time it was making pies). The young people not only learn about operating a business by doing it, they make a substantial profit each year (often more than a thousand dollars). This money goes into a foundation they've created, to which other classes in the school and members of the community may apply for grants of $100. The young people award the grants, most recently to a local nursing home for music on records and tape (J. Lewicki, personal communication, Nov. 17, 1992).

Aside from the obvious economic benefits to communities as they gain goods, services, and a new appreciation of the skills and capabilities of their young people, other strengths of this model are that it provides real work experience that is relevant and transferable. Unlike simulation programs (Junior Achievement, DECA), students themselves analyze the market and determine needs and strategies to fill those needs. Students discover sources of capital, write business plans, and own and operate the businesses, assuming all the risks that accompany every economic endeavor. It is the student owners who make decisions about the business. The immediate relevance and potential payoff make this approach very appealing to a wide variety of students, particularly those whom the current system neither fits nor values.

The model teaches the importance of context and helps young people look closely at, understand, and value their local communities.

Entrepreneurial approaches are not without problems, and each set of sites deals with them in different ways. Liability issues are a concern, particularly where heavy equipment or student travel are concerned. Superintendents with entrepreneurial projects in their schools suggest that boards of education pass resolutions expanding the mission of the school to include economic (or preferably the larger term, community) development. Then, as school-sanctioned activities, projects are covered under existing school insurance policies. Competition with local merchants can be another concern, particularly in the early stages of entrepreneurial activity when the directions that student efforts will take is not clear. Occasionally grumbling about spending public money to "subsidize" enterprises arises. Again, board of education policies of no competition can allay those fears, as can informational meetings between students and local business and service clubs. Since one objective of these projects is to improve the community through studies of which services and goods are locally needed, making research results publicly available is another strategy to gain local support. As a cautionary note, however, there have been instances where local politics make some kinds of businesses unworkable or when young people have been exploited by adults, raising a whole set of moral issues and conversations.

Educational accountability is also important. Parents, community members, and other teachers may ask, "How can we be sure that students are really learning?" There are two ways. The first is that each teacher will analyze the basic skills and competencies for which they are regularly responsible and make plans to be sure they are covered (a pragmatic, sensible approach is outlined in *Sometimes a Shining Moment* [Wigginton, 1985], and summarized in Nachtigal et al., 1989). The second way is even more compelling. Students enthusiastically show and tell adults with whom they are interacting how much they are learning. Parents report that conversations at home have moved from monosyllables to excited outbursts of new information regarding issues such as the social boundaries in the communities, the county system for licensing and permits, the history and settlement patterns of the town, the recalcitrance of the state fire marshall, the problems of cash flow, and the surprising number of existing businesses in the county.

Community perceptions can be problematic, as adults are not accustomed to seeing young people downtown during school hours and often assume students are goofing off when they are collecting information or doing research. Community meetings; articles in the local papers, on the radio, and in newsletters; conversations at churches about community needs; appearances at service clubs; and word of mouth can all be channels for information that will eliminate misunderstandings. School secretaries will get some calls and should be primed to answer them, as should all school staff and faculty.

Finally, what if the student business fails? Statistics on small business failure rates are familiar and gloomy. Many of those failures are attributable to poor preparation and the lack of a business plan. Careful attention to teaching how to create a business calls forth skills that will serve young people whenever, wherever, and if ever they decide that working for themselves is what they want to do. If after all the careful planning and work, a business fails (or the student decides to go to college, move away, stop doing it), then that is a lesson to be learned as well. The business owners involved with these programs appreciate that students are aware of and willing to assume risks. That is, they say, the exchange for the potential to make a profit. After all, student knowledge is the point of these projects. When interpreted by a talented teacher, failure is also a learning opportunity.

As we have seen, entrepreneurial notions are evolving into a dynamic new balance between the needs of individuals and those of the community. The final model involves the creation of community development partnerships with the schools and expands community-based opportunities for students beyond the economic realm to include community service.

Schools as Partners in Community Development

Ideas that inform this model come from the environmental movement and its notion of the "web of life," from agriculture's emerging emphasis on sustainability, and from communitarian thought. Its roots go deep into educational reform traditions, back to Dewey (1939), community-based education, and the philosophies of writers with a particular interest in the importance of context, including Wallace Stegner (1985), Wendell Berry (1990), and William Least Heat-Moon (1991).

In this model, the purpose of the school is to prepare young people to be economically and civically productive citizens and to contribute to the development of the community. Both individual and collective benefit are emphasized. Teachers act as information givers, organizers, coaches, strategists, and co-learners. Students are seen as activists, advocates, community contributors, economic modelers, and learners responsible for monitoring their intellectual growth and the psychosocial concomitants of that growth. Parents become partners in the student's education and learners as well, providing rich out-of-school experiences and reflections on prior knowledge.

> It is characteristic of that form of knowing which Dewey located in the household and the neighborhood that one learns, not through accumulating tested propositions about the objective world, but through participating in social practices, by assuming social roles, by becoming familiar with exemplary narratives and with typical characters who illustrate a variety of patterns of behavior. One does not feel like an autonomous subject learning specific facts about an objective world out there. One becomes what one knows. That is how one learns in the family, on the job, and largely, in church. (Bellah et al., 1991: 158)

Communities in this model become a locus of learning. The community is the context in which learning takes place and is shaped. Community members are coaches and mentors. The community provides opportunity for service, sites for research and analysis, and a fellowship of adults who value knowledge and continue learning themselves. The learning community is rich with contact between young people and adults.

The curriculum is interdisciplinary, focused on the explicit learning skills as well as content areas. It is production oriented and grows out of learners' interests. Local events and geography provide examples and inspiration for the curriculum. The curriculum is experiential, hands-on, and project-focused. It deals with real problems in real time.

Contextualizing Education: Looking at the Local Environment

A revitalized sense of community, of cultural endowment, not only touches the inchoate yearning for belonging that is part of the human condition, it also makes us more responsible for the world in which we live. As Wendell Berry says,

> Local living is not less necessary for city people than for country people. All of us, in city or country, must learn to shorten our supply lines and live as much as we can from nearby

sources that we can see and know and thus, we must hope, learn to take care of. (Berry, 1990: 4)

An example of how this emerging research informs action can be seen in Parrish, Alabama. Parrish is an old coal mining and railroad town. It has an unusually high level of learning and behavioral problems among students, which community residents and teachers suspect might be attributable to lead poisoning. Parrish High School has proposed a project which will involve students in a variety of lead-testing and community cleanup efforts. Working with a faculty physician assigned to the PACERS Cooperative by the University of Alabama, students will devise a health screening questionnaire to assess symptoms of lead poisoning in children and adolescents. Students will try to locate the source of lead contamination and plan to test water, paint, and soil samples from homes around the community. If lead contamination is indicated, students and community leaders will seek federal and state funding for a full-scale lead decontamination effort. Because twenty percent of Alabama's public school students have degrees of lead poisoning severe enough to cause neurological damage, the work of Parrish High School students will be immediately transferable around the state.

In Soldier's Grove, Wisconsin, fourth-grade students created their own opportunities to improve the environment. The small village (300 residents) is in a flood plain. In a terrible 1979 "hundred years' flood," the business district was submerged. The buildings were leveled and the downtown moved several blocks to the east to get away from the river. What remained when the water subsided were a few old trees and bare land that the city called a park. James Lewicki's fourth-grade students saw the dreary area each day as they went to school, a block and a half away. They divided into four teams, mapped the area, and decided what each of the quadrants needed to become a real park (an ash tree for shade near the playground, a swamp oak for a wet area next to the river, etc.). They wrote proposals to the village board, received approval for their project and minimal funding, negotiated with the Wisconsin Department of Natural Resources for surplus tree stock, and spent several weeks digging three-foot-by-two-foot holes for the trees. In the process, they became archaeologists, finding foundation stones and debris left from the previous inhabitants. This led them to conversations with older residents of town who could recreate the buildings and their functions. A very dry spring followed, and the fourth graders spent their recess time at the park, lugging heavy buckets of water to the thirsty trees. During the first summer, students who lived in town volunteered to continue the watering, which has since been taken over by the village.

In its "Triangle and Trees" center, Alabama's W. S. Harlan Junior High School is planning an all-in-one contextualized science, outdoor education, recreation, and town beautification facility. Developed on property adjacent to the school, it will have several sections including a native growth and forestry management area, a vegetable producing area, and a flower and shrubbery area. The center will include a greenhouse and a semioutdoor classroom which can double as a community amphitheater. Triangles and Trees will also have a walking and fitness trail providing a safe area for the community's many widows to walk and facilities for more vigorous fitness activity. Students will identify, mark, and provide basic information on trees, underbrush, other plants, and soil types. Each class will have a vegetable patch and a flower bed for which it is responsible. In addition, students will survey area residents to obtain requests for plants with the goal of having a student-provided plant in every home, yard, or garden in the school district.

Other Alabama projects take widely varying approaches to environmental issues. Students at Mellow Valley school are conducting an energy audit of their school buildings, then planning and carrying out the retrofit construction that will not only reduce the school's fuel bill but also serve as a model and resource to community residents. Oakman students are studying the quality of water in the county and sources of pollution in an interdisciplinary project involving science, math, and vocational agriculture. Collinsville has raised $5,000 for land for an Animal Husbandry Center and made alliances with the mayor and some elderly volunteers to help with its development. Bibb Graves High School is purchasing land for a school and community park.

The cultural environment is no less important to community development than the economic or physical environment, yet many of us live in communities where the cultural endowment has been devalued and stripped away by inattention, competing priorities, and the seductions of the mass media. As in Upper Sand Mountain, Alabama, one good way to begin to recapture the cultural endowment of a community is to ask simple questions: "What can the grandparents of the young people who live here do that their grandchildren can't? What do they know that these children don't?" The list of lost skills and knowledge becomes the beginning of project designs that intend to redevelop and renew the rich local culture of the area. Community histories, created with written, audio, and video media, can aspire to be more than anecdotal (the richest examples are found in the twenty-year history of Foxfire). They provide cultural analysis based on information given to student compilers. Students use photographs for documentary and artistic expression. School and community newspapers which cover local news are, according to the Freedom Foundation, "at the cutting edge" of student journalism. Where no official library exists, computer technology placed in empty storefronts or unused classrooms and operated by volunteers have created community study centers that link poor, isolated communities to public libraries and other information sources (and give young people a very clear message about the importance and joy of learning).

Linda Abboud, a practicing artist and art teacher working in Nebraska, has sought to instill in her students the joy of making art and bringing an aesthetic celebration to their town's public space. Twelve years ago she began to examine the way she taught. Dissatisfied with her courses' product orientation, organizing principles, emphasis on labels, smatterings of various media, and a brief bow to art history, she developed ways to connect the joy she felt in her work with the everyday lives of her rural students. This is how she tells the story:

> I began to see true art as the communication of meaning—the meaning of social systems, of beliefs and rituals, and of ideas about human relationships. Art spoke through the use of tangible materials such as paint, charcoal, clay, brick, stone, metal, glass, fiber and the like. I asked myself what this organization of materials in form and texture and color could communicate in different times and places and cultures. (Center for Rural Affairs, 1992: 17)

Linda's reflections led to a restructuring of her junior high classes. She learned to coordinate her work with the student's work in social studies classes, so that students studying the Roman wars might also be designing bridges in clay, coliseums and temples in cardboard, and frescoed murals in one or another paint media.

She also found opportunities to move into the community. Her students became involved in designing and painting a 200-foot supergraphic design for a gym wall and two mosaic wall panels for the city auditorium. These panels incorporate the agricultural symbols of rural community life and provide opportunities to make meaningful connections between the symbols on the mural—water towers, church rituals, fat cattle, and corn—and symbols significant to agricultural peoples in other places, times, and cultures. The work took five years to design

235

and execute. Students undertook serious writing projects, comparing their sense of the meaning of life with that of people in other ages as they explored issues of peace and justice, ecology and the environment, and perhaps most important, community survival (Center for Rural Affairs, 1992: 10–11).

Successful projects begin with respectful and patient listening to the experts, the people who live here.

> Inhabitants of the area are relatively well acquainted with its conditions, and they are very capable of contributing to improvements in their own way and in the interest of the community. In this way, a community grows from the inside with the help of its own residents and in harmony with its particular characteristics. This type of community development must, of course, occur in balance with regional, national, and international conditions, but it should be primarily driven by the local inhabitants. (Olivegren, 1986: 15)

Because successful community development involves a wide range of people, this model may require the most diverse and flexible instructional strategies. Instruction takes place in large groups, small groups, cooperative task forces and teams, and individually as appropriate. The emphasis is on teacher-student consultations on progress and cooperation, rather than individual isolation and competition. This form of instruction is specifically designed to incorporate practice in skills that reflect how adults work together.

> These [skills] include team problem-finding and solving; communication; decision-making; commitment; confidence in abilities; and boldness in developing ideas and approaches. Learning activities should be presented as real-life problems: full of ambiguity; bound to specific circumstances and constraints; dependent on formal knowledge *and* creative "figuring-out"; and with important consequences. (Jeannie Oakes, quoted in Berryman, 1987: 8)

Instruction is a shared responsibility, directed at times by the teacher but at other times by expert community members and by other students. The learner is helped to develop skill in the art of reflection and self-assessment. Because in many instances this role is new to them, students need help getting started in assessing (and valuing) their existing knowledge and competence. In and out of class, students need frequent opportunities to perform and receive suggestions for improvement from a variety of perspectives. At various points during their academic careers, and at the end, students need a chance to reflect on what they have learned, what they still need to know, and how to assess themselves.

Instruction and assessment are performance-based and tasks are transparent so that the entire community can judge their value and level of accomplishment. Performance is a public event. The community is interested and anxious for opportunities to see (and evaluate) for themselves the returns on their education investment. In some schools, performance-based final exams attract audiences that rival attendance at athletic events.

Time schedules and class organization are determined by the demands of the kind of learning taking place. The school day is typically divided into larger blocks of time, and both the school day and school year may become longer than current practice. Teachers team with one another and stay with a cohort of students for large amounts of their academic careers. Teachers and students experience more autonomy in decision making. All school inhabitants see themselves as learners and contributors to the health of the community of which the school is a part.

Finally, funding: many of the community development projects don't require additional funding. Several of the experiments are the result of a single teacher deciding to use existing resources differently, like Linda Abboud. Within a single building, a group of South Dakota teachers and their principal worked together to revise the schedule to provide longer blocks of instructional time by team teaching. Some sites, like Oakman, have found sympathetic board of education members who engineer an expansion of the mission of the district that provides opportunities for community-based activities.

Funding beyond the school budget can also be located. The diversity of ways to get additional resources mirrors the diversity of the efforts. The PACERS Cooperative has gathered support from state and federal housing agencies, from the state library system, from local, regional, and national telephone companies, and from foundations by working to make the boundaries between youth-serving and other kinds of public and private agencies more fluid. Their strategy works because they are able to identify mutual interests and persuade others of their value. REAL is supported by grants and contributions from foundations and individuals, and hopes that eventually its members will make it self-supporting. Some schools have begun school foundations, particularly appealing to alumni who have prospered elsewhere. Model school foundations have been established in Coffee Springs and Spring Garden schools in Alabama and more than $25,000 in contributions gathered. Smaller, family-directed foundations with regional or local roots and interests are likely sources. Finally, local resources should not be overlooked. Cris Anderson, superintendent of Presho, South Dakota, created a revolving loan fund for student entrepreneurs from small local donations (none of which could be over $100 in order to expand the number of contributors). Additional support can come from in-kind contributions from community businesses and members.

Environmental and public service work can also access a variety of goods, services, and funds. One vocational agriculture class has a contract with the New Mexico Game and Fish Division to care for wounded animals and assist with national forest management. Wisconsin's Department of Natural Resources contributed more than 800 trees to the park planting project undertaken by fourth graders in Soldier's Grove. As noted, Alabama students are accessing federal low-cost housing funds from the Farm Home Administration for solar construction and retrofitting home projects, and other Alabama schools are saving more than seventy-five percent of their distant learning line charges because of a special educational telephone rate negotiated on behalf of the PACERS Cooperative. One set of experimenters in South Dakota created an invisible college by using small amounts of outside funding from a regional educational laboratory to rent a meeting room so they could come together to plan, encourage, and share with one another.

Lessons Learned and Suggestions for Sustainable Education

Real reform in education requires a paradigm shift from the technical perspective that arose from the factory model with its emphasis on standards, on measurable outcomes, and on control to a more holistic view of the role of learning in the lives of individuals. Traditional education has been, for much of America, an extractive industry, based on models that ignore local contexts, local strengths, and local needs. We are in the process of creating another, more sustainable model for education that uses the interactions between individuals and their social context to teach how to accumulate and apply knowledge in community. This new model stresses the responsibilities we have to ourselves and our multidimensional personal growth and the responsibilities we have to one another in society. It is a series of lifelong, often difficult and simultaneously joyous experiences that stress our interconnections with the future, as well as with the past and the present. We begin with the lessons learned across all of these naturally occurring experiments, some of which tend to ratify some things that the change literature has been saying for a number of years, some of which are surprising, and some of which confirm hunches. As a whole, these findings begin to bring to the surface the principles of a new model for education.

What Works: Ratifying What We Know about Change

The first thing that these grass-roots experiments have in common is that they have precious little in common. Each is unique and appears to be successful to the extent that it meets the needs of its unique context, whether that context is on the prairies of western Minnesota or in the Appalachian "hollers" of Alabama. Second, each experiment has at its center an individual or small group of individuals investing enormous amounts of energy. Sometimes that person is a teacher, like Dave Versteig or Robert Youngblood or Linda Abboud, who is looking for ways to bring meaning to the practice of his or her profession and to her or his students. Sometimes it is a principal or administrator looking for a way to reconnect the school and the community and to provide better service to both. And sometimes the spark is carried by outside helpers such as the Mid-continent Regional Educational Laboratory (McREL) Rural Institute program, REAL Enterprises, the Center for School Change, or the Program for Rural Services and Research. No surprises here. Significant, lasting change adapts to local conditions and needs a champion to get started.

What Works: Surfacing Surprises

What is surprising, what is counterintuitive, is the role of expertise. Each experiment is led by a teacher or a group of teachers, working with other innovators and "making it up." These aren't folks who have all the answers. They are people willing to risk operating at the edge of their competence, not from the center. "It's given us the courage and support to dream," they say. They give up what they are comfortable doing and knowing to learn new ways of relating to students and other adults. This means examining assumptions, thinking hard about the purposes of activities and events, risking failure, and being willing to expand and shift rules, roles, and relationships. One teacher speaks for many when she says, "We're learning we have to back off and let students make mistakes, but it's helped us see students as problem solvers, rather than problem makers."

What Works: Confirming Three Hunches

Three hunches get confirmed when analyzing what works. The first is about rewards. Rewards are not what the society usually values. They aren't money. There is no big sugar daddy, no great monetary reward or merit salary increase built into any of these efforts. Nor are the rewards in leisure time or graceful pace. Much of this work takes place in addition to already full schedules, during after-school hours. It takes extra effort, concern, dedication on the part of teachers. Planning, thinking, reflecting on, and building new relationships is slow, patient work that takes long periods of time. McREL's Rural Institute has been working with schools for twelve years, PRSR for ten, and REAL Enterprises for eight. Nevertheless, it is rare program planners who allow themselves the time necessary to put successful efforts in place. My personal hunch is that all social service–type jobs have a built-in martyr culture, where one's commitment to the cause is measured in the amount of fatigue one endures and the number of bags under one's eyes. Human service workers are so busy caring for others, they don't treat themselves humanely and are often too exhausted to celebrate and enjoy the fruits of their labors.

The rewards are also not fame. Because these projects operate well outside the existing establishment paradigm of how schooling should happen, the meager establishment reward systems that do exist (state "Teacher of the Year" recognition programs, for instance) ignore these teachers and programs. Often the attention that does accrue to teachers working in innovative ways is unwelcome as it may cause trouble with colleagues.

Nevertheless, the rewards are very real. The teachers involved in these experiments say that they are the most professionally fulfilling experiences of their careers. "If you ask enough people, you'll get help. We've learned how to ask and we're willing to ask." The rewards are in the growth of the students, the new spirit of confidence and optimism in communities, and in the teacher's professional and personal growth. "It's been a real catalyst to think about things." "This is reform in the best sense. It's not alienating to us either. We're creating it." Recognition, affiliation, and support are rewards that can come from interactions with other teachers and concerned adults working on similar projects in similar ways. Networks are springing up across the country of people reaching out to one another, investing energy in a common cause. A typical sentiment is, "Being together and seeing what other people are doing ignites your mind."

The second hunch is about the power and joy that come from understanding common cause and collective action. Acting together brings participants a power that none of them experience individually and the strength to bring about important changes. Because there are thirty members of the PACERS Cooperative, the Alabama Public Library Service was willing to engage in a pilot program to link small schools with inadequate library holdings with the resources of the system, leapfrogging them into the information age. Similarly, the number and diversity of PACERS schools made them attractive as outlets for state agencies to increase their service penetration into rural Alabama. Finally, the PACERS model of collective action (one school providing computers for all schools, while another prepares and prints instruction manuals and warranties, and a third markets the computers outside the network) is attracting national and international attention, forcing the state Department of Education to reconsider their assumptions about these schools and communities having little to offer. After a decade of strident, rampant individualism, people are ready and willing to work together again.

A corollary of this hunch is that the joy and power of collective action extend beyond the borders of organizations and agencies. When community members see young people doing things that benefit the community, when learning becomes concrete and real instead of abstract and foreign, they are enthusiastic about helping, financially and with their time and expertise. For instance, the county board in Monroe County donated land to the Monroe Senior High School for an expanded play and recreation area and the proposed gardening/marketing project. When public agencies sense that schools want to work with them for mutual benefit, they find creative ways to redistribute attention, priorities, and resources. When private concerns can see mutually rewarding relationships with schools, they enthusiastically invest in local communities. Phone carriers have reduced rates to schools using their lines for distance learning by thousands of dollars each year and are negotiating with the public service commission to create special, low-rate educational service areas. Boundaries are becoming less defined, less like barriers to action as we all scramble to understand our place and contributions in the information age.

The final hunch builds on the second, and is about the interconnections between parts of the system. Regardless of where they begin, each of the sites has a worldview or paradigm that understands that the world operates more like a hologram than a clock. Everything is connected to everything else. To provide the room to operate, to create change, requires loosening up the system by simultaneously working from the top (where policies are set and public perceptions created) down and from the bottom (where work is accomplished and lives lived) up. So, the Center for School Change works on legislation at the same time it sponsors alternative school models with an economic and community development focus. The Family Resource Center schools provide before- and after-school care for young people and provide employment training for parents as a concrete way to break the poverty cycle. REAL Enterprises has state affiliates and local members in states where action on the state level is not yet possible.

What's Next: Suggestions About Sustainable Education Reform

Education that suited an industrial society was an extractive industry, taking local property taxes and investing in training young people who left the area, making their contribution elsewhere. An intuitive understanding of this phenomenon contributes, I think, to the reluctance of many communities to pass bond issues and otherwise increase funding for education. We need to think about making education sustainable in communities rather than a drain on them. It is this kind of shift in perspective that represents real education reform. To begin that discussion, this chapter concludes with some emerging design principles that might be incorporated in plans for the future of education.

Sustainable education reform is a process. It builds on the strength and knowledge of local people, giving them the tools to accept responsibility for their future and fate. It requires learning a balance between self-sufficiency and the savvy to create enough space in the existing system to do what you need to do. It also seeks a balance between private gain and public value.

Sustainable education is diverse and not generic. It will become manifest in different ways in different communities.

Sustainable education reform is concrete. It values its local, unique context and considers the community a laboratory in which the most rigorous of academic lessons can be learned and evaluated in authentic and public ways. It prepares young people to live and work as adults, giving them opportunities to practice adult ways of working, learning, being responsible, and participating in the community. Based in a real community, it is practical. It recognizes real limits and operates within them.

Sustainable education reform is multifaceted. It attends to issues of purpose, content, rules, roles and responsibilities in dynamic, iterative ways that act upon the knowledge that everything is connected to everything else.

Sustainable education reform is inclusive. It involves all members of the community and recognizes each young person as having unlimited and undetermined value and potential. It does not set up organizational mechanisms to sort children into winners and losers.

Sustainable education reform is rigorous. It is intellectually grounded in research on cognition (how people learn) and in instruction (how they are most effectively taught). Learning to learn is as important as learning specific content.

Sustainable education reform is deeply moral. It is driven by a fundamental trust and belief in the capacity of people (young and old) to identify and celebrate local strengths and resources, to identify and solve their problems, to create a mutually reinforcing balance between benefits to the individual and to communities. As Cornelia Flora (1992) says, "It is socially just, environmentally sound, and economically viable."

Notes

1. Data sources included a subsample of the NELS:88 survey of 25,000 eighth-grade students, a review of some 250 schools which were nominated to participate in a study of restructured schools, and more than 100 proposals for school restructuring submitted to a quasi-public funding organization called the New American Schools Corporation.

2. Other PACERS Cooperative themes are "The Genius of Place," which studies and documents community history, and a third program component called simply "Joy" (aimed at making rural communities and schools happier places through celebration and aesthetic development).

References

Bellah, R. N., Madsen, R., Sullivan, W. M., Swidler, A., and Tipton, S. (1991). *The good society*. New York: Knopf.

Berry, W. (1990). Nobody loves this planet. *In Context* 27: 4.

Berryman, S. (1987). *Shadows in the wings: The next educational reform.* Occasional Paper no. 1, National Center on Education and Employment. New York: Teachers College Press.

Center for Rural Affairs (1992). *A school at the center: Community-based education and rural development.* Walthill, Neb.: Center for Rural Affairs.

Center on Organization and Restructuring of Schools (1992). Estimating the extent of school restructuring. *Brief to Policymakers* 4. Madison, Wis. Center on Organization and Restructuring of Schools.

Dewey, J. (1939). The school and society. Reprinted in J. Dewey, *The child and the curriculum and the school and society.* Chicago: University of Chicago Press, 1956.

Flora, C. (1992). Presentation at the McREL Invitational Conference on Sustainability, October, Estes Park, Colo.

Gibson, D. (1991). Footprints. *Rural Electrification* (Fall): 12–14.

Grunwald, H. (1992). The conservatives' morning after. *Time,* November 30, 82.

Haas, T. (1992). *Unearthing abundance.* Final report to the Ford Foundation of the PACERS Small Schools Collaborative Grant. New York: Ford Foundation.

Hinz, L. (1991). *Students as entrepreneurs: Building academic skills and strengthening local economics.* Minneapolis: Center for School Change, Humphrey Institute of Public Affairs.

Kreck, C. (1992). A Family Affair. *Denver Post Magazine,* November 29, 12–17.

Lambert, R. (1992). *Proposals to the Ford Foundation.* Tuscaloosa, Ala.: Program for Rural Research and Service.

Least Heat-Moon, W. (1991). *PrairyErth.* Boston: Houghton Mifflin.

Nachtigal, P., Haas, T., Parker, S., and Brown, N. (1989). *What's noteworthy on rural schools and community development.* Aurora, Colo.: Mid-continent Regional Educational Laboratory.

Olivegren, J. (1986). How a little community is born. *In Context* (Autumn): 15.

Orr, D. (1990). What is education for? *In Context* 27: 54–55.

REAL Enterprises (1989). REAL Enterprises to be nationalized. *The REAL Story* (Athens, Ga.) 2 (1): 2–3.

REAL Enterprises (1990). Shoe repair business has lots of sole. *The REAL Story* (Athens, Ga.) 3 (2): 1.

REAL Enterprises (1992). REAL sweeps 15 states! Landslide imminent? *The REAL Story* (Athens, GA.) 4 (1): 1.

Schlechty, P. (1992). Speech at the summer meeting of the North Central Accreditating Association, June 25, Breckenridge, Colo.

Simon, P. (1975). *Kodachrome.* NY: ACSAP.

Stegner, W. (1985). *The sound of mountain water.* Lincoln: University of Nebraska Press.

Walberg, H. J. (1992). *On local control: Is bigger better?* Paper prepared for the Hubert H. Humphrey Institute for Public Affairs and the North Central Regional Laboratory.

Wigginton, E. (1985). *Sometimes a shining moment: The Foxfire experience.* New York: Doubleday.

Index

Contributors

TERRILL BUSH is Special Assistant to the President of Hostos Community College, a bilingual college in New York City. She holds a master's degree from Teachers College, Columbia University and has taught ESL in New York and Bogota, Colombia.

ROBERT B. EVERHART is Dean of the School of Education and Professor of Education and Sociology at Portland State University. He is the author of *Practical Ideology and Symbolic Community* (Falmer) and *Reading, Writing, and Resistance: Adolescence and Labor in a Junior High School* (Routledge).

TOM GREGORY has taught at Indiana University for twenty-four years. He conducts research on, consults with, and writes about public alternative schools. He is co-author (with Gerald Smith) of *High Schools as Communities: The Small School Reconsidered* (Phi Delta Kappa), which describes the power of alternative public schools and argues for the transformation of all schools into small, close-knit communities.

GRACE PUNG GUTHRIE, Senior Associate at Far West Laboratory, is author of *A School Divided: An Ethnography of Bilingual Education in a Chinese Community* (Erlbaum) and co-editor of *Culture and the Bilingual Classroom: Studies in Classroom Ethnography* (Newbury House).

LARRY F. GUTHRIE directs the Students At Risk Program at Far West Laboratory in San Francisco. His current research focuses on ways in

253

Contributors

which interagency collaboration and school restructuring can improve educational and social outcomes for children and families.

TONI HAAS helps people think about how to make education sustainable and appropriate to their communities and children. She consults with foundations, federal and state agencies, individuals, and communities from her office in Denver, Colorado.

DAVID HAGSTROM is the Director of the Alaska Center for Educational Leadership and an Adjunct Professor at the University of Alaska-Fairbanks. He is the former principal of the Denali Elementary School in Fairbanks, Alaska.

ARNOLD LANGBERG was the Principal of High School Redirection in Denver, Colorado, and the founding Principal of the Jefferson County Open High School, also in Colorado. He is currently one of the three directors of MINDS UN-LIMITED, a company that provides support for authentic heroism on issues relating to education, the arts, and the environment.

DAVE LEHMAN is the Principal of the Alternative Community School in Ithaca, New York; ACS is a member school of the Coalition of Essential Schools. Dr. Lehman's articles have appeared in *Holistic Education Review* and *Changing Schools*.

ROBERT PETERSON teaches fifth grade at La Escuela Fratney in Milwaukee, Wisconsin. He is also an editor of *Rethinking Schools* and co-chair of the National Coalition of Education Activists.

MARY ANNE RAYWID is a Professor of Education in the Department of Administration & Policy Studies at Hofstra University, where she is also the founder and director of the Center for the Study of Educational Alternatives. School reform and restructuring have been a primary focus of her work for a number of years. She has long been interested in and associated with alternative schools—in the several roles of researcher, developer, evaluator, participant-observer, and friend—and she has studied and written extensively about them.

GREGORY A. SMITH is an Assistant Professor of Education in the Graduate School of Professional Studies at Lewis and Clark College in Portland, Oregon. He is the author of *Education and the Environment: Learning to Live with Limits* (SUNY) and a co-author of *Reducing the Risk: Schools as Communities of Support* (Falmer).

MARY ELLEN SWEENEY was an advisor in an alternative teacher education program at Regis University for three and a half years. She is the managing editor of *Changing Schools*.

254